The Emergence of Modern Hebrew Literature in Babylon from 1735-1950

Shofar Supplements in Jewish Studies

The Emergence of Modern Hebrew Literature in Babylon from 1735-1950

Lev Hakak

Purdue University Press / West Lafayette, Indiana

Printed in the United States of America.

Library of Congress Cataloging-in-Publication Data
Hakak, Lev.
[Nitsaneh ha-yetsirah ha-'Ivrit ha-hadashah be-Bavel. English]
The emergence of modern Hebrew creativity in Babylon from 1735-1950 / Lev Hakak.
p. cm. -- (Shofar supplements in Jewish [studies])
ISBN 978-1-55753-514-6
1. Hebrew literature--Iraq--History and criticism. 2. Hebrew language--Iraq--History.
I. Title.
PJ5049.I68H3513 2009
892.4'099567--dc22

2009006178

Dedication

To Mr. and Mrs. Yair and Sara Samrai, for their love of Babylonian Jewish heritage which they carried from Babylon, to Israel, and finally to America; and for their exemplary dedication to family life.

Contents

Acknowledgments

Special thanks to The Babylonian Jewry Heritage Center and its Chairman of the Board, Mordechai Ben-Porat, for permission to publish the English version based on the original Hebrew version. I also thank the Center for allowing me to use their image archive. I thank Dr. Zvi Yehuda, the Research Institute Director of the Center, for his tireless support of this project. I thank the University of California, Los Angeles, for supporting the preparation of the manuscript. I thank Leonard Binder, the former Director of The Von Grunebaum Center for Near Eastern Studies, for his support of this project. And I thank Tina Lewin Wellman for her style editing efforts.

Introduction

A. A Brief History about the Jews in Babylon

Sumerians, Acadians, Babylonians, Assyrians, and Neo-Babylonians ruled Babylonia during man's history. Babylon was the birthplace of the Patriarch Abraham, who emigrated from Mesopotamia to the Promised Land in accordance with the command of the Lord (Genesis 12: 1-5). In 732 B.C., the children of Israel were exiled to Babylon (in this book I will use the name Babylon for Iraq, Mesopotamia; and Israel also stands for Palestine and Erets Yisrael), and in 721 B.C., there was an additional exile. The Assyrians exiled ten Hebrew tribes from Palestine (more than 27,000 Jews). This brief history about Babylonian Jews will serve as the context for the Hebrew creativity discussed in this book. In presenting this brief history, I rely on Shohet (see Bibliography, Shohet) and his numerous sources.

In 597 B.C., Nebuchadnezzar exiled about ten thousand Jews from Jerusalem to Babylon (exile of Jehoiachin). The end of the Kingdom of Judah and Jerusalem came in 586 B.C. (the exile of Zidqiah) when the Babylonians destroyed the First Temple and exiled about forty thousand Jews. The exiled Jews adjusted to their new place. They multiplied, prospered, and enjoyed freedom.

The Persians ruled Babylon from the sixth century B.C. King Cyrus allowed (in 538 B.C.) the Jews to return to Palestine. In 458 B.C. and 444 B.C., many Jews returned to Judea under the leadership of Ezra the Scribe and Nehemiah, and the Second Temple was built in Jerusalem. Still, some Jews remained in the Babylonian exile.

The end of the Persian rule came in 331 B.C., when the Greeks conquered Babylon under the command of Alexander the Great. The Babylonian Jews adapted themselves to the new reality. Jews who escaped from the Greeks' oppression in Palestine found shelter with the Babylonian Jews. When the Greeks' control in Mesopotamia weakened, the Hellenistic period ended. The Persians reappeared and ruled Babylon (as the Parthians) from 139 B.C. to 226 C.E. During this long period, the spiritual and economic life of the Babylonian Jews thrived.

There were three independent Jewish mini-states in Babylon. In 25-40 C.E., two Jewish brothers who rebelled against the Parthians established a mini-state in a fortress in Babylon. Another mini-state began when the king and people of the kingdom from the state of Adiabene (northeast of the Tigris River) converted to Judaism. The queen and her son supported the Jews in Palestine and then immigrated to Jerusalem and fought against the Romans. In 116 C.E., the Romans destroyed the kingdom of Adiabene. Another mini-state was established in Babylon in 495 B.C. by the Head of the Exile, Mar Zutra II, who rebelled against the Persians to avenge the killing of his father by the Persian King. After seven years, the Persians destroyed this mini-state and crucified Mar Zutra.

The Persian rule of the Parthians (139 B.C.-226 C.E.) was followed by the rule of the Persian fire worshippers and fanatics, the Sassans (until 635 B.C.). The Sassanid era was restless. Some kings from the Sassanic Persian Empire imposed various limits on the Jews, and some were moderate.

During the Persian rule, Babylonian Jewry became the center for world Jewry. The years 219-500 are known as the period of the Amoraites (Interpreters) who were Talmudic sages that interpreted the words of the Tania (the teachers-authorities quoted in the Mishnah). The Amoraites created the Babylonian Talmud. The Jews of Babylon compiled the Talmud (the commentaries on the Mishnah; the commentary and the Mishnah) in about 500 C.E. This version of the Talmud, the Babylonian Talmud, is considered the most authoritative source for Jewish law throughout the Diaspora. Besides law, it comprises commentary, legends, folkloristic materials, history, and much more.

The Babylonian Talmud mentions about two hundred towns in Babylon where the majority of the populations were Jews whose towns were home to organizations for charity and education similar to those in Palestine. The Jews at that time were craftsmen, farmers, exporters, and importers. Some were landowners.

The years 500-589 were the time of the Saboraim (Talmudic teachers after the Amoraim and before the Gaonim) who explained the Babylonian Talmud.

In 638 B.C., the rule of the Sassanic Persian Empire ended, with the Muslim Arabs conquering Babylon. They renamed the region Iraq and made Islam its official religion. The Jews embraced the Arab rule and paid poll tax. In turn, the Arab rulers treated the Jews with tolerance and inspired a spirit of freedom. The yeshivot ("Yeshivas," Talmudical Colleges) resumed their role in Jewish education, and the new ruling party recognized the important role of "The Head of the Exile," the leader of the Jews, who had both secular and religious authority. In fact, until the eleventh century, he held a prestigious office, collecting taxes and appointing Jewish judges and the rabbinical schools' spiritual leaders.

The Jews were treated well during the Arab rule. Instead of the Aramaic language, they spoke Arabic, and they moved from the countryside to the city. They particularly flourished during many centuries of the Abbasid Kingdom (750-1258), during which some Jews held high positions. During the Abbasid Kingdom Jews were physicians, engineers, astronomers, translators (to Arabic), traders, and craftsmen. The years 589-1038 are known as the time of the Babylonian Gaonim ("Geniuses," talented, highly learned, Gaonites), who were the heads of the Babylonian Yeshivot. The end of the Gaonim period was also the end of Babylon being the spiritual center for world Jewry.

In 763, Baghdad was built on the banks of the Tigris and became the capital of the Abbasid Kingdom. "The Head of the Exile" moved to Baghdad. From that time until the exodus of the Jews from Iraq, Baghdad was home to more Jews than any other place in Iraq (about Baghdad in the twelfth-eighteenth centuries see Yehuda, 2002). Some Caliphs (such as Harun a-Rashid) declared oppressive actions against Jews and other religious minorities while other Caliphs were tolerant.

The years 1055-1508 marked many centuries of change under Iraqi rule. In 945, Shi'ite Muslims, known as Buwaihids, conquered Iraq. Then, in 1058, the Turkish Seljuqi invaded that country. In spite of the hardships inflicted by these changes on the Jewish population, evidence shows that in 1170, Iraq had great religious scholars. The 40,000 Jews who lived in Baghdad had twenty-eight synagogues and enjoyed good life.

The Mongols conquered Iraq in 1258 and slaughtered most of its inhabitants. Yeshivot were destroyed and the position of "The Head of the Exile" was eliminated. The surviving Jews attuned themselves to the rule of the Mongols. Some Jews were appointed to very high positions (such as Chief Vizier, Governor of Baghdad) and were later accused of various crimes and executed. During the conquest of Timurlang, thousands of Jews were murdered. There were other dark times in Jewish life during that era. In 1508, Shi'ite Persians conquered Baghdad.

After the above mentioned volatile regimes, the years 1534-1918 were the time of the Ottoman rule. Under the Ottomans, the Turks sent a ruler to Iraq ("Pasha"). The Jews were awarded religious freedom and were represented by their president. When the Persians conquered and ruled Iraq again (1623-1638), 10,000 Jews fought with the army of the Turkish Sultan who took over Iraq. From 1750-1831, the Mamluks occupied and ruled Iraq. The Mamluks were slaves from Georgia who accepted Islam. The time of the Mamluks was marked by a revitalization of Torah studies, new Hebrew publications, and economic comfort for the Jews on the one hand, and extortion, plagues, flood, persecutions, blood libels, and sometimes anti-Semitic regulations on the other. The president of the Jewish community was its leader. In addition, he often also served as the chief banker and an assistant to the governor.

Sheikh Sassoon ben-Salah, the founder of the Sassoon Dynasty, was one of these presidents. The richest man of his time in Baghdad was the businessman David Sassoon (1792-1864), who knew many foreign languages. The Queen of England decorated his son, the philosopher, businessman, and philanthropist Sir Albert (1817-1897). David Solomon, who owned the biggest collection of Jewish manuscripts, and Siegfried, an English infantry officer, a poet, and a writer, are more recent descendents of the Sassoon family.

In 1831, the governor ("Wali") of the central Ottoman government overpowered the Mamluk ruler. The Turkish rulers appointed forty-two rulers in Iraq ("Walis") in 1831-1917. During the time of the Walis, more children in Iraq received an education, newspapers and books were published, and the telegraph and postal services were instituted. During the rule of some Walis, the Jews enjoyed equality, while under the rule of other Walis, the Jews experienced persecutions. Regardless of hardships, under the rule of the Walis the Jewish people experienced progress in their educational system, economic life, and civil rights. The school system continued to be modernized. This included the establishment of the Alliance school system in 1864 in Baghdad and the enrollment of Jewish students in Turkish, French, and schools in other countries. There were prosperous times during this period. For example, during this time, the Suez Canal (1869) opened. The Jews enjoyed progress in their civil rights due to the 1839 declaration of human rights by the Sultan and the 1869 reforms of Midhat Pasha.

Menahem Salah Daniel, an educated philanthropist and businessman, represented the Jews of Baghdad in the Turkish House of Representatives in Constantinople in 1876. Later, after the establishment of the Iraqi kingdom, he became a senator.

About two thirds of Iraq's 80,000 Jews lived in Baghdad at the beginning of the twentieth century. The position of Chief Rabbi ("Hakham Bashi") was substituted by the position of the president of the Jewish community. Beginning in 1909, Jewish men had to serve in the Turkish army or pay an annual tax in lieu of the service. In the last stage of the Turkish Empire, the Jews suffered a decline due to natural disasters and to the large payments and taxes imposed by the Walis, who also imposed an anti-Semitic policy.

In World War I, Turkey declared war against Britain, France, and Russia. Jewish leaders were arrested, and Jews were accused time and again of causing the Turks' economic hardships. Thousands of Jews were drafted to the army without training, and many of them died in the fight against the Russians. Many Jews became officers and assumed combat or administrative military duties. During the War, some Jewish schools were converted to hospitals, and some Jewish businessmen's properties were confiscated to support the war. Before the British captured Baghdad in 1917, the Turks arrested and murdered many Jews, and later they allowed the looting of Jewish stores.

The British occupation of Iraq ended in 1918. The Jews viewed the British occupiers as liberators, welcomed, and aided them. In 1920, Britain was given a mandate over Iraq and ruled Iraq until 1932. In 1925, there were 90,000 Jews in Iraq, including 60,000 Jews in Baghdad. At the end of the 1920s, there were about 80,000 Jews in Baghdad and about 120,000 Jews in Iraq. Jews were the most important minority in Iraq. Thousands of them worked for the British government in public service, including in the police and in the army, because of their knowledge of languages. In addition, they held important positions in banking and in export and import.

The Jewish community improved its services to its members in areas such as medicine, schools, religion, and charity. The Zionist movement was legalized, and the community established contacts with various organizations in Palestine. Jews participated in journalistic and literary Arabic publications.

In 1918, independence was granted to the occupied countries. Christians and Jews did not support the desire for an independent Iraq, but they agreed to an Arab rule based on the British promise that the minorities would be safe in Iraq. In 1920, Iraq was declared a democratic state, with a constitution, parliament, cabinet, and king. The first king of Iraq (Faisal) supported equality among all citizenry and was considerate and appreciative of the Jewish minority. As a religious minority, the Jews had representatives in the parliament, and they also had a senator.

Iraqi Jews also immigrated to Israel beginning in 1818 (see the chapters about the Mani brothers) and founded Yeshivot there. From 1919 until Israel was established in 1948, about 8,000 Jews emigrated from Iraq to Israel. In the 1920s, the Zionists in Iraq became organized. In the 1920s until 1936 (the arrest of Aharon Sason), there were Zionist activities in various towns in Iraq. In 1921, an official permit was given to the Zionist Society for its activities, but the permit was not renewed. Nevertheless, Zionist activity was allowed.

Iraqi Jews were concerned less with developing Zionist thought and more with partaking in Zionist activities such as sending donations to Palestine, aiding immigration, purchasing land, and promoting Hebrew language and literature. New Jewish schools were founded, including a school in which all the studies were conducted in Hebrew and another school that promoted teaching Hebrew in Hebrew. Babylonian Jews kept longstanding, strong ties with Palestine. Emissaries came from the land of Israel to Iraq, and the Jews of Iraq sent rabbis, volunteers, and financial contributions to Palestine.

Since 1912, Aharon Sason (refer to Chapter 3 about his poetry) is considered to be the founder and the father of the Zionist movement in Iraq. In 1920, a Hebrew literary society was established. It attracted hundreds of members within a few months, and it offered a Hebrew newspaper club, guest lectures, a library, Hebrew language classes, and a Hebrew publication (refer to Chapter 10 about *Yeshurun*).

In 1929 (a year of riots against the Jews in Palestine), Zionist activity was prohibited, and the teachers who were sent from Palestine to Iraq were expelled. In that same year, a Zionist group of teenagers ("Ahiever") began underground Zionist activities, including maintaining a Hebrew library, teaching Hebrew, sponsoring lectures in Hebrew, donating money to Palestine, assisting in immigration to Israel, and actually immigrating to Israel. There were other Zionist organizations in Iraq, among them the Hebrew Book Distributors (established in 1930) and the Hebrew Youth Organization.

Until 1931, two committees managed Iraq's Jewish community. They were the Committee for Spiritual Affairs, which was in charge of such aspects of Jewish life as education, religion, rabbinical schools, synagogues, and dietary laws, and the Committee for Material Affairs, which was in charge of Jewish operated hospitals, charity, community finances, and property. The head of the community was the Chief Rabbi (Hakham Bashi), with a board of sixty lay-leaders and twenty rabbis (see the chapter about *Yeshurun*). In 1931, the government enacted the "Jewish Community Law." A position for the Head of the Community was added, making it possible to have one person hold both titles—Chief Rabbi and the Head of the Community.

The Jewish community in Iraq had many synagogues, charitable organizations, and social clubs. In the cities of Baghdad, Basra, and Mosul, there were rabbinical courts dealing with matters of domestic law, as well as other disputes. Additionally, there was a Court of Appeals in Baghdad.

Sir Sassoon Yehezkel was the Finance Minister during five cabinets, the Acting Prime Minister, and the British king granted him the title of "Knight of the British Empire." Jewish students majored in fields such as education, medicine, and law. Jews and Muslims had good relations. The British Mandate was terminated in 1932, and the nationalistic elements in Iraq became more powerful. In 1933, King Faisal died and his eighteen-year-old son (Razi) became the king until he was killed in a suspicious car accident in 1939. At this time, Iraqi radical nationalists made their admiration for the Nazis known, the civil rights of minorities were repealed, and the king did not give the same consideration to the Jews as his father had.

The first Arabian country that supported Arabs carrying weapons in Palestine was Iraq. In the 1930s, there were Arabs who demanded to kill Jews as a revenge for Zionism and Arab fatalities in Palestine. Teachers in Arab countries spread anti-Semitic ideas. There were press campaigns against the Jews in Iraq, pro-Nazi organizations were founded and circulated Nazi propaganda, the Mufti of Jerusalem came to Iraq to promote the enmity against the Jews, and the German Consul in Iraq promoted hatred for the Jews. As a result, the economic condition of the Jews in Iraq was weakened. Jews who did not serve in the army paid a special tax. Their mail was censored. The number of students admitted to post-elementary schools was limited, and teaching Hebrew and Jewish history in Jewish schools was prohibited. Jewish publications in Arabic and in Hebrew (*Yeshurun*) were eliminated. Several Jews were murdered in various towns. Jewish leaders declared, as requested, loyalty to Iraq, and Jews participated in Iraqi nationalism, but this did not mitigate the terror. The Zionist movement that was legal in Iraq in the 1920s went underground in the 1930s. However, at the end of the 1930s and during the beginning of the 1940s, it ceased operating in Iraq, and the leaders of the Iraqi Jews were vulnerable and powerless, at the same time that the German military power occupied Egypt.

On the first and second day of June in 1941, there was a pogrom against the Jews in Iraq as a result of Nazi incitement using propaganda and nationalistic-religious instigation. This pogrom was known as "Farhood," robbing and looting by rioters (see Moreh). Rashid Ali Al-Kilani opposed the pro-British policy of the royal family of Iraq and the Government of Iraq. He led a military revolt and established a pro-Nazi military dictatorship. Muslims prepared to begin a pogrom against the Jews. The British army invaded Iraq, Rashid Ali escaped, and a temporary government was established. The Jews rejoiced over the reestablishment of the pro-British government. Incited Muslims, who already prepared for a pogrom against the Jews, were disappointed. On those first June days, during the Jewish holiday of Shavu'ot (Pentecost, Feast of Weeks), Jews were injured and murdered and Jewish women were raped. Jewish property was looted and Jewish houses were burned down. At least eighteen babies, sixty-two young, single men and women, forty-eight fathers, nineteen mothers and thirty-two old men and women were murdered. 850 to 2,118 Jews were injured; 600 to 2,371 stores and 875 to 1,000 houses were looted; and 6,558 houses were damaged. It was difficult to know the number of those murdered and injured Jews and the extent of the damage to their property, because it was impossible to thoroughly investigate what took place. In addition, there were missing Jews. Various aspects of the pogrom were researched (see Bezalel, *Pe'amim,* no. 8). The Jews of Iraq commemorate the pogrom by reading the lamentation of Rabbi Shelomo Ben-Salih Shelomo Gabai (refer to Chapter 3) "I Will Roar Like a Lion."

The alarmed Jews in Iraq considered various ways of preventing future pogroms, which included joining Iraqi nationalism movements, assimilating into the Iraqi culture, joining the communist party, or immigrating to other countries to further Zionism. The Zionist movement, with its desire for an exodus to Palestine, was the strongest direction. Several Jewish organizations were established by young people, and later joined by adults, striving for self-defense and immigration to Palestine. Beginning in 1942, they were assisted by emissaries from Palestine. They assisted in establishing the underground movement of "He-Haluts" (refer to Chapter 12 about *Derekh He-Haluts*) for members who were at least fifteen years old, while the younger members were organized into other groups. The members of this movement were given Hebrew books and publications, held meetings, studied Hebrew, and often spoke Hebrew among themselves. They also had classes for Jewish studies, including Jewish history and the geography of Palestine. They raised funds for Palestine and held conventions in order to set the movement's goals. Among those goals were promoting the Hebrew language, preparing for self-defense, including the use of arms, immigrating to Palestine, liberating Jewish women, and training for vocations. In 1946, in Baghdad alone, the movement had one thousand members. In 1948, the movement had more than two thousand members, both men and women, in Iraq. The members and the Iraqi cities that had branches of the movement were given Hebrew nicknames.

By asserting Zionist ideas, the movement influenced Jewish schools' curriculum. From 1942 through 1951, the movement transported illegal immigrants to Palestine, in spite of the fact that there were smugglers who robbed, raped, and murdered some of the people that they were hired to guide. During the last two years of this operation, fifteen thousand Jews emigrated from Iraq to Palestine illegally.

The second wing of the movement was an organization that was in charge of defending the Jews in Baghdad and in other cities when needed ("Ha-Shura"). Arms such as guns and hand grenades were purchased from Iraq or received from Palestine. Ha-Shura existed in Iraq until the end of 1950. Beginning in 1951, Jews began immigrating from Iraq to Israel.

At the end of World War II, during the time of Palestinian battles, Iraqi pro-Nazi leaders returned to power and restarted an anti-Semitic campaign. Jews in public positions were discharged. Zionism became a crime, and business licenses were not given to Jewish merchants. Additionally, contacts with Palestine were banned. The Iraqi press was hostile to the Jews. There were demonstrations against Zionism. Public schools did not admit Jewish students, and only religious studies and prayers were allowed in Jewish schools. The government of Iraq was the first to implement the Arab governments' 1946 decision to end Jewish activities in Arab countries and to fight Zionism. The Jews were called "hostages" by the Iraqi government. Their exit from Iraq was restricted and illegal immigration ended.

In 1947, Iraq experienced a famine. The Jews became the victims of rage against the Iraqi government, communism, British Imperialism, and Zionism. Also during that year, various libels were circulated against the Jews. They were accused of contaminating the drinking water in Iraq and giving poisoned candies to Arab children. That same year, the General Assembly of the United Nations called for a Jewish and Arab State with a partition in Palestine. Participants in mass demonstrations in Iraq declared a holy war (Jihad) against the Jews. Volunteers were enrolled for it, and some leaders called for the annihilation of the Jews. The government even sent volunteers to the Palestine Liberation Army. The news about Jews winning battles in Palestine resulted in further hostility against the Jews in Iraq. Such hostility was also encouraged by the government, by the imams (preachers in mosques), and by the media.

The State of Israel was declared on May 14, 1948, and extremists in Iraq declared that the Jewish people were doomed to go into the sea or to their graves. Jews did not go out of their homes, and the Jewish underground was prepared for a defense. However, the government prevented provocations, although it announced that Iraqi troops were sent to Palestine to destroy the State of Israel. Martial law was declared, and Jews were under surveillance. They were extorted, fined, and arrested. Some were charged with treason and tortured to death. Jewish homes and clubs were confiscated. Zionist activity and Communism were declared as criminal, dangerous offenses. When the 1948 War of Independence ended, and the defeated Iraqi troops returned to Iraq, more Jews were dismissed from public work. Many Jews were unemployed. Jewish banks could not conduct foreign trade. Arabs did not shop in Jewish stores, and Jewish students were advised to leave public school for their safety.

Shafik Adas was an Iraqi Jew who employed thousands of people as the main importer of Ford in Iraq and in his other businesses. He was not involved in Zionism, and he had friends holding the highest positions in Iraq. He was arrested, charged with treason without a defense, and hung in front of his mansion (to the joy of 12,000 spectators). His body was mutilated and his property confiscated. Many Muslim citizens voiced disapproval of this trial that was covered by the world media.

In October 1949, many members of the He-Haluts were arrested. The Jews declared a strike protesting the arrest and weakness of the head of the Jewish community (Rabbi Sason Kaduri). About 1,550 Jews were sentenced to jail, 1,450 of whom were sentenced to three to ten years. In 1950, when immigration to Israel became legal, there were about 3,000 Jews in jail.

Mass escape of the Jews from Iraq to Palestine began again in December 1949. When martial law was abolished in Iraq, in March 1950, the Jews were allowed to leave Iraq. Every Jew who left Iraq had to leave all valuables in Iraq, except fifty dinars and thirty pounds of baggage. While the new law caused the Jews to rejoice, it angered the anti-Semites, and some Jewish property was destroyed by arson.

Within three months following the publication of the new law, the overwhelming majority of the Jews in Iraq registered for immigration to Israel and sold their property for a fraction of the real market price. The Iraqi government expected about 8,000 Jews to immigrate. However, at the beginning of 1952, only 6,000 Jews were left in Iraq. 108,000 Iraqi Jews—not including illegal immigrants—immigrated to Israel. 123,371 Jews emigrated from Babylon to Israel in the years 1948 to 1951. They did so in spite of the fact that their community property and personal property were confiscated. From 1952 through 1960, 2,989 Jews emigrated from Babylon to Israel, and in the years 1961-2001, 4,504 immigrated.

The unexpected mass exodus of Jews from Iraq impacted the Iraqi economy and public service. There were incidents of Jewish casualties as a result of terrorists' bombing of Jewish places. Iraqi police searched and found arms and documents of the underground movement. Jews were arrested, and two of them were sentenced to death and executed in a street in Baghdad. Following the mass immigration, the Iraqi government froze and seized all the property of the immigrants, including substantial amounts of money in banks. Jewish residents with foreign citizenship were ordered to leave Iraq.

In 1963, there was a new Iraqi government. Twenty Jews were killed or could not be found. From 1963 through 1965, substantial property of Jews who did not return to Iraq on or before a date specified in their passports was confiscated. At the time of the 1967 Six-Day War, there were 3,000 to 3,500 Jews in Iraq. Many were arrested, and new discriminatory laws constrained their civil rights. About one tenth of Iraqi Jews were in jail from 1967 through 1969. In December 1968, six Iraqi soldiers in Jordan were killed in combat with the Israeli Defense Force. Subsequently, tens of thousands of Iraqis demonstrated, demanding revenge. About a month later, nine Iraqi Jewish citizens were hung. The United Nations Secretary General, the Pope, some Arab countries, and other entities denounced this act, but a few months later, two more Jews were hung. The 1970 appeal by various countries and the United Nations to allow the Jews to leave Iraq was rejected. In 1971, there were 1,000 to 1,500 Jews in Iraq. In 1973, 400 Jews were left.

From 1972 through 1973, the Iraqi secret police killed twenty-three Jews, in addition to the fifteen Jews who had disappeared. From 1973 on, sick Jews or those over sixty-five years old could leave Iraq if they paid £1,500. In 1975, the Iraqi government invited the Jews who left Iraq to return, but this welcome did not trigger the return of a single person.

Among the many great rabbis of the nineteenth and early twentieth centuries were Rabbi Abdallah Somekh (1813-1889) and Rabbi Yosef Hayyim (1835-1909, refer to Chapter 4). At the same time, there were well-known Jews who made meaningful contributions to Iraqi law, and others were among the pioneers of modern medicine. There were also well-known Jewish journalists and writers who wrote in Arabic. Fifty Jewish singers in Arabic were famous in Baghdad, and Jewish musicians performed regularly on the Iraqi radio. In addition, Jews were the pioneers of the dramatic arts in Iraq and were among the pioneers of painting schools.

During the Iraq Liberation War, there were about thirty-five Jews in Iraq. These individuals were old, and twenty-six of them were airlifted from Baghdad to Israel in 2003.

In Israel, there were about 243,500 Babylonian Jews in the year 2005. Collectively, they constitute the third largest Israeli community. 72,200 of them (about thirty percent) were born in Iraq, and the rest were born in Israel. Iraqi Jews won the Israeli prize in the fields of religious literature, Arabic linguistics, science, and research of the Middle East—three of them for special contributions to Israeli society and to the state of Israel. Thirty Iraqi Jews served in the Keneset (Israel's parliament). The Israeli Sephardic Chief Rabbis came from families of Iraqi origin, and Iraqi Jews were appointed as judges to the Israeli Supreme Court and other courts. Among the government positions held in Israel by leaders of Iraqi descent are those of the Israeli Defense Force Chief of Staff, the Defense Minister, and the Minister of Trade.

B. The Essence of the New Hebrew Creativity in Babylon

The Jews of Babylon lived there for more than 2,500 years, until the 1950-1951 Operation Ezra and Nehemiah, when the majority of them, 123,000, immigrated to Israel. This was the oldest community in the Jewish Diaspora and was the spiritual and religious center of the Jewish people for a period of more than one thousand years. This community's literary works were not given any role in the history of modern Hebrew literature.

My goal is to present secular Hebrew literature written by the Jews of Babylon from 1735-1950. If my goal is achieved, it may result in additional research of Hebrew creativity in other countries, including Middle Eastern countries that today do not play any part in the history of modern Hebrew literature. In writing the history of literature of any people, one has to recognize not only the mainstream literature in which that literature was conceived, but also what was created in the outlying areas.

There were many Hebrew liturgical poets who wrote in Babylon until the first half of the fourteenth century and, while very little remained of the works written from that time until the beginning of the eighteenth century, there are many poems from the beginning of the eighteenth century until 1950-1951. The Jews of Babylon authored far more than 1,200 liturgies and poems in the 250 years that preceded Operation Ezra and Nehemiah. Medieval Hebrew poetry influenced those works, the minority of which is secular. Drawing on a variety of themes, there was religious poetry, such as poems praising God, Sabbath poems, poems for holidays and festivals, and days of fasting and of troubles. It also includes poems of love and those that express yearning for Jerusalem, Didactic poems, and poems expressing gratitude to public figures such as kings, donors, and rabbis. Other poems were written in the context of public events, such as the dedication of a new synagogue, the completion of studying a tractate in the *Talmud, (Talmud* is the codification of Jewish law. The second part of the *Talmud* is *Gemara*, which provides commentary on the first part, *Mishnah*), or personal events, such as marriage, birth, circumcision, Bar Mitzvah, or dedication of a house. There were many poems about biblical characters, particularly about Ezra and Ezekiel, whose graves were in Babylon, according to tradition.

During this period, the Jews of Babylon also wrote secular Hebrew poetry about the same themes as the secular medieval Hebrew poetry such as poems of Praise, Lamentations, Cogitation, Love, Complaints, and Riddles.

Most of the Hebrew literature, written or published by the Jews of Babylon, was about religion and Jewish Law. Biblical interpretations, prayer books (that sometimes included Hebrew liturgical poetry written in Babylon), sermons, Jewish Law compilations, and Jewish mysticism dominated their writing. However, the Jews of Babylon wrote secular literature, too. Besides secular poetry, they published folktales, textbooks, stories, articles, and even a play, all in Hebrew. There were also people, such as Rabbi Shalom Bekhor Hutsin and Yisrael Katan, who published journalistic articles in various Hebrew periodicals that appeared in other countries at that time, particularly in Europe and in Israel, such as *Ha-Havatselet, Ha-Tsefira, Ha-Levanon* and *Ha-Maggid.*

Jewish authors who wrote in Arabic had a potentially large number of readers, while authors who wrote in Hebrew, particularly those who wrote for the local readers in Babylon and did not publish in Hebrew periodicals that appeared in Europe or Israel, addressed a small number of readers. These Hebrew authors made a conscious decision marked by commitment to the Hebrew culture. It is a cultural task to ensure that authors who dedicated their life to writing in Hebrew be acknowledged.

The main Hebrew literary productivity in Babylon was in poetry. Few of the poems appeared in Hebrew poetry books of their perspective authors. Other poems appeared in prayer books and in songs books published in Babylon, India, Israel, Italy, and other countries. There were poetry volumes of one poet or of various poets, and other poems were published in periodicals or found in manuscripts. Some poets left us many poems and liturgies while others were less prolific. Of course, this does not include all the Hebrew poems and liturgies that were written by the Jews of Babylon. There were poets who were born in Babylon (mostly Baghdad), and immigrated to Israel, India, China, the United States, and other countries, where they continued their Hebrew creativity. Medieval Hebrew poetry influenced the poetry not only through its themes, but also through its form and content. Hebrew poetry, written in Europe at that time, was another source of influence.

During this period, poets such as Shaul Yosef and David Tsemah maintained the content and form of the versatile literary tradition of medieval Hebrew poetry with its "ornamented speech," while other poets such as Saliman Mani and his brother, Avraham Barukh Mani, were influenced by Hebrew poetry of their time.

The themes of medieval Hebrew poetry were conventionally fixed, reflecting on wine and passion, friendship, complaints of a personal nature, chastisement and satire, condemnation, boasting and self-praise, personal dirges and official ones, orations, wisdom, and ornamental epigrams.

The meter of Hebrew poetry written in Spain was quantitative. The metrical system and the poetic language of this poetry spread to Egypt, Yemen, North Africa, the Ottoman Empire, and Babylon, until the immigration to Israel. Even nowadays there are poets, such as Amnon Shamosh, who continue to write according to this system. The poetic language and metrical system of Hebrew poetry in Spain also dominated Hebrew poetry in Provence, then spread through Europe and ruled Hebrew poetry in Italy until the nineteenth century.

The quantitative meter in Hebrew is based on regulated "pegs" (Hebrew: "Yetedot") and cords (Hebrew: "Tenuaot"). It is not based on a pattern of stressed and unstressed syllables, but on a pattern of short and long syllables. There are dozens of regular quantitative meters. A "foot" (Hebrew: "Regel") is a recurring group of syllables. The basic form of the poem is a distich (Hebrew: "Bayit"), consisting of two lines, the first one is called a door (Hebrew: "delet"), and the second one is called closing (Hebrew: "soger"), ending with a rhyme, which in some poems links it to the whole poem. The poetry written by the Jews of Babylon was influenced also by the imagery, word play, puns, homonyms of Spanish-Hebrew poetry, and by the various biblical allusions and meter of Spanish-Hebrew poetry.

A notable work in the field of Hebrew liturgies and poetry published by the Jews of Babylon may be seen in Ben-Yaacob's book (Ben-Yaacob, 1970). Ben-Yaacob published about 460 of these liturgies and poems, about one third of the poems he knew of at that time. He wrote an introduction about every poet and added footnotes to the poems, including many biblical allusions (some of the poets in Babylon presented the allusions to the reader in their footnotes). Ben-Yaacob's valuable book established the foundations for further research and work in the field.

I have introduced Hebrew poems written in Babylon from 1735, and I included authors who were born in Babylon and immigrated to Israel or to other countries. In other publications (Hakak) I have discussed the Hebrew literary works written in Israel by Jews from Babylon.

In this book, I will also illustrate the Hebrew poetry written by some of the poets who were mainly prolific in Babylon, and they continued their work in Israel. I have not included literary works written in Arabic, but only in Hebrew letters. Jewish authors who wrote in Babylon in Arabic (such as Meir Basri, Anwar Shaul, Murad Mikh'ael, Ya'acov Bilbul, Shalom Darwish, Avraham Ya'acov Ovadia, and Shalom Katav) addressed the Arabic readers, most of whom were Muslims.

As to Babylonian Jews' folk literature, which is a rich field by itself, I have only illustrated it by translating for this book some of Rabbi Yosef Hayyim's folktales, for which I also wrote a brief introduction.

In this field of folktales, there are books published in Hebrew in Babylon, such as the three volumes published by Rabbi Shelomo Hutsin (Hutsin, 1890), which include many folktales, and folktales collected from the books of Rabbi Yosef Hayyim (Hayyim, 1912 and 1913). A variety of folktales about Babylonian Jews appeared in Israel in various books. Yitshak Avishur published in Heda Jason's book a list of books published by Babylonian Jews, which included folktales and books about Babylonian Jews that were collections of Iraqi Jews' folktales (Jason, 1980, 17-26). Avishur, an important scholar in the field of Babylonian Jewry, also published two volumes of folktales of Babylonian Jews, a selection that originated in their manuscripts (Avishur, 1992).

As to the poetry discussed in this book, I focus on secular Hebrew poetry in Iraq. One can distinguish between secular poetry and liturgical poetry by the differences in their forms and style, objectives, attitude and tone of the poetic speaker, and the poem's disposition (Pagis, 1970, 22-24). Liturgical poetry was used for prayers and penitential prayers (hymns). One must remember, however, that the Jews of Babylon were people of deep religious faith, and therefore, religious expressions and ideas from prayers played a role in many of their secular works. In some instances, their poems can be classified as both secular and liturgical.

The classification of the majority of their poems is clear. The objective of liturgical poetry was to accompany the prayers and make them more vibrant, written for the public and not for the individual, while secular poetry was written for its own sake (Shilowah). The secular poetry often followed up the poetics of secular poetry and its genres, structure (an "introduction" related to any subject; "transition verse"; the "body" of the poem itself, about the actual theme), conventional phrases and imagery, colorful kaleidoscope of style, motifs, and meter. Liturgical poetry was not subjected to these rules. Liturgical poems alluded to the place in the prayers where they should be connected, while secular poems stood by themselves and did not depend on a permanent, pre-existing text. The themes and perspective of liturgical poetry were different from those of secular poetry, which also helps in differentiating between them.

Modern Hebrew literature influenced the Iraqi Jews' writing in various ways. Babylonian Jews interacted with Jews from other communities, traveling from Iraq to other countries, and Jews from other countries visited the Jewish community in Iraq and worked there. The Jewish community invited teachers from Israel and other countries in various fields of expertise, including Hebrew. Jews from Baghdad subscribed to Hebrew periodicals published in Europe and Israel, served as journalists and reporters for those periodicals, and published articles in the area of Jewish law as well as in other fields. There was a group of cultural activists who were interested in Hebrew culture and contributed money and articles to Hebrew periodicals. In addition, the Jews of Iraq published some Hebrew periodicals of their own. Another opportunity for interaction was modern Jewish schools in Iraq, the curricula of which included, aside from Hebrew and Jewish studies, secular studies and foreign languages.

Yitzhak Avishur (1995, 235-254) discussed transformations in Jewish literature written in Hebrew and in Judeo-Arabic and Arabic in Babylon in 1750-1950. In the first one hundred years of that period, canonical religious Jewish literature in Babylon was written in Hebrew, while the non-canonical literature such as folktales, stories, poems, and proverbs was written in Judeo-Arabic. The second period, the second half of the nineteenth century, was a time in which Jewish literature in Hebrew and in Judeo-Arabic flourished. This was a period of significant rabbinical literature, and in addition to the genres written earlier, the authors of this period wrote about Jewish mysticism, biblical interpretation, and interpretation of prayers. Hebrew literary works were translated into Judeo-Arabic. Journalistic articles, liturgies and moralistic literature, and a short-lived periodical were published. In the third period, which was the first half of the twentieth century, the literary Arabic of the Jews of Babylon repressed the productivity in Hebrew and in Judeo-Arabic. The reasons for this were the multiplication of printing houses and Jewish authors who wrote in Arabic, the increased status of the literary Arabic in comparison with Judeo-Arabic, and the fact that the rich community leaders dominated the spiritual ones.

Hebrew language was a fundamental part of all Jewish school programs in Babylon. A large number of the relatively small Jewish community's members in Babylon (at its peak did not exceed 130,000 Jews) knew Hebrew. Some of them mastered the language to a spectacular degree. Their Hebrew language has deep roots in various sources, particularly in the Bible. The vocabulary that was available to them was substantially more limited than the one available to contemporary Hebrew authors, but their knowledge of the Bible and the rabbinic literature made it possible for them to express all feelings and thoughts.

When it comes to evaluating the literature of the Jews of Babylon, particularly their poetry, it would be wise to apply both relative historical standards and poetic standards of our time. We should, for example, consider the distich as the basic form of the poem consisting of two lines ("door" and "closing"; "delet" and "soger") and the literary dynamics between the two parts, but we can evaluate the aesthetic achievements by contemporary standards as well. In these poems, the use of the conventions of medieval Hebrew poetry, by themselves, does not determine their aesthetic achievements. When contemporary Israeli poets used such conventions (examples include Amnon Shamosh and Ratson Halevi), they did not serve as the basis for evaluating their poems.

In this book, I have also discussed some folktales of Rabbi Yosef Hayyim, a missive by Rabbi Ya'acov Hayyim, a short story and a report by Rabbi Saliman Mani, Hebrew periodicals that included reporting, stories and a play, and articles and journalistic writing. Everything presented here is not necessarily an important piece of literature. However, in some cases, it provides an illustration of the substantial Hebrew cultural activity in Babylon in modern times.

Scholars and historians of Hebrew literature, including Yosef Klausner, P. Lahover, H. N. Shapira, Baruch Kurzweil, Shimon Halkin, Dov Sadan, Avraham Sha'anan, Eisig Silberschlag, Abraham Holz, and Gershon Shaked, argued about the question of the exact beginning of modern Hebrew literature. The various definitions of the new Hebrew literature of these scholars cannot explain why the literary productivity of the Jews of Babylon, as peripheral as it may be, was not incorporated into the history of modern Hebrew literature. The secular literature of the Babylonian Jews did not strive to undermine the tradition. It was not void of God's holiness as they strived for aesthetic achievements. The history of Hebrew literature should not account for the centers of Hebrew literature only (Italy and Holland from the 1720s until the 1770s; then Germany; Austria [Galicia] from the beginning of the nineteenth century until 1840; afterwards Poland, Lithuania and Ukraine until 1917; then Israel) but also for outlying areas, such as Babylon.

C. Jewish Education in Babylon

In Babylon, children could start attending Jewish day school at a very young age. By the end of the thirteenth century, Jewish education moved to private religious elementary schools ("heder"). In these schools, a teacher ("melammed") prepared four- to six-year-old pupils (mostly boys) to read the Bible and the prayer book ("Siddur"). The Hebrew letters were taught by pointing out the visual shape of a letter, for example, the *Heh* ה was described as "leg amputated." Then the students learned the vowels and were able to read the Pentateuch with the melody determined by the cantillation signs of pointed text. Older students read the Bible and could chant the Pentateuch. They read the weekly Portion of the Pentateuch and the corresponding parts from Prophets and Hagiographa.

The children learned to read applying the eight biblical tunes of the Jews of Babylon. The teaching of reading, understanding, and interpreting the Bible was a fundamental goal. The teachers accommodated the parents who requested that their children be taught the translation of the Bible to Judeo-Arabic.

There was a more advanced "heder," in which the *Gemara* was taught, that prepared the students for rabbinical schools. The teachers taught beautiful, fine penmanship, handwriting that escalated from fonts to words to sentences and then to writing business letters and other letters.

Some teachers had one or two assistants. Teachers were highly respected and maintained close relationships with the students' families. Underachieving students were punished for staying behind the class in their studies, for sloppy homework, and for school misconduct. On the other hand, students' efforts and accomplishments were recognized in various ways, including awards given to them by their teacher. Most of these awards were religious Hebrew books. Only a minority of students left school after three to four years.

In addition to private elementary religious school (private "heders"), there were public Jewish religious schools (general "Heder": "Talmud Torah" and "Yeshiva"). The first of them was established in Baghdad in 1832. It was for boys only, beginning at the age of four. Jewish communities in Babylon followed this system and established their own public schools (Yehuda, 1996, 9). The enrollment in the public school, including lunch, was free for those who could not afford it and, over time, became free for all the students. The school had twelve grades, beginning with classes in which the Hebrew alphabet was taught and ending with classes in which *Gemara* was taught. In each class there were fifty to sixty students.

In 1860, there were less than eight hundred pupils in the heder. In 1876, there were several thousand of them. The curriculum of the heder was eventually incorporated into the curriculum of the modernized Jewish schools.

In 1840, a rabbinical school, headed by the highly erudite Rabbi Abdallah Somekh, was established (Yeshivat Bet Zilkha). Students were prepared for admission into a special program, taught by a high caliber teacher, and only outstanding students of religious schools were admitted. About twenty years after its establishment, thirty rabbis taught in this rabbinical school. Rabbis, religious judges, other important community leaders, and ritual slaughterers graduated from Yeshivat Bet Zilkha.

A second Yeshiva was established in 1906. The public schools were gradually modernized and secular disciplines were increasingly included in their curriculum. The classroom space was enlarged. The curriculum included Bible study, Talmud, Arabic, and Hebrew. In 1886, the rabbis agreed to include foreign languages, such as French, as well as arithmetic. Music teachers organized student choirs.

In 1864, the first Alliance Israelite Universelle School was founded in Baghdad. Its curriculum contained Jewish religious studies and general studies, including Hebrew and foreign languages: Arabic, French, English, and Turkish. In time, more Alliance schools were established, and thousands of students were enrolled. The Jewish community objected to the Alliance representatives' attempt to change the Babylonian Jews' traditions and customs (see Yehuda, *Bateh*, 1996; and "Yehudeh," 1996; Stillman, 100-101) and to inculcate Western French education. As a result, over time, the Jewish community developed its own educational system, which was more progressive than any other Jewish educational system in the Middle East, and disengaged from Alliance.

At the end of the nineteenth century, enrollment in religious private and public Jewish schools decreased. New laws required that teachers become accredited, and parents wanted to provide progressive modern education for their children. Beginning in the twentieth century, the Jewish community founded schools following the public school curriculum, as well as Jewish religious studies, so that students could be admitted to public high schools.

At the beginning of the twentieth century, Babylonian Jewish communities started establishing modern schools that accommodated most of Babylon's Jewish students. By 1907, the Jewish community appointed a committee for Jewish schools, which established many new elementary, middle, and high schools, both private and public (Ben-Yaacob, 1979, 293).

In 1920, there were twelve Jewish schools in Babylon, and by 1936, there were seventeen of them. In 1920, 4,030 boys and 1,481 girls studied in the Jewish schools. Ben-Yaacob (ibid, 294-299) provided information about thirty-seven Jewish schools in Baghdad alone. Fifteen percent of Baghdad's university students were Jews in 1943.

The educational standards of the Jewish schools were high. Ninety percent of their students passed their high school graduation examinations. The students received medical services, physical education classes, and grants from the community.

In 1949 and 1950, there were 19,000 Jewish students in Babylon, one third of whom were female. Most of their teachers had higher education. In 1950, for example, approximately 120 Jews received their degrees in law, medicine, pharmaceutics, engineering, and calculus, and fifteen of them were women.

D. Hebrew Teaching and Hebrew Knowledge in Babylon

In this context, it is pertinent to look at the place of Hebrew in the curriculum of the Jewish schools. The roots of Jewish education were in Hebrew as taught from the Bible and other religious books. Therefore, knowledge of Hebrew was anchored to knowledge of these sources. Until 1912, teaching Hebrew was achieved by teaching the Bible. This explains, to a large extent, why Babylon's Hebrew poets used biblical allusions in a highly creative way that demonstrated their superb knowledge of biblical texts. It also explains why they could presume that their readers should be able to grasp these allusions without any need for an interpreter. Many Jews knew biblical verses by heart, and when they conversed in Judeo-Arabic, they used biblical verses and language and phrases from the Talmud and other Jewish sources.

Babylonian authors and readers were familiar with the vast traditional Jewish literature created over a period of more than 2,000 years. They knew the Bible, the Talmud, the Talmudic legends, the Midrashic commentaries, the Prayer books, medieval Hebrew poetry, and the poetry of the Enlightenment period. They also read contemporary Hebrew periodicals.

As a result, the authors expected the readers to be affected by the original phrase or even word, idea, story, condition, or feelings to which they alluded. While Western literature evoked traditional context without the walls of nations, Hebrew poets alluded to their own tradition, and their allusions were indivisible from it. Any translation of these works that ignores the allusions will alter and belittle the original.

Beginning in 1906, Midrash Talmud Torah began replacing the public heder. Its curriculum included general fields of study, particularly languages (English, Turkish, Arabic) and mathematics.

In 1912, Shelomo Salih Shelomo and Moshe Gorgy co-authored a Hebrew textbook (*Ha-Mathil*) for beginners, and in the same year, a Hebrew textbook (*Lekah Tov*) for advanced students was co-authored by Salim Yitshak Nissim and Yehezkel Haham Shemuel. In 1919, Dr. Rabbi Moshe Ventura wrote a book about teaching Hebrew in Hebrew. In 1927, Moshe Sofer and Ya'acov Tsion Mu'alim Nissim published a Hebrew book of fables that included a dictionary.

Hebrew was taught in all the Jewish educational institutes. Students studied the Bible, prayers, and translation of the Bible. In 1903, in Baghdad, Aharon Sason was known for teaching, reading, writing, and speaking in Hebrew. From 1917 through 1919, Dr. Rabbi Moshe Ventura taught Hebrew in Baghdad, trained tens of Hebrew teachers, and in 1919, published a Hebrew textbook (see Ventura, *Ivrit Be-Ivrit*, Hebrew in Hebrew), one of several Hebrew textbooks published in Baghdad from 1906 through 1927. From 1919 through 1935, Hebrew flourished in Babylon. In 1920, a Hebrew literary association was established in Baghdad that spread language and literature through Hebrew books.

In 1924, Aharon Sason established a Zionist Hebrew school (Pardes Ha-Yeladim) in Baghdad, in which he lectured in Hebrew on various subjects. The student body numbered 350. They had access to a Hebrew library, learned Hebrew language and literature, and acted in Hebrew plays (Cohen, 85-89). After the third grade, the students continued studying Hebrew through high school in the public Jewish community schools (Rahel Shahmun and Shammash).

The Hebrew teaching standards in Jewish schools were high. Nearly every child in Babylon understood Hebrew, and many of them could speak it. For one decade, beginning in 1925, the Jewish community invited teachers from Israel to teach Hebrew language, literature, and Jewish history, and they remained mainly in Baghdad. There were also local teachers of Hebrew. The teachers organized Zionist youth groups, producing the first Babylonian Jewish pioneers in Israel (Schayyik, 146). Textbooks were ordered from Israel as well (Ben-Yaacob, 1979, 301-302).

Sometimes the community leaders who were afraid that they might be charged with Zionism and Nationalism (ibid., 89-90) treated the teachers from Israel coldly. The first teacher from Israel in Baghdad was Moshe Sofer, who taught Hebrew in the school Rahel Shahmun, where he established a Hebrew library of 3,000 books, including modern Hebrew literature. And, within time, persecution against Zionists began. The Iraqi Ministry of Education prohibited the teaching of Hebrew and Jewish history in Jewish public schools, and the last teachers from Israel were deported in 1935. This year also marked the end of Zionist education in Jewish public schools. Religious studies were limited to few weekly hours of Bible studies (see ibid.).

Avraham Rozen, a poet and an educator, was another teacher sent from Israel to Baghdad. He taught (in Shammash) Bible, Hebrew language, and literature, including modern Hebrew poetry. At this time, a group of students organized a literary and sports association, whose members spoke amongst themselves only in Hebrew. The students presented Hebrew plays (of Dov Berkovich and Yisrael Dushman) and gathered to sing in Hebrew. Rozen encouraged the establishment of 'Ahi'ever, an association for spreading Hebrew books. In his publication (see Rozen), Rozen stated that knowledge of Hebrew in Baghdad was not less, and perhaps more, than knowledge of it in other Jewish communities. Almost every child knew Hebrew. The young Jewish people were sharp and energetic. There were Hebrew speakers of all ages. Jewish schools conducted parties in Hebrew. Young people subscribed to books and journals from Israel. Jewish students excelled and were recognized in public schools.

Zionism and Hebrew were interrelated. The Zionist activity from 1918 through 1935 was intensive and included the publications of Hebrew pamphlets. Zionist youth organizations also were founded. In 1947, the teacher Ezra Haddad, with the authorization of the government, published a book for Hebrew reading instruction and a book in Arabic for Bible instruction.

Among the Babylonian Jews there were those who subscribed to Hebrew publications mainly from Europe, but also from other countries, and ordered Hebrew books published in Europe and in Israel. Babylonian Jews also wrote for Hebrew periodicals (including *Ha-Havatselet, Ha-maggid, Doar Ha-Yom, Ha-Tsefira, Ha-Perah, Ha-Tsvi, Ha-Levanon*). Rabbi Shelomo Bekhor Hutsin from Baghdad (1843-1892) published many journalistic articles and also some poems. He was the representative for *Ha-Havatselet* (published in Jerusalem), *Ha-Levanon* (published in Jerusalem and Paris), *Ha-maggid* (Lyck), *Ha-Tsefira* (Warsaw), *Ha-Melits*, (Saint Petersburg), *Ha-Mevasser, Perah and Maggid Meshrim* (these three Hebrew periodicals were published in Calcutta). Jacob Obermeyer, an Austrian Jew who lived in Baghdad, (1869-1880, see Obermeyer) spoke of hundreds of Jews in Baghdad who read *Ha-Levanon* and *Ha-Maggid* and of many additional people in the community who knew these publications.

E. The Hebrew Press in Babylon

We did not know about Jews from Baghdad who authored books from the fourteenth century until the beginning of the eighteenth century. During this time, Jewish communities were destroyed, and manuscripts were lost due to calamities, plagues, and wars (Benayahu, 9-21). In the eighteenth century until the middle of the nineteenth century, the rabbis of Babylon printed their books in Constantinople. This is what the poet and Rabbi Ezra Habavli (see henceforth) did with the publications of his 1738 and 1742 books, and Rabbi Moshe Binyamin with his 1735 book (*Ma'aseh Rav*). Afterwards, the authors sent their books to Livorno.

Access to printing houses was difficult. There were authors of manuscripts who were modest and did not seek fame or recognition. In addition, there were highly knowledgeable teachers who were more interested in devoting their time to instructing students directly, rather than producing books. In addition to calamities, plagues, and wars, robberies were largely responsible for manuscripts not reaching printing houses. In the introduction to his book, Moshe Binyamin tells the reader that he sent a complete manuscript to print, but it never arrived due to a robbery. Of course, there were other manuscripts that were sent for printing but never reached their destinations (Ye'ari, *1940*, Vol. 2, 100).

In his book, Ye'ari lists (ibid., 106-159) more than four hundred Hebrew books published in Iraq. He then updated his list (Ye'ari, "Tosafot"), and Ben-Yaacob ("millu'aim") as well as other scholars added to it. The Babylonian Jewry Heritage Center owns about 250 different Hebrew books published in Iraq. Ya'acov Zamir (see Zamir) published the titles of nineteen books out of this collection that Ye'ari did not mention. Benayahu (27-28) mentions many more, stating that most of the Hebrew books published in Baghdad were liturgical textbooks, castigation books, folktales, and translations. Even after 1863, the year

Hebrew printing was established in Baghdad, authors sent their manuscripts to Livorno, where books could be produced in better printing quality, and to Constantinople.

Barukh Moshe Mizrahi established a printing house in Baghdad in 1863. Beginning that year, some of the Hebrew books authored in Baghdad were published there. Barukh Mizrahi published Hebrew books (Ye'ari, 106-107) and also his Hebrew journal *Ha-Dover* or *Dover Mesharim* (1863-1871). For some sixteen years, from 1866 through 1882, the printing house of Rahamim Ben Reuben Ben Mordekhai and his partners Moshe and Aharon Ptaya, published fifty-five books (Ye'ari, 107-117), some of which were reprints. Among the Hebrew books that were published were books of folktales and fables and various volumes of liturgical poetry. Just a few years after this printing house stopped publishing, there was no active Hebrew printing house in Baghdad. From 1888 through 1913, Rabbi Shelomo Bekhor Hutsin established a printing house where a total of more than seventy books of folktales, Jewish law, homiletical interpretations, liturgies, and prayers (Ye'ari, 117-131) were printed, first by him and then by his son. The books that were printed in this printing house included the first published manuscripts by rabbis from Iraq, prayer books and liturgies for the Jews of Iraq, and reprinted Hebrew books that were published in various places, such as Amsterdam, Vilna, and Berlin. Rabbi Shelomo Bekhor Hutsin (see Hakak, "Shelomo Bechor"; and Hakak, *Iggerot*) produced books with no printing errors and in a beautiful format. After Hutsin's death, his son Yehoshua continued this activity from 1894 until 1913.

In 1904, Ezra Dangur and his sons established a Hebrew printing house where they edited and printed about 150 Hebrew books (Ye'ari, 131-146). Dangur held high positions in the Jewish community, among them was Chief Rabbi of Baghdad (1923-1927). In the 1906 *Sefer Ha-Shirim* ("The Book of Poems"), he collected 415 liturgies that were known to the Jews of Iraq, many of them composed by Babylonian Jews of his generation or from previous generations. The themes of the liturgies were many and covered the entire events of the year. While some of the Hebrew printing houses did not attach their names to the book due to fear of the government, in this book Dangur specifies that it was printed with the permission of the Bureau of Education in Baghdad. The five issues of the periodical *Yeshurun* (that will be presented later in this book) were also printed in this printing house, as well as a collection of Hebrew songs and liturgical poems (*Shireh Rinnah,* 1906), a collection of Sabbath and circumcision songs (*Shireh Shabbat U-Milah*, 1906), many of which are sung today by Babylonian Jews, and a book of Jewish law. In this Hebrew printing house, Moshe Ventura's textbook *Ivrit Be-Ivrit* (Hebrew in Hebrew), was published in 1919, as was the highly treasured Jewish law volume of Yosef Hayyim (*Ben 'Ish Hai, 1912*).

While Dangur's printing house was active in 1922, Zion Ozer established another Hebrew printing house that published about thirty Hebrew books (Ye'ari, 148-150). Two years later, in 1924, Elisha Shohet launched an additional Hebrew printing house (Ye'ari, 150-157). He published various Hebrew poetry volumes, including the works of poets such as David Tsemah, Shelomo Salih Shelomo, Eliyahu Nahum, Menasheh Salman Shahrabani, Sason Yisrael, who will all be discussed in this book, along with other authors.

There were other, smaller Hebrew printing houses. Except for the first one, all the Hebrew printing houses mentioned here, that is, Rahamim and Ptaya active in 1866-1882; Hutsin active in 1888-1913; Dangur active in 1904-1936; Zion Ozer active in 1922-1927; and Elisha Shohet active in 1924-1937, published Hebrew books in years that overlapped the Hebrew publishing activity of one another. This may serve as one of the indicators as to the Babylonian Jews' demands for these books.

F. The Hebrew Creativity of Near Eastern Jews and the History of Modern Hebrew Literature

While I am not claiming that the poets presented here produced Hebrew poetry of higher aesthetic accomplishment than that of their contemporaries in Europe, I am suggesting that they should be recognized and made part of the history of Hebrew literature of their time. The exploration of Hebrew creativity in various countries has to continue, especially in the Near Eastern countries, where there has been considerable Hebrew culture that has been neglected. Until this is done, the mapping of Hebrew literature in modern times will be lacking.

The current accounting of Hebrew literature includes authors whose aesthetic achievement was not distinguished, the inclusion of which supports the presentation of the historical literary string. For example, not every chapter in the Hebrew enlightenment literature attests to high inventive and imaginative endeavor, yet that is important to Hebrew literary history. The claim that Jews in Near Eastern countries were, until a later stage, out of the dynamic processes of Western Jews does not do justice to the Jews from the Near East (Hakak, *Yerudim*, 28-29).

The important editor (of *Pe'amim* and more) Yitzhak Bezalel (see Bibliography Bezalel) is one of those who insisted that the Hebrew literature of Near Eastern Jews was not researched enough, that there are many manuscripts that have to be explored and many authors are unknown to us. We do not have a systematic presentation of the literature in any of these countries, as the need to research the literary activity in them was not acknowledged. As a result, the map of Hebrew literature is incomplete, as is the presentation of the Jews from the Middle East. This work focuses on one of these countries only.

The literary works discussed in this book are presented for their own merit, but also for substantiating the argument that there was ample secular Hebrew creativity in Middle Eastern countries. By doing this, Hebrew literature will receive its due and be canonized appropriately in history.

Part 1: Poetry

Chapter 1: Pathfinders and Explorers in the Eighteenth and Nineteenth Century Hebrew Poetry in Babylon

Modern Hebrew poetry began at the end of the eighteenth century as European Jews began to become part of the modern world. Although the Bible includes magnificent poetry, there were periods that were almost entirely lacking in Hebrew poetry, such as the Talmudic period (70-500). Hebrew poetry later reappeared in Byzantine Palestine (sixth to eighth centuries) and in Babylon (eighth to tenth centuries). Spain's "Golden Period" (tenth to fifteenth centuries) produced both religious and secular poetry. The Spanish Hebrew poetry adapted the conventions of Arabic poetry, which followed in Provence, Italy, and other places. However, the medieval Hebrew poets in central Europe wrote sacred poetry until the breakdown of the religious tradition in Central and Eastern Europe in the eighteenth and the nineteenth centuries, when the writing of secular poetry became predominant.

The Enlightenment movement, which began at the end of the eighteenth century, strove to enlighten the Jewish people, to modernize and reform their life, and to bring political and social emancipation. The Enlightenment period poets wrote in a style that lacked in vocabulary and flexibility. Within time, The Enlightenment movement had taken a romantic and nationalistic direction. The new nationalism found its expression in the Zionist movement. Hayyim Nahman Bialik (1873-1934) came to the poetic scene at the culmination of the Enlightenment, and modern Hebrew poetry began with him and his contemporaries. Words were invented, and the poets were free from the rhetoric and didactic inclinations of the Enlightenment poetry. In addition, new themes, language, and poetic techniques were introduced.

Babylonian secular poetry was influenced by biblical poetry, medieval Hebrew poetry, poems of the enlightenment period, and Bialik's generation. These various influences will be illustrated in the course of the presentation of the poems discussed in this book. The influence of medieval Hebrew poetry was particularly strong. At the beginning of the eleventh century, the center of Jewish learning moved from Babylon to Spain. Hebrew poets were influenced by Spain's Arabic poetry, embracing its form, meter, rhyme, themes, and content. During a period of 500 years, the Spanish Hebrew poets wrote thousands of poems about the aforementioned themes. From the twelfth to fourteenth centuries, the Babylonian poets were influenced by Spain's Hebrew poetry. The secular poetry that was written in Spain was a new phenomenon in Hebrew, because until that time only liturgies were written in Hebrew. There are no existing Hebrew liturgies or poetry from Babylon that were written after this period until the eighteenth century, due to calamities, such as floods and plagues, and also due to the absence of a local printing house. During the last 250 years in which the Jews lived in Babylon, there were many local Hebrew poets and liturgy authors (more than seventy). Many of them were influenced by Spanish Jewish poetry and by the well-known poets who were influenced by that poetry.

A selection of Babylonian Hebrew poetry written about various themes is featured in this chapter. The styles and contents of the poems, their dispositions, and the positions of their respective speakers and their audience are secular. These poets possessed a great knowledge of Jewish sources. They were rabbis and sages, and their poetry, although sometimes minuscule, was part of their intellectual and spiritual life.

I draw special attention to the publications of Ezra Habavli (1735, 1742) and suggest that castigating poems of this almost anonymous poet were among the most distinguished poetic accomplishments of Hebrew poetry in both the eighteenth and nineteenth centuries. His rich, imaginative style, his striking use of allusions, and his detailed ingenious images are some of the typical elements that make his poetry distinctly vibrant. By all criteria, his work clearly should be part of the Hebrew literature canon.

Further in this chapter, I present a jubilant, playful poem by Rabbi Moshe Hutsin (who died in 1810) that was written for Purim (a Jewish festival commemorating the deliverance of Jews in ancient Persia).

Saleh Matsliyah (who died in 1785) wrote many poems, and I will also introduce and illustrate their poignancy and their didactic mission. His son, Rabbi Nissim Matsliyah, published poems until 1816. There are also poems with elegant puns that are attributed to him and his father.

Rabbi Sason Ben-Mordekhai's (1747-1830) poems are about poetic and thematic issues and leave readers a poetic credo endorsing the frugal use of words and a belief in the educational mission of poetry. His "sweet" poetic cover draws the reader in by his usage of complex poetic devices, including notable poetic openings and closures, ingenious images, symbols, parables, homonyms, internal rhyming, repetitions, partaking of all the human senses in the poetic experience, and allusions. When the "sweet" cover unfolds, the reader encounters "bitter" reprimands and moralistic demands.

Rabbi Mordekhai Ben-Sason (who died in 1852), the son of Rabbi Sason Ben-Mordekai, demonstrates consciousness of poetic language, melodic aspects, and linguistic effects.

Rabbi Moshe Ptaya (1830-1905) presents a poem comprising meticulous structure, vigorous rhythm, and dramatic suspense until its closure with the good prevailing over the bad.

Rabbi Yosef Hayyim (1820-1911), one of the highest Jewish religious authorities of his time, was consumed by religious and national issues and the writing of liturgies.

Rabbi Sason Yisrael (1820-1911) wrote about the eternity of heaven and the mortality of man. In order to convey his messages, he employed rhetorical questions, creative images, a decisive discourse, allusions, and a dynamic poetic rhythm.

The translations in this book are verbal. They do not capture the rhyme, the meters, and the homonyms of the original Hebrew poems. The translations reflect the allusions used in the Hebrew texts, where the allusions are in harmony with the text. The translations are not a fair representation of the aesthetic poetic achievements of the original text.

◆ ◆ ◆

There are other poets who wrote secular Hebrew poetry in Babylon in the nineteenth century, such as (see Hakak, 2003, 71-80) Rabbi Moshe Ptaya (1830-1905), Rabbi Yosef Hayyim (1834-1909), who was the most prominent rabbi in Babylon during the last generations when the Jews lived there, and Rabbi Sason Yisrael (1820-1911). The learned Jews in Babylon knew Hebrew thoroughly and considered writing Hebrew poetry as part of their creativity. They wrote liturgies and poems with national themes, and they also wrote secular poetry. The division between the religious and the secular is often challenging, because the religious and moralistic aspects were always central to the thinking of these rabbis.

Rabbi Ezra Habavli: The Debate of Man and his Earth

Rabbi and poet Ezra Habavli, who lived in the first half of the eighteenth century in Babylon, was born to a well-learned and religious father. His book *Tokhehot Musar* ("Moral Reproof"), completed in 1731, was published in 1735, in Castaneda (Hakak, 2003, 45-49). In 1742, he published his book *Netivot Shalom* ("Peace Paths"), which included castigations, homilies, and biblical interpretations. (Ben-Yaacob, 1970, 227; 1979, 97).

The goal of Habavli's didactic poems is to guide his readers so that they live an ethical life and refrain from walking the wrong path. The book has seventeen castigations, a broad introduction, and a conclusion. The general structure of the castigation includes a brief opening in praise of the power of the specific castigation itself, presentation of the punishments the reader will face if he does not change his sinful way of life, then the poetic speaker demands that his admonished reader repents and describes the reward that a life of faith and ethics will bring him. Each one of the castigations focus on one issue, such as the importance of praying, the evil of slandering, the dangers in being envious, the sin of cursing, the harms in being arrogant, the harms of the addiction to food, and the harms of the addiction to alcohol. The book has 216 pages, and each one of the lines has two parts.

One of Habavli's castigations is a debate between man and Earth. This is not, of course, a Jewish theme but one that embraces all people. I will illustrate the poetic flair of this poet by a close reading of a part of this castigation. Habavli's style is intensive and powerful, his imagination is encapsulating and capturing, his soul is tempestuous, his arguments are poignant, and his rationales are touching. He powerfully defines the sorrow of human existence with his poetic strict scheme of rhythm and rhymes.

The opening of the poem (distich 1-9, a distich consists of two lines, the second of which ends with a rhyme) presents the topic and the subject matter. The first part is a monologue in which man talks to the Earth. In the second part (10-37) man is admonished by the Earth for being proud, unashamed, and ungrateful, and for ignoring his mortality. The poetic speaker intervenes again and describes the man's fury after listening to the Earth (38-40). He defends himself to the Earth (41-230), claiming that he treats it kindly, while the Earth itself is treacherous, cruel, revengeful, and destroys its inhabitants, eternally burying everyone in it. The poem's closure is man's prayer to stop the Earth from ruling man, to gather his people (the Jews), and a plea to the Earth to grant man the blessings of the land and to cease its curses (231-240).

In order for one to get a sense of the poem's form and content, I will now illustrate Habavli's poetics with some of the distiches. This is the beginning of the statement the Earth makes to man (10-16). A translation can hardly capture the beauty of the language in these distiches. In addition, the translation is subject to interpretation, because the Hebrew poem demands a careful reading and rich vocabulary in order to appreciate it. The homonyms and meter are lost in the translation, and while some distiches are easy to decipher, others are difficult. Here is the original Hebrew text:

בֶּן אָדָם אֵיךְ תְּהַלֵּךְ בְּיָד רָמָה
וְלֹא תִכָּלֵם מִלִּפְנֵי שׁוֹכֵן רוּמָה
מָחָר אֶת אִישׁוֹן עֵינֶיךָ תֹּאכַל הָרִמָּה
וְיִצְרְךָ הָרָע יִרְדֹּף אַחֲרֶיךָ עַד חָרְמָה
וְאַחֲרָיו תָּבוֹא אֵלֶיךָ הָאָרֶץ הַנְּשַׁמָּה
וּבַעֲפָרָהּ תַּדְאִיב מִגּוּפְךָ אֶת הַנְּשָׁמָה
תַּשְׁפִּיל מֵעָלֶיךָ אֶת גֹּבַהּ הַקּוֹמָה
וְלֹא תַשְׁאִיר לְךָ שְׁאֵרִית וּתְקוּמָה
הִיא וּשְׁתֵּי כַלּוֹתֶיהָ עִמָּהּ
וְתַשְׁחִיר פָּנֶיךָ לְנֶגֶד עַמָּהּ
אָכֵן הָסֵר מֵרֹאשְׁךָ אֶת מִצְנֶפֶת הָאֲדֻמָּה
וְאַל תִּתְוַכַּח בְּעַזּוּת פָּנֶיךָ עִם הָאֲדָמָה
אֲשֶׁר מִמֶּנָּה לֻקָּחְתָּ
וְלִבְגָדֶיךָ בִּבְשָׂמֶיהָ הִרְקַחְתָּ

Man, how are you walking with a high hand
And you are unashamed in front of Him who dwelleth on high
Tomorrow the worm will nibble the pupil of your eyes
And your evil will chase you even unto Hormah
And then will come to you the desolate land
And with its soil it will dissolve your soul in your body
It will lower your stature
And will not leave any residue or revival of you
She and her two daughters-in-law with her
And will insult you in front of its people
Behold, remove the red mitre off your head
And do not argue insolently with the earth
That out of it wast thou taken
And scented your clothes with its fragrances

The Earth wonders how it happened that man is walking proudly and unashamed ("with a high hand," Exodus 14:8) in front of God in heaven "who dwelleth on high" (Isaiah 33:5), while man's days on Earth are short, threatened by his own mortality, and he is punished for his evil inclination that will chase him to the bitter end. Then he will arrive to the country of desolation ("the land that was desolate," Ezekiel 36:34), and the destruction that will inflict suffering and pain on his soul ("...and chase you...even unto Hormah," Deuteronomy 1:44) will humiliate him and not leave any remnant of him. The Earth will inflict all of this on man while "her two daughters-in-law are together with her." In Ruth (1:6) we are told that Naomi "went forth out of the place where she was, and her two daughters-in-law with her." The biblical Naomi did so after the death of her husband and two sons, Mahlon and Khilion (names that semantically remind us of illness and death), when she heard that there was no hunger in the land any more. The Earth with three widows who experienced the death of their loved ones will inflict destruction on man. The desolate land will put man, who is walking with courage, with "a high hand," to shame. Man must remove the cap ("the mitre shall be removed," Ezekiel 21:31) that he wears with coquettishness, act humbly, and not treat the Earth with insolence. He must be grateful to the Earth ("for out of it wast thou taken," Genesis 3:19), as it is responsible for creating him, and for the scented clothes he wears with fragrances that grow upon it.

All the distiches (distich, "bayit") above the first line (delet) rhyme with the second line (soger). In addition, we find many internal rhymes in the lines due to grammatical suffixes, such as "'aenekha" (your eyes)-"'aharekha" (behind you). Most beautiful are the rich rhymes at the end of the lines as the poem is cautiously rhymed and rigorously metered. It does not have one rhyme throughout the poem. The biblical meter clearly impacts the poem. The number of words in the first line of the distich equals the number of words in the second line of the distich.

Here Habavli proves that he is a virtuoso of the Hebrew language. Like medieval Hebrew poets who employed an adroit variety of homonyms ("tsimmudim"), he too, employs homonyms and a fully inspired command of the language. In many distiches, the first and second lines end in homonyms. There are various kinds of homonyms in the poem, such as complete words, or homonyms with one different vowel. Some of these homonyms are "neshamma" (desolate)-"neshama" (soul), "'immah" (with it)-"ammah" (its people), "adumma" (red)-"adama" (Earth). These are homonyms that differ from each other by one vowel. We also find "shatahta"-"hittahta" (homonyms with one different letter), "Rama" (height)-"rumma" (high, "shokhen ruma" refers to God who "dwelleth on high," Isaiah 33:5)-"rima" (worm, especially in a grave), "koma" (stature)-"tekuma" (revival, recovery)-homonyms with one word that have an additional letter.

The two participants addressing each other in the second person dramatize the debate. The reason for the question posited by the Earth at the beginning (10)—how did it happen that man is walking proudly—is reinforced by pointing out the weakness of man and emphasizing the Earth's might. The Earth is powerful and active, and man is passive. The Earth will decrease man's height, will lower his stature, it "will blacken" his face (will mortify him), it will insult him, and it will dissolve his soul and his body.

I will present a portion (172-195) of man's response to the Earth:

בַּחֲרוֹנֵךְ תַּשְׁחִיתִי הַמְסֻלָּאִים וְהַיְקָרִים   וּבְתוֹךְ חוּצוֹתַיִךְ כֻּלָּם מְדֻקָּרִים
הַתִּינוֹקוֹת יָבוֹאוּ אֵלַיִךְ בַּחֲצִינִים   וְלֹא תַשְׁאִירִי הַפַּחוֹת וְהַקְּצִינִים
כֹּל חַכְמֵי לֵב וְהַיּוֹעֲצִים   תַּחַת בָּמוֹתֵךְ כַּיְתֵדוֹת נְעוּצִים
הַמְּלָכִים לַעֲבוֹדַת שְׂדוֹתַיִךְ נֶעֱבָדִים   וְאֶת עֲפָרֵךְ יְנַשְּׁקוּ כָּעֲבָדִים
הַפְּגָרִים רוֹחֲשִׁים בְּקִרְבֵּךְ כַּנְּדָלִים   וְלֹא תַשְׁאִירִי הַקְּטַנִּים וְהַגְּדוֹלִים
מִתְּלָאוֹתַיִךְ יִצְעֲקוּ הָאֲנָשִׁים וְהַנָּשִׁים   וּמִקִּלְלָתֵךְ הַקְּדוּמָה הֵמָּה נֶעֱנָשִׁים
תֹּאַר חֶמְדַּת הַחֲתָנִים וְהַכַּלּוֹת   תַּחַת כַּפּוֹת מַנְעָלַיִךְ כָּלוֹת
בִּמְקוֹם מִבְחוֹר בְּרוֹשָׁם   עָפָר יָשִׂימוּ בְּרֹאשָׁם
בִּמְקוֹם הַדְרַת יְקָרָם   יִבָשׁ כַּחֶרֶס מְקוֹרָם
בִּמְקוֹם תִּפְאֶרֶת כְּבוֹדָם   רִמָּתֵךְ תְּפַלַּח כְּבֵדָם

בִּמְקוֹם מִרְקַחַת רֵיחָם   חֲמָתֵךְ שׁוֹתָה רוּחָם
בִּמְקוֹם מֵי הַוְּרָדִים   הַנְּחָשִׁים בְּגוּפָם רוֹדִים
בִּמְקוֹם נְעִילַת הָעֲכָסִים   יִשְׁתּוּ אֶרֶס הָעֲכָסִים
בִּמְקוֹם שֶׁמֶן מִשְׁחָתָם   יִפְּלוּ בְּבוֹר שַׁחֲתָם
בִּמְקוֹם הַפְּאֵרִים וְהַקִּשּׁוּרִים   בְּצִירֵי דַלְתוֹתַיִךְ קְשׁוּרִים
בִּמְקוֹם הַנְּטִיפוֹת וְהָרְעָלוֹת   יִשְׁתּוּ כּוֹס הַתַּרְעֵלוֹת
חֶמְדַּת הַשְּׁבִיסִים וְהַשַּׂהֲרוֹנִים   כְּלוּאִים בְּתוֹךְ הַסַּהֲרוֹנִים
נִזְמֵי הָאַף וְהַטַּבָּעוֹת   בְּתוֹךְ עֲפָרֵךְ טְבוּעוֹת
בָּתֵּי הַנֶּפֶשׁ וְהַלְּחָשִׁים   הַנְּחָשִׁים עֲלֵיהֶם מִתְלַחֲשִׁים
בִּגְדֵי הַמִּטְפָּחוֹת וְהַמַּחֲלָצוֹת   תַּחַת אֲבָנַיִךְ מְחֻלָּצוֹת
לוֹבְשֵׁי הַחֲרִיטִים וְהַמַּעֲטָפוֹת   בְּתַכְרִיךְ בּוּז מְעֻטָּפוֹת
אַנְשֵׁי הַתַּעֲנוּג וְהַמְּנוּחָה   תְּכַלִּים בְּיָגוֹן וַאֲנָחָה

In your wrath you will destroy those compared with fine gold and the precious
And on your streets they all are stubbed
The babies will come to you suckling
And you will not spare the governors and the leaders
All the sagacious and the advisers
Are fixed like pegs under your grave-mounds
And the kings will be servants in your fields
And they will kiss your soil as slaves
The corpses rustle in you like centipedes
And you will not spare the little and the old ones
Because you afflict them men and women will scream
And they are punished because of your ancient curse
The beauty and grace of the bridegrooms and brides
Is wrecked under the trampling of your shoes
Instead of their tall cedars
They put earth on their heads
Istead of the glory of their preciousness
Their fountain will dry up as clay
Instead of the grandeur of their honour
A termite will slice their liver
Instead of the mixture of spices for their fragrance
Their soul drinks your rage
Instead of the rose water
The snakes rule their bodies
Instead of wearing the anklets
They will drink snakes poison
Instead of their anointing oil
They will fall in the pit of their grave
Instead of [wearing] the headtires
They are tied in your door hinges

Instead of the pendants and the evils
They will drink the cup of poison
The delight of the fillets and the crescents
Is locked in the dungeon
The nose- jewels and the rings
Are submerged in your soil
The chest jewelry and the whispers
The snakes hiss on them
The cloaks and the aprons
Are taken out and placed under your stones
Those who dress with girdles and matelets
Are rapped with shrouds of contempt
The people of pleasure and rest
You annihilate with sorrow and sighing
Your evil cleaves unto them
Their tongue cleaves to the roof of their mouth
And they will groan like the wounded
And will drink the cup of your dregs

The man argues that the Earth, in its anger, wreaks havoc on precious people ("the precious sons of Zion, comparable to fine gold," Lamentations 4:2) and that they are stubbed on its streets. Death does not spare babies, sages, or honorable people, who are "fixed like pegs" under the soil. This simile refers to how firmly they are stuck in the Earth and how their value is decreased. Kings, who were accustomed to many people conducting themselves as slaves in their presence, serve and work in the fields (Exodus 1:14-15) and kiss the soil of the earth like slaves. Kings and slaves, young and old, men and women, all have the same fate on Earth since the "ancient curse," "the original sin" of Adam and Eve. They will all become corpses and transform into insects, and the beauty of the brides and grooms will be destroyed by the shoes that trample on the earth. The tall and beautiful cedars (Second Kings 19:23) they used while alive are replaced by dirt. Glory will be replaced by dryness, by death, which is the punishment of Babylon ("and make her fountain dry," Jeremiah 41:36).

In some distiches, the poet presents contrasts between what people were when they were alive to what happened to them while on Earth. These distiches begin with the word "instead." The first line of every distich rhymes with the second line, and the use of homonyms ("tsimmudim") sharpens the contrast of the significance of the homonyms. These distiches are shorter than the previous, and in the following distiches, the rhythm is faster, only to stress the gap between life and death and to deplore Earth. The first line of nine distiches begins with "instead," which is followed by a description of the enjoyment, beauty and grandeur of life, and the delights that people indulged in while alive. The second line describes the suffering of these people and their ending in the depths of the Earth. When alive, they enjoyed life with all their senses. The magnitude of their enjoyment when they were alive is identical to the magnitude of their suffering in the bowels of the Earth. Instead of the mixture of their incenses ("reham"), their spirits ("ruham") drink the rage of the Earth, and instead of smelling and tasting rose ("veradim") extract, snakes tyrannize ("rodim") over their bodies now. Instead of their anointing ("mishhatam") oil that was so pleasant to touch and smell, they will fall into their grave ("shahat") pit. The spectacular nose jewels and rings ("tabba'ot") are now invisible, for they sank ("tevua'ot") into the soil. On the Earth, senses that were used for enjoying life were converted into other senses. Dead women, instead of wearing women's jewelry that is alluring to the eyes and has a ringing sound enjoyable to the ears—ankle-bands, anklets ("'akhasim")—now drink the poison of snakes ("'akhasim"). Instead of pendants in the shape of a drop ("netifot," see Isaiah 3:19) and instead of veils ("rea'lot"), they will drink poison ("tar'aelot"). Onomatopoeia is used when the whisper of the snakes is described: "...ha-lehashim ha-nehashim...mitlahashim" ("...the whispers...the snakes hiss at them").

Many of the objects described in the poem were mentioned in Isaiah (3:18-24). Isaiah described the daughters of Zion that walked haughtily while wearing expensive clothes and jewelry and their punishment. The detailed description provided this poet with the language for many of the jewels and ornaments he mentions. In this part of the poem, however, the punishment is not the consequence of a sin, but it applies to all human beings, and unlike the prophecy in Isaiah that addresses the salvation after the punishment, there is no salvation in the poem. "Their tongue cleaves to the roof of their mouth" alludes to Psalms (137:6), but portrays death.

In the last eight distiches quoted above, the poem portrays various images that further illustrate the past while people were alive and dwelled on the Earth, and then juxtaposed to the present, when they were inside the Earth (dead).

In the distiches that describe precious garments and jewelry, the first line describes these objects and the second line describes the destiny of those who possessed them. The fillets, women's hair ornaments in the shape of the sun and crescents, and women's jewelry in the shape of a half moon ("shevisim vesaharonim," Isaiah 3:18) are locked together with rings and the nose jewels in the prisons of the Earth ("saharonim," the spelling of the Hebrew words for half a moon and jails differ, but the pronunciation of these words does not). Snakes murmur on the women's chest jewelry ("bateh ha-nefesh") and on amulets (Isaiah 3:20, "the corselets, and the amulates") with their whisper ("ha-lehashim," see Isaiah 3:20). The rhymes and internal rhyme are onomatopoeic to the hiss of a snake: "...lehashim / ha-nehashim...mitlahashim." Cloaks and festive apron attire ("ha-mitpahot ve-ha-mahaletsot") are pressed and stretched under the stones ("mehulatsot"). The despising shrouds ("ma'tafot") of the earth now cover ("mea'utafot") the people who carried purses ("haritim") or had mantles and wore beautiful covers over their clothes' mantelets. The despising shrouds may remind us how "...Mordeckhai went forth from the presence of the king in royal apparel...and with a robe of fine linen" (Esther 8:15), especially since the sound of the description of his royal robe, "takhrikh buts," is close to the sound of "takhrikh buz," shrouds of contempt.

Isaiah (3:16) described the daughters of Zion and their punishment. They were haughty, walked with wanton eyes and made a tinkling ("tea'kasna") with their feet. This haughtiness was going to be punished by the Lord, who will "take away the bravery of their anklets, and the fillets, and the crescents; the pendants, and the bracelets, and the veils; the headtires, and the armlets, and the sashes, and the corselets, and the amulates; the rings, and the nose jewels; the aprons, and the mantelets, and the cloaks, and the girdles; and the gauze robes, and the fine linen, and the turbans, and the mantles" (ibid., 18-23). In our poem, the poetic speaker uses the detailed objects. However, this is done as a necessity, for the vocabulary does not draw with it the notion of sin and punishment. While in Isaiah, the punishment is limited to the sinner women, while in the poem, it is described as the destiny of any person. Whereas in Isaiah (4), the punishment ends and there is comfort at the end, it is not so in the poem. Those who experienced delight and relaxation will end up in anguish and a sigh. Dreadful things will cleave unto them (see Deuteronomy, 28:21, "The Lord will make the pestilence cleave unto thee"); their tongue will cleave to the roof of their mouth (Psalms 137:6; also 22:15). All of the people will end groaning as those who were slain in a battle and sucking the yeast cup that was designated as a punishment for the wicked ("for in the hand of the Lord there is a cup... Surely the dregs thereof, all the wicked of the earth shall drain them, and drink them," Psalms 75:9), the soil of the Earth grinds their flesh, and a worm will eat their liver.

In the first half of the eighteenth century, when Habavli wrote this poem, he did not hear Hebrew spoken, as Hebrew was a language of sanctity only. Habavli's poem is not a liturgy, as its theme is universal and its ideas are of interest to all mankind, regardless of their religion. In the Hebrew vocabulary that existed in his time, and particularly in biblical Hebrew, he could express each one of his fine ideas, playing the language as a virtuoso. Hebrew was a fire that burned in his heart, and he expressed himself without caring how many people would be able to read and understand what he wrote. He was persecuted and found shelter in his artistic creation. His language is highly sophisticated, and his creativity is extraordinary. The reader must read the poem slowly in order to comprehend it. Numerous effects flow from every line. The images are captivating, and the lyrical cogitation dwells on a theme that is close to the human heart. More than 270 years have passed since Habavli wrote his poem, and still every line in it speaks to us vividly and emotionally.

Many literary generations passed before any poet came close to matching the stature of Habavli as a writer of Hebrew poetry. Any accounting of the history of Hebrew literature without this giant would be lacking.

"A Man Must Get Tipsy": The Call of Rabbi Moshe Hutsin

When Babylonian Hebrew poetry was discussed, the issue most deliberated was the lack of secular poetry and the presence only of liturgies. Indeed, the Babylonian Jews had deep religious convictions, and although there are far more liturgies written by them than secular poetry, they did write secular poetry as well. Religious beliefs permeated their secular poetry, too, but these beliefs did not change the secular nature, themes, purposes, individualistic expressions, and the secular position of the poetic speakers.

Moshe Hutsin (who died in 1810) wrote liturgies that were popular among Jews in Babylon and in other near eastern countries. They were sung in public. Only twenty-four of his poems survived. His poem *Maher Be-Yom Purim Kuma* ("Hurry Up and Wake Up on the Purim Day," see Ben-Yaacob, 1970, 96: Hakak, 2003, 50-52) is clearly secular. Its content and rhythm are light and jubilant. The first letter of each one of the eleven stanzas joins in an acrostic composed of his name and of the word "hazak" (be strong). Each of the eleven stanzas is composed of four lines. The four lines of the first stanza rhyme with each other, and they also rhyme with all of the last lines of the other ten stanzas. In each of these ten stanzas, the first three lines rhyme with each other. The poem is written in one of the meters of medieval Hebrew poetry.

The poetic speaker addresses the reader in the second person singular. The tasks that the speaker suggests to the reader are humorous, as if he, the speaker, is drunk. He encourages the reader to drink wine on the day of Purim (the carnival festival celebrating the rescue of the Jews of Persia as recorded in the Book of Esther).

The use of the poem's allusions is part of its whimsical spirit. The reader is encouraged to sell his possessions, his ox and donkey and garment, in case he does not have enough money to buy a lot of wine. Sell his clothes? "If thou at all take thy neighbor's garment to pledge, thou shalt restore it unto him by that the sun goeth down; for that is his only covering, it is his garment for his skin; wherein shall he sleep? And it shall come to pass, when he crieth unto Me, that I will hear; for I am gracious" (Exodus 22:25-26). A creditor who took a garment as a pledge must return it so that the borrower will have it for the night. The idea that one should sell his garment to buy wine on Purim and get drunk is a mere humorous exaggeration that suits the poem's spirit.

The allusion here does not speak in earnest. To the contrary, its effect is humorous. One must get drunk to the level of the drunkenness of "Noah the husbandman," who "drank of the wine, and became drunk" (Genesis 9:21). Noah's nakedness ended up with the curse on Noah's son Canaan, who saw his father's nakedness. With blessings on Noah's sons, Shem and Japheth, who took a garment and went back and covered the nakedness of their father. If the reader listens to the poetic speaker, he will end up in a shameful situation, drunk and naked in front of his children, but he may not find a garment to cover him. Here again, the use of the allusion is mischievous and playful. The poet was a rabbi, and the reader was not really expected to interpret the speaker's suggestions literally.

The speaker further suggests, "He who has a headache should drink wine," knowing well that he alluded to the Erubin tractate (54: 2)—"he who has a headache should be engaged in the study of the Torah." Jesting goes far, and while God "woundeth, and His hands make whole" (Job 5:18), in this poem it is the wine that has the role of making one whole, "all the wounds are naught in the presence of wine" for the wine "will make whole of all the wounds." The biblical God is supportive, and "to him who hath no might He increaseth strength" (Isaiah 40:29), while in the poem's closure it is the wine, not God, that does so.

In one of his well-known liturgies that is sung nowadays, Moshe Hutsin used the biblical language of "to him who hath no might He increaseth strength" (Isaiah 40:29)—in a context and manner that is religious and somber: "Redeeming and Deliverer King / …to him who hath no might He increaseth strength / Who holds the weak hand of the poor ones." God, not wine, is the one who gives strength.

Wine plays the role of God in a poem written by a rabbi, which was truly amazing, albeit unorthodox. The speaker's position is of a drunken man, and he aggrandizes the wine and its effects as almighty. In eighteenth century Baghdad, it took a great deal of courageous poetic license to write in this way. It is obvious that Moshe Hutsin intended to write a secular poem, not a liturgy. The poetic speaker addresses the reader in the second person, as equal to equal, without any pretentious castigating position, and he importunes him to drink until he loses his clarity of mind. But even in this poem, the speaker does not forget to explain that one is traditionally required to do so during Purim.

Didactic Poetry: Rabbi Salih Matsliyah

Salih Matsliyah, appointed as a rabbi in Baghdad in 1773 (and died in 1785), was a famous cantor and highly respected authority in Jewish law, the legal part of Jewish traditional literature. His liturgies and his son's liturgies were published in prayer and poetry books. Forty of his liturgies and poems are well-known. In one of his poems, he writes "about the theme of advice" and encourages his readers to ask for their friends' advice, because listening to good advice results in success and pride. The advice is free, while those who give the advice paid a high price for the wisdom inherent in their advice:

תְּחִלַּת דְּבָרִים   עֲצַת הַחֲבֵרִים   שְׁאַל לְךָ וְתָרִים   לְרֹאשׁ כַּנְּשָׁרִים
קְחָה דוֹד בְּחִנָּם   וְהַצְלַח, וְהִנָּם   קְנָאוּם בְּהוֹנָם   וְדָמִים יְקָרִים

The initiate of everything
Is the advice of friends
Ask so that you will lift up
Your head as the eagles

Take it free, buddy
And succeed, and it was
Acquired with riches
And with a precious price

His instructive, moralizing poem is written in the metric system of Spain's Hebrew poetry. He talks to his reader in the second person and approaches him affectionately ("dod," beloved, buddy). The fact that the advice is complimentary contrasts with the high price the advisor paid for it. The outcome of listening to the advice is described by a simile; the person who takes the advice will elevate his head like the eagles.

In another poem, the poetic speakers' friends pose the question who is he collecting his riches for. His answer is that better his enemies will inherit the fruits of his toil than having to ask a friend to give him anything.

שְׁאָלוּנִי מְתֵי סוֹדִי אֲשֶׁר אֹהֵב   לְמִי אַתָּה מְאַסֵּף הוֹן וְרֹב זָהָב
כְּלֵילוֹת כָּל זְמַנְּךָ בָּרְחוּ כִצְבִי   וּמָה לְךָ עוֹד בְּקִבּוּץ הוֹן בְּעֹז רַהַב
עֲנִיתִים: טוֹב יְגִיעִי יִנְחֲלוּ אוֹיְבַי   וְלֹא אֹמַר לְאוֹהֲבִי אֲהוּבִי הַב

My beloved confidants asked me
Who are you collecting riches and lots of gold for
Your time flees like nights and like a deer
So what are you collecting riches vigorously and boastfully
I answered: Better that my enemies inherit my toil fruits
Than my saying to my buddy, give me pal

The fleeing of the days like a deer is, of course, a faded simile. While the question is presented in an indirect way, he shifts in the last distich to a directive, presenting his response to the question. The internal rhymes ("khitsvi"-"'ohavi"-"'ahuvi") enrich the poem's melodious aspect, and they are an addition to the rhymes at the end of each of the lines of the distiches.

Rabbi Nissim Matsliyah: Playful Poetry

Rabbi Nissim Matsliyah, the son of Rabbi Salih Matsliyah, was far more capable than his father as a poet. The last poem from his poetic legacy was written in 1816. Like his father, he also employed in his poems the metric system of Spain's Hebrew poetry. His poetic sophistication, detailed attention to the aesthetic aspects of his poetry, and his succinct language is demonstrated in the following poem:

אוֹיְבִי דִמָּה   לַעֲלוֹת כִּימָה   שָׁכַח רִמָּה   וְסוֹפוֹ שְׁאוֹל
לָבוּשׁ רִקְמוֹת   גָּבִישׁ רָאמוֹת   מַעֲלוֹת רָמוֹת   נַפְשׁוֹ לִשְׁאוֹל
אִם זֶה נִגְעַל   פְּרֹשׂ שֹׁעַל   דַּלְתֵי רוּם עַל   פָּנָיו נָעוּל
שָׂם עֹל צָרִי   עַל צַוָּארִי   אֶשְׁאַל צוּרִי   עֲדֵה נָא עֹל

My enemy imagined
That he will elevate to the Pleiades constellation
He forgot the grave worms
And that his end is Sheol [grave]

Dressed with embroidery
Crystal and coral
High achievements
His soul sought

He loathed
Spreading his hands [supplications]
The doors of heaven above
Are locked to him

He put the yoke of my enemy
On my neck
I will ask God
To remove my yoke.

The enemy forgot that while man can find his way to attain precious stones, he cannot find the way to wisdom: "No mention shall be made of coral or of crystal; yea, the price of wisdom is above rubies" (Job 28:18). Thus, wearing precious stones is not evidence of possessing wisdom. The enemy that employed coquetry and relied on his materialistic possessions was sure of himself and loathed ("nig'al") spreading his hands ("peros shoal" with supplication). Therefore, his prayer will not be heard. The word "nig'al," translated above as "was loathed," is ambiguous; it can also mean "was cleansed." Applying its second meaning, the idea is that even if the enemy tries to purify himself of his attitude and conduct, the doors of heaven will be locked in front of him, because he is the one who put the repression yoke on the neck of the poetic speaker, who asked God ("tsuri") to take his yoke off ("'adeh," Proverbs, 25: 20) him. The first three parts of each quatrain (four-part) distich rhyme with each other. The rhyme of the first three parts changes from one distich to another, while the fourth parts of the distiches rhyme with each other. This rich rhyming is further enriched by homonyms ("tsimmudim"), such as "she'aol," meaning both a grave and to ask; "ramot," meaning both a precious stone and high. The close sounds of other words, such as "tsari" ("my enemy"), "tsavari" ("my neck"), and "tsuri" ("my God"), draws further attention to the poem's message. In addition, biblical allusions are employed in clever methods.

The rhythm of the poem is lively. The ambiguity of the third distich enhances the poem. The heights the enemy imagined in ascending to the stars are contrasted with the expected descent to the grave (also abyss). Precious stones worn boastfully are contrasted with the worms that will be in the grave. Putting the yoke around the speaker's neck triggers the prayer to remove the yoke. Man's days on Earth are short, regardless of what he aspires to.

There are also poems that are attributed to both Rabbi Salih Matsliyah and Rabbi Nissim Matsliyah, although each man's contributions to these poems are unknown. These poems are friendly castigations, which remain friendly even when they express sharp chastisement and hard complaints against "time" ("Atabba," poems of complaint, reproaching a friend, influenced by Bedouin poetry and melodies).

I will demonstrate the poetic sophistication of these poems by one string:

אָבוֹא שַׁעֲרֵי תְפִלָּתְךָ מְכֻתָּר
וְלִישׁוּעָה אֱהִי תָמִיד מְכֻתָּר
רְאֵה אוֹיְבַי לְעַבְדְּךָ הִמְכוּ, תַּר-
אֵינִי נִפְלָם וְשָׁכְבָם בַּעֲצִיבָה

I will come to your prayer gates crowned
And will always have the anticipation for your salvation
See how my enemies humiliated your slave
You will show me their fallen and laying in agony.

This is one of the eleven strings that constitute the poem. All the strings begin with the words "I will come to your prayer gates." The heart of the poem is the word "mekhuttar" that appears at the end of each poetic line and changes its meaning in each of them. The poetic speaker will come to the prayer gates of Jerusalem with his phylacteries like a crown on his head ("mekhuttar"). He will always be surrounded by ("mekhuttar"), the anticipation for salvation. In the third line, two words create the sound of "mekhuttar." The poetic speaker addresses God in the second person and asks him to see how the poetic speaker's enemies lowered and humiliated ("himkhu") him, and he then asks God to show him these enemies in their agony and fall. This time, the word "mekhuttar" is the outcome of the combination of the word "himkhu" ("humiliated") and the first syllable of the word "tara'eni" ("you will show me"). The fact that these first three lines rhyme, creates a melodious expectation for the reappearance of the rhyme, and its absence holds a surprise. The fact that all the last lines of all the eleven strings rhyme creates another melodious anticipation and rhyme pattern.

Rabbi Sason Ben-Mordekhai: "I am Sason a Small Minded and Short Tongued Man"

Rabbi Sason Ben-Mordekhai (1747-1830) authored many books, six of which were published and included poetry. We know of eight manuscripts that he wrote and did not publish and of other manuscripts that were burned (Ben-Yaacob, 1970, 252; 1979, 130-133). Sason Ben-Mordekhai was a rabbi, cantor, homilist, and a mystic (Kabbalist). In addition, he was in charge of marriage certificates and marriage ceremonies. He was also an artist and drew the Jerusalem Temple on a curtain in front of the Ark of the Covenant (parokhet) in a synagogue. His grandfather was the president of the Jewish community of Baghdad. More than 130 liturgies that he wrote remain with us today. Most of these are moralistic poems that were published in Hebrew prayer and poetry books in Middle Eastern countries. Benayahu (28) praises the quality of his work and his influence on other religious authorities of his time.

In 1796, Rabbi Sason Ben-Mordekhai completed his book *Kol Sason* (Livorno, 1856; Baghdad, 1891; Jerusalem, 1963). In its subtitle, the book is defined as reproachful and based on a fable and its moral. The title of the book is ambiguous: The author's first name is Sason, and the title refers to the fact that this book is his voice ("kol"). However, it also refers to "the voice of mirth and the voice of gladness" ("kol sason ve-kol simha," Jeremiah 7:24, also 16:9; 25:10, 33:11) that is sung in weddings. The first poem is also a motto poem. This poem attests to the fact that the poet considered writing a poem to be an intellectual creative process, a commitment to specific poetic standards, and an activity with a consciousness of poetic devices by which the poet reaches the hearts of his readers. It was not enough that the poem had a moralistic message. However, the poet also appears as a poetic speaker with clear poetics.

רְאוּ סֵפֶר בְּתוֹכְחַת שִׁיר מְגֻלָּה   וּמוּסָרִים מְאִירִים בָּאֲפֵלָה
עֲלֵי מִדּוֹת גְּעוּלוֹת וַחֲמוּדוֹת   לְשׁוֹן קָצָר וּבָאֵיכוּת גְּדוֹלָה
וְהַמָּשָׁל לְכָל מִדָּה בְּצִדָּהּ   לְהָעִיר לֵב, לְהוֹרוֹת אֶת שְׁבִילָהּ
וְשִׁיר חִבַּר, עֲלֵי מָשָׁל יְדֻבַּר   כְּמוֹ תֵבָה וּבְמַנְעוּל נְעוּלָה
לְאֵיכוּתִי וְלַאֲשֶׁר כְּמוּתִי   עֲשִׂיתִיהוּ לְתַקֵּן הַמְּסִלָּה
וְהוּא מִנְחָה לְיוֹרֵד לֹא לְעוֹלֶה   וּמִמֶּנָּה כְּמוֹ מַעֲשֵׂר וְחַלָּה
אֲנִי שָׂשׂוֹן קְצַר שֵׂכֶל וְלָשׁוֹן   בְּלֹא דָבָר וְמַעֲנֶה וּמִלָּה
בְּנוֹ לְמָרְדְּכַי מֹשֶׁה יְצ״ו לוֹ   מְאוֹר שֵׂכֶל וְלֵב מֵבִין וְחֶמְלָה
וְהוּא נִשְׁלַם בְּיֶרַח זִיו וּבִשְׁנַת   שָׂשׂוֹן שִׂמְחָה וְצָהֳלָה וְגִילָה

Look at the book with its opened poetic rebuke
And castigations that light the darkness
About graceful virtues and appalling vices
A concise language and a high quality
And the fable for each virtue
To awaken the heart and direct it to the virtuous path

And a poem about a fable was composed
Like a chest locked with a padlock
For a man of my qualities and those who are like me
I composed it to repair the path
It is an offering to he who ascends, not descends
And like a tithe and Hallah [bread]
I am Sason, small-minded and a short-tongued man
Empty handed without a response and a word
The son of Mordekhai Moshe may God protect him and preserve him
Who was a light to the mind and had an understanding heart and compassion
And it was completed in June in
A year of joy merriment and mirth [1796].

The poetic speaker establishes a personal communication with the readers by addressing them in the second person plural in the distich's first line: "Look at the book with its opened poetic rebuke." The allusion explains why it is better to present an uncovered rebuke than a hidden one: "Better is open rebuke, than love that is hidden" (Proverbs 27:5). An open rebuke can bring a person back to a good way of life. The poetic speaker established that his castigation is not veiled and that its goal is to light the road for the person walking in darkness. His poetry is expressed in "a concise language and a high quality." He will explain the virtues by fables in order "to awaken the heart and direct to the virtuous path." The poem's goal is "to repair the path" of people. The poem is "an offering to he who ascends, not descends," and it is an offer for a person to rise up and better his ways.

In this motto poem, the poet presents his poetic credo and immediately uses language that clears him from any claim of being boastful. He declares that he is "small- minded and a short-tongued man," the grandson of Mordekhai Moshe, who was a light to the mind and possessed mercy and an understanding heart. Here the poetic speaker becomes one with the biographical poet and portrays in a few words his grandfather, Moshe Mordekhai Shindukh, "who was a light to the mind and had an understanding heart and compassion," and was the president of Baghdad's Jewish community. The exemplary person is presented in the poem as one who has high intellect, understanding, compassion, and the ability to influence.

The poem's opening volume is a presentation of its themes and poetics. It focuses on morals and virtues, contains open rebukes, and it is an offering to the reader, who can benefit from it. The poetic speaker believes in conciseness. The fable is a device to awaken the hearts and gives the pleasure of deciphering it. As for virtues, intellect and compassion must be combined.

The fact that the poem is instructive does not imply that its author ignored its aesthetic aspects. The poem has a musical effect due to the many rhymes, not only those at the end of the second line of the distiches, but also the internal rhymes that appear unexpectedly and have melodic and semantic roles. Here we find "musarim me'airim" ("shining [illuminating] morals"), "middot ge'aulot ve-hamudot" ("fine virtues and vices"), and in an awe striking language due to its sounds and rhyme he writes: "Ani Sason ketsar sekhel ve-lashon" ("I am Sason, short-minded and short-tongued"). The appearance of the "s" in the original Hebrew version three times and then "sh" all within a five-word line and the internal rhyme ("Sason"-"lashon") are musical. The poet's creativity contrasts his humble statement.

One is tempted to demonstrate more and more the poetic richness of this Hebrew poet from Baghdad who died more than 170 years ago. The following poem, containing one of the meters of medieval Hebrew poetry, is part of the volume *Kol Sason*. It cautions the reader about where his love of pleasures might take him:

אַהֲבַת תַּעֲנוּג נֶפֶשׁ עֲרֵבָה   וְרָעָתָהּ מְאֹד גְּדֹלָה וְרַבָּה
וְדִמְיוֹנָהּ כְּמוֹ יוֹרְדֵי סְפִינָה   בְּתוֹךְ יַמִּים וְתָעוּ הַנְּתִיבָה
וְהֵם תּוֹעִים וְגַם נָדִים וְנָעִים   וְרָאוּ אִי בְּתוֹךְ הַיָּם רְחָבָה
נְטוּעִים בָּהּ דְּשָׁאִים עִם זְרָעִים   וּמַעֲדַנִּים עִם עֲצֵי תְנוּבָה
וְשׁוֹשַׁנִּים בְּרֹב מִינִים מְשֻׁנִּים   וְהָרֵיחַ לְהַנֶּפֶשׁ מְשִׁיבָה
וְצֵל נָאֶה אֲשֶׁר יֶעֱרַב לְרוֹאֶה   וּמַיִם הַמְּתוּקִים הֵם סְבִיבָה
וְעֵת רָאוּ מְאֹד תָּמְהוּ וְנָשְׂאוּ   וְיָרְדוּ וּבָאוּ תוֹךְ רְחוֹבָהּ
וְשָׁם רָעוּ וְגַם אָכְלוּ וְשָׂבְעוּ   וְסוֹף נָעוּ וְיָצְאוּ חִישׁ לְעָזְבָהּ
וְנִשְׁאַר אִישׁ אֲשֶׁר הֶחְפִּיר וְהִבְאִישׁ   וְלֹא יָצָא וְשָׁכַב מַעֲצֵבָה
לְהָאִי בָּא זְמַן הַקֹּר וְשָׁבָה   וְהָיְתָה לְבָעֵר וַחֲרֵבָה
וְסָר צִלָּהּ וְגַם פִּרְיָהּ וְהִלָּהּ   וְנִשְׁאֲרָ[ה] כְּמִדְבָּר וַעֲרָבָה
וְקֶרַח לֵיל וְחֹרֶב יוֹם אֲכָלוּ   וְנַפְשׁוֹ הִיא צְמֵאָה גַּם רְעֵבָה
וְלֹא רָאָה לְיַלְדֵי יוֹם וּבָאָה   תְלָאָתוֹ בְּלִי שִׁעוּר וְקִצְבָּה
רְאוֹת עַיִן וְחֶמְדַּת לֵב כְּאַיִן   וּמַה טּוֹבָה רְאוּת הַלֵּב לְהַבָּא

The love of pleasure is sweet
But its evil is awfully grave
It resembles voyagers
At the seas who lost their way
And they are lost and are fugitives and also wanderers
And they saw a spacious island
Grass and seeds are planted in it
And delicacies with fruit trees
And roses of many distinctive kinds
With invigorating fragrance
And a lovely shade delightful to the observer
And sweet water around
And when they saw it they were amazed and carried [their belongings]
And came down and went to its streets
And there they wandered and ate and were satiated
And then they quickly moved out and left

And one man who behaved shamefully and vilely remained
And he did not leave but laid down in sorrow
The winter came to the island and it again
Became eaten up and ruined
And its shade and fruits and praiseworthiness was vanished
And it became like a desert and wilderness
And night frost and day drought consumed it
And his soul was thirsty and hungry
And he did not foresee the turbulence [the sons of days] and faced
Innumerable and incessant hardships
The eye vision and the heart coveting are naught
But how good is the heart vision from that time on.

The poem opens with a generalization: "The love of pleasure is sweet / but its evil is awfully grave." The reader is then (distiches 2-13) presented with a tale that illustrates the opinion expressed in the first distich; lost voyagers found a magnificent island, and they rejuvenated on the island and then continued their voyage. Only one passenger did not foresee the future and remained on the island. When the winter came, he was hungry, thirsty, and lonely. The moral is presented in the last distich (14): One should not pursue what his eyes covet but should pursue what his thoughts tell him.

The first distich opens the poem with articulation and grandeur. Its two lines rhyme with each other, and it contains only one idea. The many internal rhymes (distiches 3-5) emphasize the wandering of the lost voyagers on the one hand and the splendor of the island on the other hand. Other distiches (6-8) also stand out in their internal rhymes. All the senses participate in the description of the island: vision (trees, grass, etc.), taste (sweet water), smell (roses), and touch. Intensive rhyming calls our attention to the one passenger who did not conform to the conduct of the voyagers and stayed on the island: (8-9: "hish," quickly; "'ish," a man; "hiv'aish," behaved vilely, also stunk, became malodorous). While all passengers but him left the island in a hurry, he did not leave and lay down in sorrow (Isaiah 50:11). The island no longer had shade, fruit, sweet water, or any type of food. The paradise island turned into a desert, and it was not praiseworthy anymore (distich 11, see Leviticus 19:24). Enjoyment of pleasures should be temporary, and a person who makes it a way of life will endure troubles.

The frequent use of multiple internal rhymes impacts the rhythm, repeatedly surprises the reader, and creates sounds that together with the significance of the words highlight ideas, emotions, and contrasts. The meter, ambiance, syntactical tensions, repetitions, and tone, together with the internal rhymes, define the rhythm. Within the medieval poetic scheme that the poet strictly follows, he finds creative ways of enriching his style, therefore surprising the reader and forming a distinctive poem.

The following poem (Hakak, 2003, 66) represents the poet's creative and playful mastery of the Hebrew language, while the word "khos" is a homonym that appears in seven different meanings:

מֵאָה בְּרָכוֹת תַּחֲשֹׁב הֵיטֵב וְכוֹס
תִּרְוֶה בְּיֵין רֶקַח בְּמִזְרָקִים וְכוֹס
קוּמָה חֲגֹר חֶרֶב, כְּבֹשׁ יִצְרְךָ וְכוֹס
דִּבְרֵי זְמִירוֹת אֵל הֵיטֵב הַדֵּק וְכוֹס
כָּל מַעֲשֶׂיךָ יִהְיוּ לַשֵּׁם וְכוֹס
דַּע לְךָ אֲשֶׁר אִם תִּתְאַוֶּה עֵינְךָ בְּכוֹס
דִּינֵי אֱלֹהִים לְךָ וּמִסְפָּרָם כְּכוֹס

Bless one hundred blessings a day and count them well
Be satiated of spiced wine from big cups and a glass
Rise wear your sword and conquer and slaughter your evil inclination
Distinctly express praises of God
Do all your deeds secretly for the sake of God
Know that if he covets a woman
Eighty-six of God's laws would apply and their number is eighty- six.

The poetic speaker addresses the reader in these lines. In the first line, "kos" means count (Exodus 12, 4). In the second line, "kos" means a glass. In the third line, "kos" means, as in Aramaic, slaughter (Psalms 16:5). In the fourth line, "kos" means cut, express decisively. In the fifth line, "kos" means cover. In the sixth line, "kos" means a woman, in this case a strange woman. In the seventh line, "kos" is eighty-six in numerology. The word Elohim (God) is eighty-six in numerology.

The reader's role in deciphering the meaning is substantial and is the reader's pleasure as an intellectual participant in the interpretation. The repetitious words at the end of all lines are melodic. In the second reading of the poem, the reader expects the word "kos" at the end of every line, but only its meaning is transformed. The poem is like a mysterious brainteaser in which both the reader and the poet share the same spiritual and linguistic background. Needless to say, this playfulness does not serve itself, but for this poet, it is important that his poem is edifying. The ideal reader of the poet is someone who is capable of deciphering the seven meanings of the same word.

One may conclude that the poem's didactic aspects do not imply neglecting their poetic, aesthetic aspects. These poems are challenging, and immense attention is devoted to poetic devices. At the same time, the poem is instructive, steering, reprimanding, and forewarning.

Rabbi Mordekhai Ben-Sason: His Pals Disappointed Him

Rabbi Mordekhai Ben-Sason, the son of Rabbi Sason Ben-Mordekhai, was born in the second half of the eighteenth century and died in 1852. He wrote a book about prayers according to Baghdad customs. Ben-Yaacob (*Shira*, 271-278) published his poems for the first time. He wrote poems of complaint (*'Atabba*, see above). Each stanza in his poems can be valued as a single poetic unit and they also demonstrate the poetics and thematic elements of his poetry (see Hakak, 2003, 70; Ben-Yaacob, ibid.):

וְיִשְׁתּוֹמֵם לְבָבִי בִּי עֲלֵי אָח
אִשֶׁה הִבְעִיר לְתוֹךְ קִרְבִּי עֲלֵי אֶח
וּבְהֵאָנְחִי יֹאמַר הֶאָח עֲלֵי אָח
וְנַפְשִׁי אוֹמְרָה גַּם זוֹ לְטוֹבָה

My heart is astonished about a brother
Who ignited a fire within me
And when I moaned he says unto me: "Aha!"
And my soul says, this is for the good.

In four short lines, the word "ah" is used four times, and the words play by the homonyms is the strongest characteristic here: "Ah" is a brother, close relative, a fireplace, coal-pan, a sound of moaning in pain, and a shout meaning "Hurrah! Aha!"

The speaker, however, thought that whatever happened was for the best, for reasons that the reader may consider, such as the value of the learning experience. The homonyms give prominence to make the main idea.

A similar idea is found in the following language (see ibid.):

סְבָבוּנִי אֵלִי עֲדַת מְרֵעִים
וְהֵם נִרְאִים כְּאוֹהֲבִים וְרֵעִים
וּבְהָצֵר לִי בִּתְרוּעָה הֵם מְרִיעִים
וְשָׁמְרֵנִי מִידֵי עוֹזֵר עִמּוֹ אֵיבָה

A group of friends surrounded me
And they seem loving and friendly
And when I was in trouble, they burst into shouts of joy
And shield me from a hostile helper.

The dominating word is "mereaim." In the first line, it means a group of friends, in the second, it means loving and friendly, and in the third, shouts of joy. The first three lines of each stanza rhyme with each other, and the fourth line does not rhyme with these lines. This way, the last lines craft a special attention (the last lines of the stanza rhyme with each other).

In Rabbi Mordekhai Ben-Sason's poetry, emphasis is placed on the musical playfulness of the language, on challenging the reader in deciphering the meaning, and on a message.

Rabbi Sason Yisrael Gives Advice: "For Who will You Collect Silver and Gold?"

Rabbi Sason Yisrael (1820-1911, see Ben-Yaacob, 1970, 348-362; 1979, 201) served as the Acting Chief Rabbi (Hakham Bashi) in Baghdad, but he left his position and became a Jewish studies teacher in the Alliance school in Baghdad. Some of his fifty-eight poems and liturgies that are known to us were published by his son in the book *Shireh Sason* ("Sason's Poems," 1939, Baghdad).

The following poem is typical of this poet's moralistic poetry:

שָׁאַלְתִּי אֶת אוֹהֵב כֶּסֶף וְכוֹסֵף   לְמִי תֶּאְסֹף זָהָב וְרֹב פְּנִינִים
הַתְדַמֶּה לִחְיוֹת לָעַד וְכִימֵי   שְׁמֵי מָרוֹם כֵּן עוֹד רַבּוֹת בְּשָׁנִים
הֲלֹא פֶּתַע וְכִמְעַט קָט וְתָעוּף   בְּלִי אֵבֶר לְעָמְקֵי הָאַשְׁמַנִּים
זְכֹר קֶדֶם אֲשֶׁר חָלְפוּ וְעָבְרוּ   אִישֵׁי רַהַב לְבוּשֵׁי הוֹד וְשָׁנִים
וְאָבַד כָּל זֵכֶר לָמוֹ וְנִשְׁכַּח   וְהִנָּם זֶה בְּדֵי שְׁאוֹל טְמוּנִים
וְלֹא הוֹעִיל הוֹן רַב וְזָהָב   בְּיוֹם עֶבְרָה וְחִצֵּי צַר שְׁנוּנִים

I asked a man with passion and love for money
Who do you stack gold and pearls for?
Do you imagine that you live forever and your years
Are like the years of the high sky?
Behold suddenly and swiftly you will fly
Without wings to the bottom of the dark graves
Remember old days that passed and were left behind
Boastful men dressed glamorously with silk
Any memory of them was lost and forgotten
And they are buried at the heart of the underworld
And great riches and gold profit not
In the day of wrath and of pointed enemy arrows.

The poem alludes to Ecclesiastes (5:9): "He that loveth silver shall not be satisfied with silver." The poem's rhetorical questions lead man to recognize that he is mortal, his wealth is useless in a day of wrath, and he soon will be "in dark places like the dead" (Isaiah 59:10). The reader remembers, "riches profit not in the day of wrath; but righteousness delivereth from death" (Proverbs 11:4). Wealth will not save a person facing an enemy "whose arrows are sharp" (Isaiah 5:28).

The poem is written with meter and rhymes, each distich consists of two lines, all the second lines rhyme with each other, and the rhyme links the whole poem. Each line has eleven vowels. The opening distich has a rich sound effect: "...kesef [silver] ve-khosef [and loves] / ...teaesof [stack]." The passion for money is somewhat detailed—silver, gold, and pearls. Eternity belongs to heaven, man is mortal, and the sky is high. When the wingless man flies, however, he goes to the bottom of the graves. Boastfulness and glamour end in the darkness of earth.

Chapter 2: Four Poets of Babylonian Origin

The poets Shaul Yosef, Rabbi Saliman Mani, Rabbi Avraham Barukh Mani, and Rabbi Ezekiel Hai Albeg were born in Babylon and emigrated from there.

Shaul Ben Abdallah Yosef (1849-1906) was born in Baghdad, and he emigrated from Babylon in 1868. He was a poet who emulated the style and themes of Spanish Hebrew poetry. His poetic style is rich, his knowledge of the Bible and of Spanish Hebrew poetry is meticulous, and his imagery is intense.

Rabbi Saliman Mani (1850-1924) immigrated with his family to Israel during his childhood. He held important rabbinical positions in Israel and wrote Hebrew poetry, stories, and fables.

Rabbi Saliman Mani and his brother, Rabbi Avraham Barukh Mani, were pioneers of Babylonian Jewish modern Hebrew literature, and both wrote poems expressing personal experiences. Saliman Mani's poetry employed rhetorical questions, puns, biblical and medieval Hebrew poetry contents and poetics, and original similes and metaphors. In addition, he demonstrated linguistic sensitivity to poetic sounds and syntax.

Rabbi Avraham Barukh Mani's (1854-1882) short life story reminds us of the short life story of the Hebrew poet Mikha Yosef Levensohn, who also died in his youth and left us beguiling lyrical poetry.

Rabbi Ezekiel Hai Albeg (Babylon, 1910-U.S., 1995) migrated from Babylon to Israel in 1925 and from Israel to the United States in 1933. He lived first in New York and then in Los Angeles. In Israel, he studied at a Talmudic college (Yeshiva). Albeg published eight books. Many of his poems were liturgies. In America, he was a proofreader of Hebrew books and a cantor. He wrote a play about a Jewish Babylonian wedding, he was an editor and a publisher of Jewish prayer books, and he was recorded reading the Torah (Ben-Yaacob *Introduction to Albeg's Divan*, 6-15).

The fact that these poets were born in Babylon clearly impacted their poetry in various ways related to both contents and forms. They all share a thorough knowledge of Jewish sources and have deep religious feelings. They knew medieval Hebrew poetry and emulated it (see below the poem of Shaul Yosef about this subject) to one degree or another. Some of their poems are set in Babylon. The Arab world was not strange to them. Shaul Yosef proudly claimed his understanding of it and its literature. Rabbi Saliman Mani wrote a poem about a beautiful Arab woman, and Albeg wrote poems of adoration about the Tigris River's beauty and a poem welcoming Shabbat in Baghdad.

Shaul Yosef: An Enlightened Poet

Shaul Yosef (1849-1906) was born in Baghdad to parents of noble lineage. He had both a traditional Jewish education in a religious school (Talmud Torah) and a secular education (in Alliance). In 1968, he went to Bombay where he continued his education, married, and had four children. In 1883, he went with his family to Hong Kong where he was a businessman until his death in a shooting accident. His friend, Z. S. Gabai, published a brief biography about Shaul Yosef (Abulafia, I-IV). He was a religious man, known for his strong memory, speaking abilities, and his knowledge of the Old and New Testament and the Koran. David Yelin published a detailed article about Shaul Yosef (ibid., Vol. 2, XLVIII-CII) revealing him as an author, scholar, poet, and enlightened man who spread enlightenment. Yelin acknowledged Yosef's great talents and skills in interpreting medieval Hebrew poetry and correcting its printed texts.

A remarkable man, Yosef's main interest was Hebrew literature, and he wanted to establish methodical editions and well founded interpretations of medieval Hebrew poetry. He represented with modesty the knowledge and skills that he possessed in the field of medieval Hebrew poetry. Additionally, he supported Hebrew periodicals that were published in Europe by getting them new subscribers (for *Ha-Tsefira* for example) or new members (for *Mekitseh Nirdamim*). Yosef also published seven articles in *Ha-Tsefira* in the field of medieval Hebrew poetry. The articles are important for their content, style, and also for the expression of the struggle of a Jewish man from Baghdad who strove to make a meaningful contribution to the research of medieval Hebrew literature. In this chapter, I will present only one of Shaul Yosef's poems, and in a later chapter, I will discuss his articles.

In his poem "Leshon Ha-Meshorerim" (The Language of the Poets"), Yosef wrote about the deterioration of Hebrew poetry, the gap between the self-image of Hebrew poets and their real image, and about the gap between their poetic accomplishment and their hopes.

לְשׁוֹן הַמְשׁוֹרְרִים אֻבְלָה וְנָבְלָה   וְלִפְצֹחַ שְׂפָתֵימוֹ עֲרֵלָה
סְכָלִים הֵם, אֲבָל לֹא כֵן יְדַמּוּ   וְלִבָּתָם אֲמוּלַת, מַח אֲמוּלָה!
וּמִשֵּׂכֶל, אֱמֶת, צָפוּן לְבָבָם   וְאַף אִם לַכְּסִילוּת יֵשׁ תְּעָלָה
וְיֵשׁ מֵהֶם אֲשֶׁר קִוָּה לְהַעְפִּיל   שְׁחָקֵי שִׁיר, וְהוּא חָתַר שְׁאוֹלָה
וְיֵשׁ מֵהֶם בְּפֶה רָחָב מְדַבֵּר   וְהוּא מַרְעִים וְנוֹתֵן קוֹל הֲמֻלָּה
וְיֵשׁ מֵהֶם בְּצָעְדוֹ מַעֲלוֹת שִׁיר   וְעֶרְוָה בַזְּמִיר עֵרָה וְגִלָּה
אֲבוֹת הַשִּׁיר אֲזַי הָיוּ וְעָלוּ   בְּמַעְלוֹת הַמְּלִיצָה עַד לְמַעְלָה
כְּבֶן-עֶזְרָא וְהַלֵּוִי יְהוּדָה   וְעוֹד לָהֶם מְאַת יָד בַּתְּהִלָּה
נְגִיד הַשִּׁיר שְׁלֹמֹה בֶּן-גְּבִירוֹל   וְרַב טֵדְרוֹס סְגֻלַּת כָּל סְגֻלָּה
מְלִיצַת מַעֲנֵיהֶם לֹא תְסֻלֶּה   בְּכֶתֶם טוֹב וְשֹׁהַם הַחֲוִילָה
עֲלֵי מִלֵּאת חֲרוּזֵיהֶם כְּתַרְשִׁישׁ   עֲנָק עַל צַוְּארוֹן עַלְמָה בְתוּלָה
וְכַמָּה מִמְּתֵי שִׁיר אַחֲרֵיהֶם   וְזִמְרָתָם לְמוּלֵיהֶם שְׁפָלָה
וְהַיּוֹם שָׁב זְמִיר הַשִּׁיר מְקוֹנֵן   וְנִיבוֹ יַעֲנֵהוּ קוֹל יְלָלָה

אֲבוֹי עַל תּוֹפְשֵׂי כִּנּוֹר בְּנוֹת שִׁיר   וְהִשְׁחִיתוּ וְהִתְעִיבוּ עֲלִילָה
וְתָעוּ מִמְּסִלַּת שִׁיר, וְאָרְחָם   עֲקַלְקַלּוֹת וְדַרְכָּם לֹא סְלוּלָה
וְרַגְלָם מִנְּתִיב זָמִיר רְחוֹקָה   וְנָעוּ מַעְגְּלוֹתָם בַּמְּסִלָּה
וְנִלְאוּ מִמְּצֹא פִּתְחוֹ, וְהֵמָּה   יְגַשְּׁשׁוּ כְּעִוְרִים בָּאֲפֵלָה
עֱלֵי שִׁיר יֶהֱמֶה לִבִּי כְּחָלִיל   וְצִירַי נֶהְפְּכוּ עָלַי כְּחוֹלָה
עֱלֵי זֹאת אֶפְרְשָׂה כַּפַּי לְמַלְכִּי   וְאָבוֹאָה שְׁעָרָיו בִּתְפִלָּה
עֲדֵי יָחֹן וְיַחְזִיר הָעֲטָרָה   אֱלֵי יְשָׁנָהּ וְכַאֲשֶׁר בַּתְּחִלָּה
וְיָרֹן שִׁיר, וְאַל נָא יֹאמְרוּ עוֹד: "לְשׁוֹן הַמְשׁוֹרְרִים אָבְלָה וְנָבְלָה"

The language of the poets fainteth and fadeth away
And they are of uncircumcised lips
They are imprudent, but they don't think they are
And their hearts are weak, how weak!
And truly, their heart is distanced from sense
Even though there is a cure for foolishness
And there is among them one who hoped to soar
To poetic skies, but dug into the netherworld
And there is among them one who speaks with a wide mouth
And he thunders and sounds
And there is among them one who while ascending by steps to a poem
And he exposed and revealed nakedness of the nightingale
The poetry forefathers existed and ascended
High in the poetic steps
Like Ibn Ezra and Judah Halevi
And they have a hundred parts in the glory
The poem ruler Shelomo Ibn Gabirol
And Rabbi Tudros the treasure of all treasures
Their ornate style cannot be valued
With good gold and Onyx of Havilah
Their rhymes [beads] are fitly set like topaz
A necklace on a neck of a virgin girl
And [there were] some poets after these forefathers
And their juxtaposed poems are lowly
And today the poetic nightingale is lamenting again
And it is responded to by a sound of wailing
Woe to the holders of the violin muse
And they have dealt corruptly, they have done abominably
And they went astray from the poetic path, and their mode
Crooked and their route unpaved
And their foot is far away from the nightingale path
And they circulate around and around
And they wearied themselves to find the door, and they
Grope like the blind in the darkness

My heart moaneth for the poetry like pipes
And my pains came suddenly upon me like a sick woman
Because of this I will spread out my hands unto my King
And enter His gates with the prayer
Until He graciously restores the crown
To its pristine splendor as before
And a poem will resonate, and they will not say anymore:
"The language of the poets fainteth and fadeth away."

This poem focuses on the deterioration of the poetic achievements in Hebrew poetry. The great Hebrew poets were the Spanish Hebrew poets in medieval times, while those who came after them only hoped to attain what they accomplished. Although they imagined that their poems attained meaningful aesthetic achievements, they did not.

The style of the poem is biblical, and it follows the forms of medieval Hebrew poetry. It has a quantitative meter based on a pattern of one short and three long syllables. The distich consists of two lines ending with a rhyme, which link it to the whole poem.

The poem's translation reflects the intense use of biblical language; The poets "are of uncircumcised lips," reminding us of Moses telling the Lord, "Behold, the children of Israel have not yet hearkened unto me; how then shall Pharaoh hear me, who am I of uncircumcised lips?" (Exodus 6:12).

The poem applies only the shortcoming of the verbal abilities of the poets. The description "their hearts are weak, how weak!" echoes "how weak is thy heart" (Ezekiel 16:30) about Jerusalem and its inhabitants. However, the poet's aesthetic shortcomings are not treated as a moral religious sin. In the poem, "there is among them one who hoped to soar / to poetic skies, but dug into the netherworld," which echoes "though they dig into the netherworld, thence shall my hand take them" (Amos 9:2)—the sinners will not be able to hide from the punishment of the Lord. However, once again, the use of the language in the poem does not relate to sin and punishment by God.

The poet "who speaks with a wide mouth" reminds us of the verse, "Yea, they opened their mouth wide against me" (Psalms 35:21)—only as to the action of using a "big" mouth. The poet who "while walking up by steps to a poem / and he exposed and revealed nakedness of the nightingale" reminds us of the command: "Neither shalt though go up by steps unto my altar, that thy nakedness be not uncovered thereon" (Exodus 20:26). The "nightingale" is the poem that exposes the "nakedness" of its author.

The medieval Hebrew poets had a "hundred parts in the glory" of poetic accomplishments in comparison with their followers. This reminds us of the language: "We have ten parts in the king" (Second Samuel 19:43)—the men of Israel felt that they had more rights under King David than the men of Judah.

Todrus Abulafia's poetry was the "treasure of all treasures," reminding us of the language "I gathered…treasure" (Ecclesiastes 2:8). However, while Koheleth found his treasures as vanity, the poetic speaker views poetry as a treasure.

Wisdom "cannot be valued with gold" (Job 28:16), and in the poem, the Jewish Spanish poet's "ornate style cannot be valued with good gold and Onyx of Havilah," the "land of Havilah," is "where there is gold…onyx stone" (Genesis 2:11-12).

The rhymes of the medieval Hebrew poets "are fitly set like topaz," reminding readers of the beauty of the beloved man whose "eyes like doves…fitly set" (The Song of Songs 5:13). The Jewish Spanish poets' rhymes (beads) are "fitly set like topaz / a necklace on the neck of a virgin girl," and the echo of "thy cheeks are comely with circlets, thy neck with beads" (The Song of Songs 1:10) is clear.

The poets after the Jewish poets of Spain "have dealt corruptly, they have done abominably," like the fools who "have dealt corruptly, they have done abominably" (Psalms 14:1). The Hebrew poets who wrote after the medieval Hebrew poets "wearied themselves to find the door, and they / grope like the blind in the darkness," like the men near the door of Lot's house "they wearied themselves to find the door" (Genesis 19:11) and like the Children of Israel that "grope like the blind in the darkness" (Isaiah 59:10).

The quality of the post-medieval Hebrew poetry hurts the poetic speaker, his "heart moaneth for the poetry like pipes," which reminds us of God's words "…my heart moaneth for Moab like pipes" (Jeremiah 48:36) for the punishment that is awaiting it. "Pains came suddenly upon me like a sick woman," states the poetic speaker, reminding us of Eli's daughter-in-law, Phinehas' wife, whose "pains came suddenly upon her" (First Samuel 5:19). The speaker prays for better Hebrew poetry, "I will spread out my hands unto my king," reminding us of "…I will spread out my hands unto the Lord my God" (Ezra 9:5). He will "enter His gates with the prayer" (see "Enter His gates with thanks-giving," Psalms 100:4).

In addition to biblical allusions, the poem alludes to medieval Hebrew poems, including poems of Yehuda Alharizi and Moshe Ibn Ezra. Ideas are emphasized by repeated words or themes. We find homonyms—"sekhalim" (imprudent)-"sekhel" (sense) and "kesilut" (foolishness).

The first two lines (a distich) present the poem's main idea, and they are the only two lines in the distich that rhyme with each other. In addition, the first line has an internal rhyme in accordance with its biblical Hebrew origin. The distich presents a complete idea.

The situation of the later poets becomes clear by the contrast between reality and self- image and between desires and real achievements: On the one hand—"imprudent," "foolishness," "netherworld" and "nakedness"; on the other hand—"sense," "poetic skies" and a "nightingale." The later poets' attempt to ascend poetically ends with a shameful exposure in the poem's first part. These poets' tongue (language), lips, heart, and mouth as well as various images that relate to their poetic way represent their poor achievements. The first part of the poem contrasts the second part that describes Spain's Hebrew poets who truly ascended and rose up in the poetic ladder. After praising the Spanish Hebrew poets, the speaker continues his criticism of those who came after them.

Hebrew poetry is precious for the poetic speaker, who can distinguish between poetry, thunders, and sounds. He can only express his pain and pray. The poetic closure of the poem returns to its opening and is as equally compelling as the poem's opening.

Rabbi Saliman Menahem Mani: From the Bonds of the Conventional to the Personal Articulation

Rabbi Saliman Menahem Mani (who was born in Baghdad in 1850 and died in Hebron in 1924) came from Baghdad to Hebron in 1856, with his father, Rabbi Eliahu Mani, who assumed the position of Hebron Chief Rabbi for fourteen years (1865-1879) where he founded a Yeshiva. Eliahu Mani wrote important books in the field of Jewish law, and he was a mystic man, ascetic and charitable.

Rabbi Saliman Mani served in various positions. He was senior president of the Rabbinical Court of Hebron, Chief Rabbi of Hebron, Acting Chief Rabbi of Jerusalem, and more. He published rabbinical questions and answers (Responsa), corresponded with poems of friendship and polemic with other sages, and traveled to various countries. He wrote about one hundred poems of love, friendship, complaints, love for Zion, praise, lamentations, cogitation, and riddles. Of these poems, he published only four during his lifetime. He and his brother, Avraham Barukh Mani, were among the pioneers of modern Hebrew literature among Babylonian Jews.

In 1894, Saliman Mani was in Tunisia where he wrote the following poem:

לוּ תָפוּץ אֶרֶץ תַּרְשִׁישׁ זְהָבָהּ וְיַהֲלֹמָהּ
וּתְהוֹמוֹת יַמִּים לֶשֶׁם שְׁבוֹ וְאַחְלָמָה
מַה לִּי וְלָהֶם ? וְלִשְׁאֹל בַּעֲדָם לָמָּה ?
הֵן בְּעוֹדִי חַי לֹא אֶחְסַר לֶחֶם צְנוּמָה

וּבְמוֹתִי אֶמְצָא קֶבֶר, וּצְבָא חֶלְדִּי כַּמָּה ?
וּלְהַזִּיל נַפְשִׁי הַיְקָרָה [ ] אשמָה
עַל כֵּן לֹא אֲבַקֵּר בֵּית שׁוֹעַ וְלֹא אֶטַמָּא
בִּלְשׁוֹן חָנֵף, וְלוּ כַּחוֹל יַרְבֶּה לִי עַד מָה

If Tarshish would hand out its gold and diamonds
And the deep waters a jacinth, an agate, and an amethyst
What does it have to do with me? And why should I ask for it?
While I am alive I will not be short of a crust of bread
And when I will die I will find a grave, and how long would I live?
And to denigrate my precious soul is a fault
Thus I will not visit a rich man's house and will not be impure
By a flattering tongue, even if he would give me riches like sand.

This is a poem about pride and frugality. The speaker does not need the precious stones of Tarshish (Jeremiah 10:9), the land of silver and gold, or the precious stones of the ocean ("And the third row [of the "breast-plate of judgment"], a jacinth, an agate, and an amethyst" Exodus 29:19). All he needs in his short life is a piece of bread, and when he dies, a grave. His pride and honesty are more precious for him than treasures. Unlike the poems of praise in Jewish

Spanish poetry that glorified the rich, generous man, this poem takes away the rich man's power, because there is no use for what a rich man can offer. The poem does not follow the structure of Spanish poetry. All the lines of the poem have the same rhyme, and the style is emotional. The names of precious stones are detailed, wealth is treated with derision, and the speaker's needs are scanty.

The poem, "the zeal of a man's rage," is surprising in its content. It describes the adultery of a wife, and the rage is directed not against the wife but against the man with whom she committed adultery:

אֵיזֶה עַוָּל יָהִין עֲלוֹת עַל סַף בֵּיתִי   וְחֶרֶב חֹרַב עֲנָק לְצַוָּארִי מֵעוֹדִי
וְאֵיךְ יָעֹז זָר לַעֲרוֹת מַעֲרָתִי   וְלֹא אָעִר נַפְשִׁי, וְנָקָם אֶלְבַּשׁ לְמַדַּי ?
וְאִם צוֹעִים צָעוּ יְצוּעֵי שֵׁגְלָתִי   לְמוֹקְדֵי אֵשׁ אַקְרִיב דָּמִי וְדָמַי וּמְאֹדִי
אָמוּת מוֹת גִּבּוֹרִים, וְהִיא תְהִלָּתִי   כִּי אֶתֵּן כְּבֵדִי וּכְבוֹדִי פִּדְיוֹן כְּבוֹדִי

What an unrighteous man would dare go on my threshold
While I have always worn a sword like a necklace
And how a stranger dared to expose nakedness that is mine
And I would not awaken my soul and not put on garments of vengeance for clothing?
And if degenerated people slept with my consort
To the fire I will sacrifice my blood and money and myself
I will die a heroic death, and it will be my glory
To give my liver and my wealth as ransom for my honor.

The poem focuses on revenge against the stranger or strangers for humiliating the speaker by sleeping with his wife. The speaker wonders about the imprudence of those people, who ignored the fact that the speaker is conspicuously a man of the sword. He poses two questions with a parallel syntactic structure. The use of the Hebrew language is playful throughout the poem. The unrighteous man ("'avval") dared to go up ("'alot") on the speaker's home threshold. We may be reminded, "his home is his wife" (Yoma 1:1). The sword is also a phallic symbol, and the speaker wears the sword as an "'anak," which means both a necklace and a giant in Hebrew. The question, "And how a stranger dared to expose nakedness that is mine," is more loaded in Hebrew; "La-arot maarati" means to expose the woman's nakedness that belongs to me, but it may also remind us of spilling ('leha'arot) into a female organ. The language is innovative: "I have always worn a sword like a necklace"—the literal translation should read: "A sword was always sworded like a necklace to my neck." "Sworded" is used with a poetic innovative license. Other playful usages of the language are "tso'aim tsa'au yetsu'aeh," translated above as "degenerated people slept with my consort," "dami vedamai" translated above as "my blood and money," and "kevedi u-khevod…kevodi" translated above as "my liver and my money...my honor." The sound participates in the creation of various meanings along the poem—anger, silence, screeching, and rage. The poet also employs a variety of homonyms ("tsimmudim")—"dami vedamai" ("my blood and my money"), "kevedi u-khevodi" ("my liver and my honor"), among others. It is noteworthy that this poet also employs biblical allusions such as "but the unrighteous knoweth no shame" (Zephaniah 3:5) "and He [God] put on garments of vengeance for clothing" (Isaiah 59:17). These examples illustrate how little justice can be done in a poetic translation.

Mani was falsely charged (Ben-Yaacob, 1980, 90) with bribing officials so that he could get out of trouble, and he was sent to prison in Damascus from 1880-1883. It is a unique situation to find a rabbi writing Hebrew poems in jail about the subject of jail. In one of his poem's introductions, he mentions "imprisonment in Damascus," written in 1882, "when I was a prisoner in prison in Damascus":

יְמוֹגְגֵנִי זְמַנִּי כְמוֹ יַחְשְׁבֵנִי לְאוֹיְבוֹ
וִיתַד שִׂנְאָתוֹ תָקַע בְּמוֹ לִבּוֹ
וְכָל יוֹם יְשַׁחֲרֵנִי בְּצָרָה חֲדָשִׁים לַבְּקָרִים
וְכִשְׁבוּי חַרְבּוֹ יְסוֹבְבֵנִי בְּעָרִים

אִם יוֹרֵנִי נַחַת, כְּמוֹ רֶגַע יָסֹב עָלַי עֲקֵבוֹ
וּכְנָמֵר יַהֲפֹךְ חֲבַרְבּוּרוֹתָיו כֵּן נִיבוֹ
וְחֶבֶל דְּלִי תִקְוָתִי פָּסַק תּוֹךְ בּוֹר דֻּבִּים וּנְמֵרִים
אֶרְעֶה צֹאן תְּלָאוֹתָיו עֲדָרִים עֲדָרִים

My time melts me away as if it considers me its enemy
And it stuck its hatred peg in its own heart
And every day and morning it will seek me earnestly
And as its sword prisoner it takes me round from town to town
If it gives me contentment in a moment it turns around
And like a leopard it changes its spots and words
And in a hole of bears and leopards it cut off the rope of my hope bucket
I will tend the flocks of its quandaries.

Various biblical verses echo in the poem, such as "all the inhabitants of Canaan melted away" (Exodus 16:15); "they will seek me earnestly, but they shall not find me" (Proverbs 1:29); "they [the Lord's mercies] are new every morning" (Lamentations 3:23); and "Can the Ethiopian change its skin, or the leopard his spots?" (Jeremiah 13:23). The personification of "time" (Arabic-"Alzaman") and "his children" is common in medieval poetry. "Time" and his "children" become metaphoric entities that inflict wandering and old age. Time appears as a destiny, a concealed power that triggers various circumstances without any clear reason. "Time" terminates everything, and it is the source of all troubles, the destiny that fights man ceaselessly and inflicts troubles on him. Contrary to the good people, who are persecuted by time, it bestows its favors on the injudicious ones.

Sometimes poets expressed their faith in their power to defeat the Time. It separates friends and brings about loneliness and one has to pray to be freed from its impact. The figure of Time was the figure of blind destiny that arbitrarily plagues people and tortures them. Time is bad, unfaithful, evil, poisonous, ill willed, and its children are carnivorous. It gives plenty to the evil people and takes away from the good ones, abolishes and uproots and grabs, gives and immediately takes back; one cannot escape it and the death that Time inflicts (Pagis, 1970, 294-295; Levin).

Similarly, in Mani's poem, Time is a powerful figure. It weakens the speaker, it behaves as the speaker's enemy—if it does any good deed with the speaker—it reverses it and it gave the speaker's hope to the beasts. Time is personified throughout the poem and it melts the speaker away, considers, sticks a peg, and it has a heart. Various acts of time reflect the Time's power, while the speaker is passive in comparison to it. The metaphor "hatred peg" in the first line is expanded: "And it stuck its hatred peg in its own heart." Allusions are used in an innovative way, for example, "they will seek me earnestly, but they shall not find me" (Proverbs 1:29). Here time seeks and finds the speaker. Unlike the biblical leopard that cannot change its spots (Jeremiah 13:23), time can change its spots and words. However, the poetic speaker did not lose his faith or hope in prison.

Mani's poem is written in the Sephardic accentuation. It rhymes (aa, bb, aa bb), and it does not follow the structures and meters of medieval Hebrew poetry, but it is clearly influenced by its themes.

Saliman wrote other mesmerizing poems about the prison experience. Some followed the quantitative meter, which is based on regulated "pegs" (Hebrew: "yetedot") and cords (Hebrew: "Tenu'aot") and is not based on a pattern of stressed and unstressed syllables, but on a pattern of short and long syllables. He also left poems of love for Zion, departure and longing for Zion, poems that portrayed prototypes such as liars and lazy people, a poem about a beautiful Arab woman, and more. It is clear that many of his poems did not follow any of the conventional themes that he was very familiar with, but they were particular expressions.

A Lyrical Poet Who Died While Still in his Prime: Rabbi Avraham Barukh Mani

Avraham Barukh Mani (Baghdad 1854, Hebron 1882) was four years younger than his brother Saliman Mani, who lived forty-two years after his death. Avraham Mani lived only twenty-seven years, during which time his two children died. Nevertheless, he left a meaningful poetic legacy behind. Avraham Mani was an educated man. He read Hebrew poetry of his time and had an interest in Jewish law. After his death, some of his work was published in his father's book (see Mani, Avraham). He published an introduction to a book and a poem following it, a moving lamentation about Rabbi Avraham Ashkenazi, which is evidence of his prominent poetic genius. He published in his life only three of the forty poems that reached us and were published after his death. Avraham Mani wrote lyrical poetry, lamentations, and poems about illness, love poems, riddles, humorous poems, and sonnets.

Of the two manuscripts he left behind, one was buried with him in accordance with his will, and the other one was not published (Ben-Yaacob, 1970, 191-193; Ben-Yaacob, 1980, 99-100). In *Sefer Barukh Avraham* (1987), lamentations, poems, legends, and other works of Avraham Mani, as well as proverbs of wisdom and morals, were published.

Here is a sampling of some of his proverbs: "Do not treat lightly a light [insubstantial] man who hates you, because man's arm cannot be weighed with a balance;" "When a tree bears edible fruits, all the birds swarm to it; but when its leaves wither get away from it;" "It is good to roister among roisterers, and it is wise to hide wisdom away from them, because in the chaos of the wilderness what good is topaz for, even moldy bread is better than it;" "A coat of arrogance will reveal the pubes, and righteous humbleness will cover all deformities;" "Many will live because one quack doctor died;" "On a floor of gold and silver will not grow any plant, and a heart covetous of lucre will not bear fruits of mercy and truth;" "The swindling of a swindler will wipe out the swindler, and the deceit of a man of intrigue will humiliate the deceiver."

One of his long poems (twenty-five stanzas) is about the illness of the poetic speaker, and it is an autobiographical poetic expression of the anxiety and the horror of death inflicted by his illness that forced him to be uprooted from his place (Mani traveled in order to seek medical advice). Hebrew literature experienced lyrical expressions over fear of death at a young age due to illness. I will mention as examples the medieval Hebrew poet Shelomo ibn Gabirol; the enlightenment poet Mikha Yosef Levensohn; and the poetess Rahel in the Palestinian period. In his poem, Mani expresses the poetic speaker's hopes for happiness, his understanding that sadness would not provide a cure for illness, his inability to apply this understanding to his own situation, and his becoming a victim physically, socially, and intellectually to his sadness. He knows that his death is coming soon, and he relates to this fact with horror and panic. However, he finds a way to give confidence to himself, to treat the death threat merely as a dream, and to throw the sadness out of his life. I will present a detailed analysis of this poem (Hakak, "Laatesevet"), and in the frame of this work, I will only point out some of its artistic devices.

The poem's first stanza presents the dichotomy between the existing "spirit of sadness," metaphorically "poisonous snake," to the desired "spirit of joy." The next three stanzas excel in a quick rhythm of rhetorical questions, all leading to the speaker's recognition that he has to distance himself from the unbeneficial "sadness." He wonders:

הֲיִרְפָּא הֶעָשָׁן עֵינַיִם כָּאֲבוּ?
אוֹ חֹמֶץ נִתְעָב - שִׁנַּיִם נִרְקָבוּ?
מֶלַח וּרְסִיסֵי חֶרֶס - מַכֵּה חֶרֶב?
שֶׁלֶג וּכְפוֹר עַז - כְּרָעַיִם וָקֶרֶב?

Would smoke cure aching eyes?
Or would repellent vinegar [cure] decayed teeth?
Salt and splinters of clay - [would they cure] a fatality of a sword?
Snow and robust frost – [would they cure] legs and bowels?

In the fifth stanza, the speaker wonders why he is sad in spite of his understanding that sadness has only harmful outcomes. These questions create a highly emotional style, and from the sixth stanza to the tenth stanza, the speaker describes the evil doing of the sadness. His passiveness and sadness impacts his blood, heart, arteries, vigor, and bones and darkens his shiny sun. It blocks the gates of wisdom and leads to folly, social conflicts, laziness, and aging.

Sadness is personified as a woman: "Laziness is her hire, and her gain—the mourning" (Isaiah 23:18). Even the speaker's dreams are strongly impacted by it, and when he wakes up he panics (fourteenth stanza):

מַה הַחֲלוֹם הַזֶּה! מַה אֲשֶׁר חָלַמְתִּי
בְּיַד אַכְזָרִית מַתִּי וְהִנֵּה נָפַלְתִּי

What is this dream? What have I dreamed?
By a cruel hand I died and behold I fell down.

Jacob rebuked Joseph's dream saying, "What is this dream that thou hast dreamed?" (Genesis 37:10), but the dream came true. The panic is expressed in the intense questions, the many verbs in this stanza, the wondering content, the quick rhythm, the frequent internal rhymes (in Hebrew), and the absence of a regular order of the events—he first died and then he fell down. He reminds himself that it was only a dream (sixteenth stanza), and then (stanzas seventeen to nineteen) he describes the evil rule of the sadness that appears in the character of a woman, who is a frightening, deadly maidservant that became a queen. The speaker sends away the sadness (stanzas twenty to twenty-two). He talks to it directly, calling it "malevolence" and "leprosy," and he commands it to get out of his life, using a chain of verbs in imperative:

לָכֵן צְאִי רִשְׁעָה, צְאִי מִפֹּה, מִסְפַּחַת
צְאִי וְאַל תָּשׁוּבִי הֲיִי אַךְ בּוֹרַחַת
אֶרֶץ שְׁאִיָּה לְכִי, אַךְ רְפָאִים בָּךְ גָּרוּ
חַבְּקִי הָרֵי חֹשֶׁךְ סְלָעִים נִתָּרוּ.

Thus get out, malevolence, get out of here, leprosy
Get out and do not return, just run away
Go to a land of ruins, inhabited by ghosts only
Embrace mountains of darkness and tumbling rocks.

He asks earth and heaven (the last three stanzas) to assist him in chasing his sadness away. He will divorce the sadness. "Earth and sky" will witness the divorce instrument, and he asks God to help him:

גַּם מַחֲלָה אֲחוֹתָהּ מֶנִּי הָסִירָה
וּמִיֵּינָהּ אוֹתִי עוֹד לֹא תַּשְׁכִּירָה
עָלֶיהָ צַו מַלְאָכֶיךָ: שִׁמְטוּהָ
פִּקְדוּ אֶת הָאֲרוּרָה וְקִבְרוּהָ.

Also take away from me her sister the illness
And do not make me drink of its wine again
Command your angels against it: Throw her down
Look now after this cursed one and bury her.

The sadness will have the same destiny as the wicked Jezebel: "Throw her [Jezebel] down…Look now after this cursed woman, and bury her" (Second Kings 9:33-35).

In this poem, Mani orchestrates a variety of poetic devices that include numerous allusions, rhymes at the end of the poetic lines, internal rhymes, rhymes connecting between stanzas, shifting rhythm that participates in creating meanings, personifications, a variety of homonyms, syntactic structures of parallel interrogative sentences, spoken Hebrew and elevated biblical Hebrew, rhetorical questions, and short and long sentences. The artistry in using these devices as well as other ones constructs a poem with high poetic achievements.

I consider Avraham Mani's 1880 lamentation of the Chief Rabbi Avraham Ashkenazi one of the peaks of his poetic achievements. Avraham Mani was a friend of the Chief Rabbi's son. Avraham Ashkenazi stood up for Avraham Mani's father, Rabbi Eliahu Mani, in a community dispute in Hebron.

It is reasonable to assume that Avraham Mani was familiar with the lamentations of medieval Hebrew poetry, including the poetic conventions of the lamentations that expressed public mourning of sages and public figures. This lamentation, however, is a personal expression even though it includes common, non-personal praises. Similar to lamentations in medieval Hebrew poetry, this lamentation, too, includes praises to the deceased, but it does not follow the structure of the medieval Hebrew lamentations, which consists of a short opening, transition, the main part, and the finale. Similar to the biblical lamentation, Mani's lamentation also includes the elements of praising, lamenting, and consoling. Mani begins the lamentation at the outset of the poem without any introduction, without any pensive part at the end of the introduction, and without the transition that explicitly presents the subject of the poem and the name of the person that the poem references. All of these are unlike the conventional lamentation in medieval Hebrew poetry. The praising of the deceased does not appear as a separate part in the poem but is mixed in the poem with the mourning. The language of praising the deceased is not taken from the themes and metaphors of medieval Hebrew poetry. Here, too, nature is involved in the mourning, but unlike in many medieval Hebrew lamentation poems, it does not do so by itself but does so at the request of the poetic speaker. Like in the lamentations of medieval Hebrew poetry, people play important roles in Mani's lamentation, and they are inferior to the deceased.

We do not find in Mani's lamentation a description of the burial, gravediggers, or grave. In Mani's poem, like in the medieval Hebrew lamentation poems, there is a call for general mourning, but there is no messenger that carries the terrible news about the death, and there is no cursing of the day in which the deceased died or to the world that lost him. Similar to medieval Hebrew lamentation poems, we also find consolations, but they are composed of two lines only, and there is not an entire part dedicated for consolations, as in Mani's lamentation. Unlike medieval Hebrew lamentations, it does not end with blessings for the deceased.

Only a few of the poem's first lines will be translated and discussed here:

אֵיכָה נעתמה אֶרֶץ הַצְּבִי מַדּוּעַ חָשַׁךְ שמש״ה פֶּתַע וְעַמּוּדֶיהָ הִתְפַּלְּצוּ עַל מְסִלּוֹתֶיהָ קַדְרוּת, נְתִיבוֹתֶיהָ
אֵבֶל וְכָל מַחְמַדֶּיהָ נשסו

How doth the goodliest land burnt up its sun grew suddenly dim and its pillars trembled gloom on its tracks, its pathways are mourning and all its treasures rifled

The above line is composed of several biblical verses, most of them referring to destruction and lamentation. Like the Lamentations in the Bible, it opens with the famous "how doth," alluding to "how doth the city sit solitary" (Lamentations 1:1). The first word prepares us for the spirit of national mourning. The colors are dark, and nature is mourning, the land has burned up, the sun is dim, the tracks gloomy, and the pathways are mourning. The land of Israel where Rabbi Ashkenazi dies is also defined by biblical terms; it is "the goodliest land." It is written, "...I give thee [house of Israel] the goodliest heritage of the nations" (Jeremiah 3:19). This land is now "burnt up," which echoes another verse: "Through the wrath of the Lord of hosts is the land burnt up" (Isaiah 9:18). The Hebrew words for "its sun" is abbreviated "shimsha"h"—the word "shemesh" in numerology (use of letters as numerals) creates the year of the death of Rabbi Ashkenazi ("shemesh"—640, adding 1240—is 1880). The pillars of Israel trembled, alluding to the verse "and the pillars [of earth by His command] thereof tremble" (Job 9:6). Like in Lamentations where "Jerusalem remembereth...all her treasures..." (Lamentations 1:7) that she had before its fall, here, too, Israel lost its treasure, Rabbi Ashkenazi, "...and the city [Jerusalem] shall be taken, and the houses rifled" (Zechariah 14:2), in this poem "all its treasures rifled."

The style is highly emotional. Mourning biblical language is used in a mosaic fashion. The rhythm is quick and lacks punctuation. Written this way, it expresses the shock of the mourners. Intensive verbs are introduced to create the expressions of destruction, and in some cases, the absence of a verb creates strong metaphors: "Its pathways are mourning" (in Hebrew he uses "mourning" as a noun), "gloom on its tracks."

The poem shifts to the people's mourning:

בִּרְחוֹבוֹתֶיהָ קִינִים וְהֶגֶה אוֹי נַאֲבוֹי שְׁעָרֶיהָ לְזֶרֶם דִּמְעָה הָיוּ אֲפִיקֶיהָ נְחָלֶיהָ דָּם וָאֵשׁ.

In its broad places lamentations and moaning and it wept and spread its arms alas and alack its gates its riverbeds became a stream of tears its rivers blood and fire.

Moab's punishment became the punishment of Israel: "...in the broad places [of Moab]...there is lamentation every where" (Jeremiah 48:38). What Ezekiel could find in the roll of a book given to him exists now in Israel for the death of Rabbi Ashkenazi—"lamentations and moaning": "... [A roll of a book] and there was written therein lamentations, and moaning, and woe" (Ezekiel 2:10). The emphasis shifted from nature to the mourning of the people on the streets. In the gates of a city used to sit honorable, wise men, judges. However, now "alas and alack its gates," nature and man mourn together: "Its riverbeds became a stream of tears" of the mourning people. Fire, tears, and blood participate in the lamentation:

גָּלָה כָּל שָׂשׂוֹן מנה וְתִתְיַפֵּחַ תִּפְרֹשׂ כַּפֶּיהָ וְתִקְרָא אַלְלַי, אוֹי נָא לִי כִּי שֻׁדַּדְתִּי.

Its mirth has gone away from it and it wept stretched out its hands and called woe unto me for I am undone

What happened to "the goodliest land" of Israel resembles the biblical punishment "...the mirth of the land is gone" (Isaiah 24:11). It is sobbing, stretching out its hands in supplication, and calling, like the punished people of Israel in the Bible, "Woe unto us [the people of Israel]! For we are ruined" (Jeremiah 4:13). The land of Israel is a metonymy of its people.

Rabbi Ezekiel Hai Albeg Carries his Legacy Overseas

Albeg wrote poems of castigation with prophetic fervor, poems of love for Zion, poems of redemption, and poems of complaint about wandering and suffering. In some of his poems, Albeg continued the medieval Hebrew prosody. Some of his poems were strongly influenced by Arabic poems. He also wrote rhymed prose. I will illustrate his poems through a few examples.

In his poetry volume *Kenaf Renanim,* he published poems of complaints about wandering and separation. The poems express love for the land of Israel, joy for seeing it, and sorrow for leaving it.

In one of his poems (ibid., 264-265) "In the Forest at Evening," he describes "sleeping in a convoy on the way from Babylon to Israel." The poem follows an Arabian melody and describes the closeness between the speaker and nature:

The eyelashes of dawn tickled his eyelashes. Nature sang and played music for him.

רַחַשׁ עָלִים הוּא כִּנּוֹרִי, עוּגָבִי
מֵימֵי בְּשָׂמִים הָיוּ לִי טַלִּי, רְבִיבִי

The murmur of the leaves was my violin, my organ
My dew my droplets was my fragrance

The nature is personified and became as dear as a family to him:

מִכָּל עֲבָרִי סַבּוֹנִי הָמוֹן יְדִידִים
בָּאוּ נִקְבְּצוּ אַחִים וְרֵעִים וְדוֹדִים
אֲהוּבִי - דֶּשֶׁא קָרָאתִי אָחִי וְרֵעִי
פַּרְפַּר שְׁאֵרִי - וּפְרָחִים - אִמִּי וַאֲבִי

From everywhere I was surrounded by scores of friends
Came and gathered brothers and uncles and buddies
I called grass my brother and the wind—my beloved
Butterfly—my next of kin, and flowers—my mother and father.

The entire nature is his ornament:

רוּחַ גָּמַעְתִּי צַח שפים וְנָקִי
שׁוֹעַ לְשׁוֹעִים אֲנִי וְכָל תֵּבֵל חֶלְקִי
סהר - רבידי עֲדָיֵי תַּכְשִׁיטַי - כּוֹכָבִי
כַּסְפִּי - אוֹר שַׁחַר
וְקַרְנֵי שֶׁמֶשׁ – זְהָבִי

I gulped fresh mountain air pure and clean
I am a nobleman of noblemen and the entire planet is my lot

The moon—is my necklace
My jewels-charms—my stars
My silver—the dawn light
And the sun rays—my gold.

He gives thanks to God for everything that God gave him:

מֶלֶךְ הָעוֹלָם מַה אַקְרִיב לְךָ חֵלֶף כָּל זֶה
אֵין לִי פַּר מַקְרִיב וְאֵין לִי חָלָב וְחָזֶה
אַתָּה הוּא הַכֹּל: אוֹרִי, לַפִּידִי, לַהֲבִי
אֲנִי חֲסַר כָּל וּתְשׁוּרָה אֵין לִי לְהָבִיא

King of the universe what will I offer you in return
I do not have a horned bull to offer and I don't have milk and breast
You are everything: My light, my torchlight, my flame
I am empty handed and don't have an offering to bring.

His only gift is his poetry.

On his way from Israel to America, he stayed in Egypt for a few months, and he described his sadness about his wandering in the world:

וְגָלוּת מְנָתִי וְהַנּוֹד חֶלְקִי -
אָמַרְתִּי אוּלַי אָבָנֶה
וּמְזוֹנִי בְּיָדִי וּמְטַלְטְלַי בְּחֵקִי
וְרַק אֶסַּע וְאַחֲנֶה
וּמֵעִיר אֶל עִיר בְּאַמְתַּחְתִּי וּשַׂקִּי
וְעִיר לֹא יָדַעְתִּי, אֲכַנֶּה
וְזֶה גוֹרָלִי וְזֶה לֶחֶם חֻקִּי -

And exile is my fate and wandering is my portion
And I thought maybe I would establish myself
And my food in my hands and my belongings in my bosom
And I will only journey and encamp
And from town to town with my pouch and sack
And I will name a town, unknown to me
And this is my destiny and my daily lot—
To shake [wander] as the reed is shaken

The speaker's wandering reminds readers of the wandering of the children of Israel in the desert on their way from Egypt to Israel. They, too, "journeyed and encamped" in many places (see, for example, Exodus 13:20): However, they were on their way from Egypt to the Promised Land, while the poet journeys in the opposite direction. The image of being shaken as a reed reminds us of the

Lord that "will smite Israel, as a reed is shaken in the water" (First Kings 14:15). The Hebrew word "nud" means not only to wander and be a fugitive, but also to lament and bemoan. The poem has a rhyming scheme (ab, ab, ab, ab) and portrays the situation of the speaker by specific images ("and my food in my hands and my belongings in my bosom") that depict the general way of his existence ("and I will only journey and encamp").

The feeling of being uprooted and estranged dominates the poem "Cain" (ibid., 143):

וּלְכָל-בְּנֵי תֵבֵל חֵלֶק וְחֶבֶל
וְרַק לִי אָיִן
וּמִמְּדִינָה לִמְדִינָה אֶמָּשֵׁךְ בְּחֶבֶל
וְלֹא אֵדַע לְאָיִן
וְאָנוּד בְּאֶרֶץ נֵכָר כִּמְצִיר וָחֶבֶל
וּכְמִתְרוֹנֵן מִיָּיִן
וְכָל רֵעַי וְיוֹדְעַי נחוּ כְּהֶבֶל
וְרַק אֲנִי קָיִן

And all the people in the world have a part and a lot
And only I don't
And from one country to another I will be pulled by a rope
And I don't know whereto
And I will wander in a foreign land as if by pangs and throes
And as one who is joyful by wine
And all my friends and acquaintances rested like Abel
And only I am Cain

The Hebrew word "hevel" at the end of the first, third, and fifth lines (ab, ab, ab, ab) functions as many homonyms. It means lot, rope, and throes, and Abel's name in Hebrew is Hevel. The Burden of Babylon, which Isaiah saw, includes a situation in which "they shall be frightened; pangs and throes shall take hold of them" (Isaiah 13:8), while in the poem the speaker is suffering from sharp pains. The Hebrew "anud" refers to his wandering; he wanders like a fugitive (Cain), but it also means "I will move." His motion resembles the motion of a drunken man.

He expressed sorrow and regret for leaving Israel (ibid., 144):

וַאֲשֶׁר נְשִׂיאִים עָלַיִךְ יַזִּילוּ, אַרְצִי-
הֵם דִּמְעוֹתַי וּמֵהֶם רְוִי
קַבְּלִים נָא כְּמִנְחָה וּבָם הִתְרַצִּי
כְּנִסְכֵי יַיִן וְשִׁיר לֵוִי
וְכַפֵּר חֵטְא בְּרִיחָתִי מִמְּחוֹז חֶפְצִי
לְאֶרֶץ רֶקֶם וְאַדְמַת אָוִי
וּפָנִיתִי לְדֶרֶךְ מִדְבָּר וְלַעֲבוֹר בְּצִי
וְאוֹתָךְ הִשְׁלַכְתִּי אַחֲרֵי גֵוִי

And that, which vapors drop on you, my homeland -
Are my tears, and be saturated by them
Accept them as offerings and be conciliated by them
Like wine pouring and a Levite's song
So that the sin is atoned: My fleeing from my destination
To the country of Rekem and the land of Evi
And I turned to walk the desert and cross by a ship
And I tossed you away behind my back

Albeg specifically uses the Hebrew word "yazzillu"-will "drop," will shed, which is connected with tears coming from the heavy clouds. Rain as tears is an image conventionally used in medieval Hebrew poetry. He hopes to water the land of Israel with his tears in order to appease it for his sin of deserting it and going to foreign lands that "...Moses smote...the chief of Midian, Evi, and Rekem...that dwelt in the land" (Joshua 13:21). "...The Lord separated the tribe of Levi...to stand before the Lord to minister unto Him" (Deuteronomy 10:8), and the speaker wished to have his tears fulfill several missions: watering the land of Israel, conciliating it as a song of a chosen Levite, and atoning for them for deserting Israel. Albeg's Hebrew is intense, his rhymes are creative, and his images are powerful. His tears drop like rain (touch, vision) and like wine pouring (taste) and like a Levite's song (hearing). He uses a name (Evi) that appears in the Bible only once (Hapax Legomena) to draw attention and juxtapose the land of Israel with the land from where he escaped. While he is in the desert he wants to water and gladden the land of Israel. The guilt for throwing the place of his destination behind his back is the cause of his tears. He describes his act of leaving Israel in terms of running away, without presenting the reason.

Chapter 3: The Twentieth Century Poets in Babylon

Many Hebrew textbooks were ordered from Palestine to Babylon. However, some felt that there was a need for books that would stimulate young students based on their specific local Jewish culture to learn the Hebrew language. Jewish educators in Babylon authored Hebrew textbooks with contents that spoke to the heart of their students and also effectuated progress in teaching the Hebrew language.

Aharon Sason (1877-1962) emigrated from Babylon to Palestine in 1936. In Babylon, he played a central role in the Zionist movement. He also founded a Jewish school and served as principal. Additionally, he published Hebrew poetry with a Zionist spirit that was influenced by Jewish-European nationalistic ideas.

Another educator, David Hai Abbudi, wrote in his introduction to *Shireh Bet-Ha-Sefer* (1930) that his book was designed to fill a need that was felt in Jewish schools in Babylon, the need for Hebrew songs written to Arabic melodies that were well-known by the students. His book included such songs and a dictionary that translated Hebrew words to Arabic and their synonyms. He understood well the need for themes and contents that would interest the local student.

In 1938, another well-educated Jew from Babylon, Shelmo Yitshak Nissim, published his book *Derekh Tovim*, which included twenty-one Hebrew songs. These songs were also written with Jewish educational ethical national goals in mind. The poems call for the Babylonian Jews to play a role in their time and place, to acquire knowledge of foreign languages and science, and to contribute again to Hebrew culture. These poems emphasize the power of the word and the importance of understanding reality. Above all, these poems uphold and promote good values such as doing good deeds, modesty, calm communication, giving respect to our fellow human beings, learning from any person, and more.

Shelomo Salih Shelomo Gabai (1896-1961) was another educator in Babylon who promoted the knowledge of the Hebrew language. Shelomo Gabay visited Palestine and its schools, and in 1923, when Kerem Ha-Yeladim school opened in Baghdad, he was appointed as the principal. Hebrew was the language of instruction at the school. He wrote poems of love for Zion, Hebrew language, and Jewish education, and he became renowned for his compelling poem about the pogrom against the Jews that took place on June 1-2 in 1941.

Rabbi Menasheh Shahrabani (1881-1960) also wrote about this pogrom. His ideas were influenced by the Jewish European enlightenment. He wrote one of the earliest poetic responses to the Holocaust by Near Eastern Jews. His poems seem lucid when they are read the first time, but this should not veil his linguistic sophistication.

Rabbi Yitshak Nissim (1895-1980), who became the Chief Rabbi in Israel, authored, in 1917, a lamentation about seventeen honorable Jewish men from Babylon, including his brother, who were tortured to death and then murdered by secret Turkish police.

David ben Saliman Tsemah (1902-1981) was the first Jewish poet from Babylon whose poetry protested the social gap and the way his community was treated in Israel. He was highly knowledgeable in Arabic literature and medieval Hebrew poetry and wrote about sixty Hebrew poems. He gave an accomplished sensitive lyrical expression to his time.

There were other Babylonian poets creating in Hebrew at that time. One of them was Rabbi Ezra Nagi Mkamal who was born in Baghdad in1912, immigrated to Israel in 1951, and died in 2000. Jewish authors in Babylon wrote in Hebrew, Arabic, English, and French. Poets such as Shelomo Zamir and Shalom Katav wrote Arabic poetry in Babylon. When they immigrated to Israel, they had to overcome the hardship of shifting to Hebrew. Rabbi Ezra Nagi Mkamal, like Rabbi Shahrabani and David Tsemah, wrote Hebrew poetry in Babylon and did not face this hardship. He immigrated to Israel in 1951, where he continued writing Hebrew poetry without being influenced by Israeli poetry and without giving a poetic expression to the life in the new land. He continued writing about themes and values that were not bound by a certain time and place, such as faith, honor to parents, and modesty.

Poets Herzl and Balfur Hakak immigrated to Israel when they were two years old. Their writing language was, of course, Hebrew. There were authors, such as the highly talented Samir Naqaash, who emigrated from Babylon to Israel and continued to write in Arabic and became famous in Israel and in Arab countries. Other writers, such as Shmuel Moreh and Sason Somekh, shifted from creative writing to research (Hakak, 1985, 20-24; Hakak, 1993, 167-169; and Moreh-Hakak).

Rabbi Ezra Nagi Mkamal was among the last rabbis who were ordained in the Yeshivat Bet Zilkha. He also was a ritual slaughterer, and in 1939, he received the title "Hakham" (sage). He taught Jewish studies and became famous for his sermons. His first Hebrew poem was published when he was fourteen years old.

One of his poems is a lamentation about the June 1-2, 1941, pogrom against the Jews in Iraq ("Farhood"). According to the author, it was written at the time of the pogrom. The poem is written in one of the medieval Hebrew poetry meters, and the first lines of the distiches rhyme with each other, and the second lines in the distiches rhyme with each other. Each four distiches begin with another letter of the words "bat Bavel ha-sheduda" ("O daughter of Babylon, that art to be destroyed," Psalms 138:8).

This poem, written by Rabbi Mkamal, was first published in my book (Hakak, 2003, 200-208). The poem opens with the Jews crying that all they can do is to supplicate God, and it closes with a supplication. It is a lamentation expressing and describing the cry and prayer of Jews and the savagery of their murderers. It vacillates between general descriptions and specific ones. The enemy defiled women and then murdered them, rioters stabbed to death young honorable Jewish men, and mothers cried aloud for their sons and husbands who were murdered along with little babies. Men who had dedicated their lives to the study of the Torah were murdered.

Shelomo Yitshak Nissim, a member of the Hebrew Association in Babylon, and David Saliman Tsemah, the first social protester poets, are the more accomplished poets in this group.

Among the various Hebrew educational publications in Baghdad were two booklets published by Histadrut Ha-Noa'ar Ha-'Ivri ("The Hebrew Youth Organization"): the booklet *Kovets Shirim Le-Umiyyim* (National Poems Collection) that included twelve well-known Hebrew poems, and the booklet *Hertsel* (Binyamin Ze'ev Hertsel, 1860-1904, was the founder of the World Zionist Organization and the father of political Zionism). In addition, there were two textbooks that were published by Ya'acov Tsiyyon Mu'alim and Moshe Azuri Sofer (see Bibliography). Moshe Ventura (see Bibliography) published a textbook in four volumes for teaching Hebrew in Hebrew, which included fifty-six questions and answers for students in religious and extricated matters (see Bibliography, *Mahberet*) and a book of liturgies and songs, twenty-six of them in Hebrew and eight in Arabic.

The Renaissance Poet Aharon Sason

In Babylon, Aharon Sason (born in Babylon in 1877, immigrated to Israel in 1936, died in Jerusalem in 1962) was called "The Teacher." Beginning in 1912, he was the Zionist leader in Baghdad. While in Baghdad, after World War I, he met Rabbi Dr. Moshe Ventura, an officer in the Turkish army. Together, they organized the Zionist movement in Babylon, and they promoted the movement and the immigration to Israel through the Jewish schools. Rabbi Ventura then went back to Turkey, and the British High Commissioner gave permission to establish The Zionist Society of Mesopotamia in 1921. Aharon Sason was the organization's president, and the movement expanded during his tenure. Its activities included collecting donations for Palestine, organizing immigration to Palestine, and advancing the knowledge of Hebrew language and literature. He was the director of the Hebrew periodical *Yeshurun* (refer to Chapter 10 about *Yeshurun*). In 1925, the Zionist society had one thousand members in Babylon.

In Pardes Ha-Yeladim, a Jewish school that Aharon Sason founded, Hebrew was taught in Hebrew, and teachers were trained to apply this method. In 1925, Aharon Sason published his Hebrew renaissance, revival poetry collection, *Shireh Ha-Techiyya* (see Sason, Aharon). The Iraqi authorities started restricting his activities and eventually banned them in 1929. In 1936, after riots in Palestine, Iraqi policemen confiscated his documents and his literary works from his home. He was arrested and charged with preaching Zionism. He stood trial with pride and was acquitted, but in 1936, he had to leave Babylon and move to Palestine for fear of his safety. In Israel, he was not made part of the Zionist organizations to which he had dedicated his life. Nonetheless, he published books about Jewish law and religion (Bibliography, *Totseot* and *Mekor*).

The poetry volume *Shireh Ha-Techiyya* begins with two Hebrew poems by Aharon Sason followed by the first part of the volume, which is a selection of Zionistic poems (1-40). The second part includes twenty poems by Aharon Sason (1-28). The third part of the volume begins with a poem by Aharon Sason's father followed by twenty-three poems by Aharon Sason.

The second part begins with poems of praise. The first of these are in praise of the leadership and generosity of Eliezer Salih Kadduri, and the second poem is in praise of the above mentioned school, Pardes Ha-Yeladim, one of the thirty-seven Jewish schools in Baghdad at that time. Eliezer Kadduri was born in Baghdad in 1865, and he went to China and became a rich man. He was an educated man, good looking and wise, who donated to many non-Jewish and Jewish charitable, educational, and cultural institutes.

The praise poem for Kadduri was sung at the Pardes Ha-Yeladim school at the time of Kadduri's visit. The poem is influenced by praise poems of medieval Hebrew poetry in Spain. Its opening praises the altruistic people in general, followed by a transitional part in which the poetic speaker specifically praises Eliezer Kadduri. Similar to medieval Hebrew praise poetry, the transition mentions his name explicitly. The praise itself is short, and it utilizes the embellished praising language used in praise poems in medieval Hebrew poetry. Kadduri is "the spring of the lights," he is "illuminating," and he is "from a lineage of philanthropists." The praising part is also personal. It addresses Kadduri individually who is "among the builders of Zion's ruins," a pillar of the Jewish revival. Then the poem blesses the praised Kadduri and his family.

The poem in praise of the school Pardes Hayeladim presents the accomplishments of the school in sustaining Jewish culture, in using Hebrew as the language of instruction, in having Hebrew as the conversation language of the students, and in applying modern teaching methods.

After these two poems, there is a collection of thirty Hebrew poems from various periods of Hebrew literature: Medieval Hebrew poetry (i.e., Yehuda Halevi), the enlightenment period (i.e., Yehuda Leb Gordon, 1830-1892), the Renaissance period (i.e., N.H. Imber, 1856-1909; M.M. Dolitski, 1856-1931), and the modern period (i.e., Hayyim Nahman Bialik, 1873-1934). The selection is based on the theme of national Jewish revival, and it demonstrates the knowledge of this poetry. The selection does not represent a chronological order. It is reasonable to assume that the author and editor of the book expected interested readership in Babylon. The poems are not vocalized.

The second part of the book includes twenty poems by Aharon Sason. Sason wrote a poem about yearnings (1-2) for Zion, and it is written as a dialogue among the Jewish people, who ask Zion to open its gates for her children, and to Zion, who is eagerly waiting for their return. The poem "Comfort" (3-4) is a dialogue between the people of Israel and God who tells her the news about the deliverance in the forthcoming "last days," when there will not be any more crime, when truth will defeat the lies and death will not exist anymore.

In the poem "Awakening" (5-7), God tells the people of Israel that the time for revival and salvation has come, and their enemies' hopes to prevent it did not become a reality. *The Homeland* (7-8) is a poem of love for the native soil, a place of heroes, success, modesty, and shelter.

"The Revival" (8-9) is a poem about the revival of the Jewish people and their return to Israel. It upholds the ideas of national unity and pioneering, in accordance with the Torah and the recognition of the world as to the rights of the Jews to go back to their homeland. The Hebrew language's revival is part of the national revival (9):

שׁוּב הַשָּׂפָה הָעִבְרִיָּה
חַיָּה בְּפִי הַיְּהוּדִים
הֻכְּרָה לְשָׂפָה רשמיה
וּשְׂפַת הוֹרָאַת הַיְּהוּדִים

The Hebrew language is once more
Alive on the lips of the Jews

It is recognized as an official language
The language with which children are taught.

"Blessing of the King" (10-11) is a poem expressing supplications to guard the king of Iraq. In the poem "The National Movement" (11-12), the speaker pleads with Keneset Israel ("keneset" is assembly, convention, "keneset" is singular feminine; here, The People of Israel) to wake up from the sleep of the Diaspora and to be active in its revival:

קוּמִי, אוֹרִי, כִּי בָא אוֹרֵךְ
הִתְנַעֲרִי מֵעֲפָרֵךְ
פַּתְּחִי אֱסָר צַוָּארֵךְ
הִנָּצְלִי מִכַּף צָרֵךְ.

קוּמִי, צְאִי מִגָּלוּתֵךְ
הִתְרוֹמְמִי מִשִּׁפְלוּתֵךְ
הִתְעוֹרְרִי מִשְּׁנָתֵךְ
הָקִיצִי מִתַּרְדֵּמָתֵךְ.

קוּמִי, שׁוּבִי לְמוֹלַדְתֵּךְ
אַל תִּשְׁכְּבִי עַל מִטָּתֵךְ
אַל תַּמְשִׁכִי אֶת גָּלוּתֵךְ
כִּי בְּיָדֵךְ גְּאֻלָּתֵךְ.

קוּמִי, רְאִי חֲבֵרַיִךְ
רֻבָּם שָׁבוּ לְעָרַיִךְ
זוֹרְעִים, נוֹטְעִים אֶת הָרַיִךְ,
בּוֹנִים, סוֹלְלִים דְּרָכַיִךְ.

קוּמִי, עֲשִׂי אֶת חוֹבָתֵךְ
אַל תִּפְרְשִׁי מֵעֲדָתֵךְ
חוּשִׁי עֲשׂוֹת אֶת מְנָתֵךְ
הִשְׁתַּתְּפִי בִּתְחִיָּתֵךְ.

קוּמִי, חִקְרִי אֶת יָמַיִךְ
הֲיֵשׁ אֵמוּן בְּשׁוֹבַיִךְ
הַאִם דוֹרְשִׁים שְׁלוֹמַיִךְ
אוֹ יְשַׁסּוּ חֶמְדוֹתַיִךְ.

קוּמִי, דַּבְּרִי בִּלְשׁוֹנֵךְ
נִטְעִי נִטְעֵךְ, זִרְעִי גַּנֵּךְ
סַקְּלִי, בְּנִי בִּנְיָנֵךְ
בְּתַרְבּוּתֵךְ הוֹרִי בְּנֵךְ.

קוּמִי, שְׁבִי בְּתוֹךְ אַרְצֵךְ
מִקְלָט, מִבְטָח, נְוֵה רִבְצֵךְ
שַׁחַר עָלָה, הֵנֵץ נִצֵּךְ
סַהַר נָגַהּ עַל חֲלוּצֵךְ.

Arise, shine, for thy light is come,
Shake thyself from the dust
Unlock the lock on your neck
Be saved from your enemy.

Awaken, get out of thy exile
Rise up from your degradation
Wake up from your sleep
Wake up from your deep slumber.

Awaken, return to your homeland
Don't sleep upon your bed
Don't drag your exile
Because your redemption is in your hands.

Awaken, see your friends
Most of whom returned to your cities
Sowing, planning your mountains
Building, paving your roads.

Awaken, perform your duty
Do not be a recluse of your community
Hurry up and do your fair share
Participate in your revival.

Awaken, research your history
Is there any faith in your prisoners
Do they look for your welfare
Or plunder your delights.

Awaken, speak your own language
Plant your plants, sow your garden
Clear the earth of stones, construct your edifice
Teach your children your culture.

Awaken, live in your country
A shelter, sanctuary, your life resort
The dawn arose, your buds bloomed
The moon shone on your pioneer.

This poem is presented for the purpose of illustrating the spirit of a good segment of Babylonian Jews during this time and not for its poetic imaginative creativity. Aharon Sason wrote about issues of his era, and he was familiar with Hebrew poetry of the enlightenment period, the Renaissance period, and the modern period. Nevertheless, his poems were written with the meters of medieval Hebrew poetry. He employs some biblical allusions, such as "Arise, shine, for thy light is come" (Isaiah 60:1) and "shake thyself from the dust" (Isaiah 52:2), but his Hebrew is the Hebrew of his time, and he uses allusions far less intensively than many of the other poets discussed in this book. The poem expresses the Zionist agenda. The first expected readers of the poems are Babylonian Jews, and the poem is an ideological call to them to contribute their fair share to Zionism. The revival is both spiritual and practical. All of the poem's lines have the same rhyme, which is a grammatical suffix, and it is not innovative or creative rhyming.

Similarly, the poem "Wake Up you the Sleeping" (14-17), is a call to the Jewish people to wake up and participate in the national revival and not only to pray and supplicate, but to follow the Zionist way and to build, sow, plant, guard, and harvest.

In these poems, one may trace not only biblical influences, but also influences of medieval Hebrew poems, not only in prosodic terms, but also in the language used. Yehuda Halevi's poem "God in All," opens with the following words: "Lord, where shall I find Thee? / High and hidden is Thy place/ And where shall I not find Thee? / The world is full of Thy glory." Aharon Sason also wrote a poem (12-13) about the same theme, beginning with the words: "Where shall I find the inventor of all/ and where shall I not find Him…" In the poem "Hast Thou Forgotten?" by Halevi, Keneset Israel (female figure for the people of Israel) asks God: "My love, hast Thou fortgotten Thy resting/ between my breasts? / And wherefore hast Thou sold me for ever to/ them that enslave me?" Aharon Sason wrote the poem "My Friend, Hast Though Forgotten" (16-17) in which God asks the people of Israel: "My love, have you forgotten your resting / on my mountains? / And wherefore have you been resting in the exile / When I am fulfilling my promise?" In Aharon Sason's poem "The Unity" (17-18), he encourages the Jews to unite through the Zionist movement and reminds them of the fact that they have the same God, Bible, language, and heritage.

In the poem "My Opponents Speak Halfheartedly," anti-Semites contradict themselves when it comes to assessing the strength of the Jew; they describe the Jew as a person who determines the fate of countries, and at the same time, they view him as a weak and insignificant man:

צָרַי בְּלֵב וָלֵב יְדַבְּרוּ,
תַּהְפּוּכוֹת בְּנוֹשֵׂא אֶחָד יַצְהִירוּ:
'הַיְּהוּדִי נִבְזֶה חֲדַל אִישִׁים,
מְזֹהָם וְאֵין לוֹ תֹּאַר אֲנָשִׁים

וְהוּא אִישׁ שַׁתְּ כֹּל תַּחַת רַגְלָיו,
צִיר הַמְּדִינוֹת יִסֹּב עָלָיו,
הוֹפֵךְ וּמֵקִים כִּסֵּא מַמְלָכוֹת,
עָשִׁיר וְחָכָם בְּכָל מְלָאכוֹת.׳

הוֹי! אִם בֶּאֱמֶת תְּרוֹמְמוּהוּ,
לְגָבְהֵי מָרוֹם תְּנַשְּׂאוּהוּ,
לָמָּה לֹא תֵּחַתּוּ משאתו,
מַדּוּעַ תִּשְׁסוּ חֶמְדָּתוֹ,

הַאִם אֵין זֹאת לְבֶצַע פְּנֵיכֶם?
דִּבְרֵי אוֹן וּמִרְמָה בְּפִיכֶם?

My opponents with a double heart do they speak
Make presumptuous [forward] statements about the same theme:
'The Jew is despised and forsaken
Filthy and his visage unlike that of men

And he put all things under his feet
The hinges of the country is turning upon him
He turns over and launches chairs of kingdoms
Rich and wise in all ingenuities.'

Woe! If you really glorify the Jew
And to the sky elevate him
Why doesn't his Majesty terrify you
Why shall you spoil his treasures?

Aren't you looking for lucre?
Aren't your words deceitful and iniquitous?

The poet employs various allusions, such as "with double heart do they speak" (Psalms 12:2), wisdom will deliver "from the way of evil, from the men that speaks forward things" (Proverbs 2:12), the nations that treated the people of Israel as "despised and forsaken" (Isaiah 43:3) find out that they erred, "his visage unlike that of men" (42, 14), "thou has put all things under his feet" (Psalms 8:6, this is what God did for man), "as a door turns on its hinges" (Proverbs 26:14), "shall not His Majesty terrify you" (Job 13:11, Job to his friends about God), and "he shall spoil the treasures of all precious vessels" (Hosea 13:15). Some of these allusions must be interpreted carefully as they are a matter of vocabulary and are a mere use of ready language that does not seek full effects. For example, the effect of the line "Why doesn't his Majesty terrify you" is not, of course, that Jews resemble God. The poem has simple, grammatical rhymes (aa, bb). It is a polemic poem with a message, and it is intended to be of national service. The presentation in first person singular of the prejudicial assessment against the Jews and the response in a second person plural toughen the encounter.

The nations push the Jew away wherever he is, and no matter what he does, he will find refuge only in Israel (20-21). The dangers strengthen the Jew, "a man whose merciless enemies are all around / Is vigilant with all his senses and does not know sleep."

In another poem (21-22), the lines opens with the speaker asking where will he run away from the nationalistic spirits that affect his life? West Europe and East Europe will not provide him with a solution. If the Jew acquires wealth and knowledge, it will evoke anger and hatred against him. At the poem's closure, he answers the question that opened the poem; only Israel is a safe place for him, where he can develop his abilities, live in accordance with the Torah, and establish a shelter for future generations. In another poem, the speaker sees that the revival of the Jews and the redemption of Israel is coming in spite of the hardships (25-26).

Aharon Sason also wrote poems that were not focused on national themes. In one of his poems, he desires to instill good values, asserting that happiness derived from good deeds is far more important than wealth ("The Eternal Happiness," 18-19). Man should not forget that he is only dust, and if he does not leave behind him a good reputation, he did not accomplish anything of significance in his life ("Good Name," 19-20). He wrote a poem of praise to God (22-23), a poem urging children to wake up and study the Torah (23-25).

The third part of the volume begins with a poem (1) by Aharon Sason's father, in which the speaker describes the afflictions of the Jews and prays for redemption. The rest of the poems, twenty-four in number, are by Aharon Sason. In these poems, the poetic speaker supplicates God to guide and redeem (2) the people of Israel. He urges man to be honest, to follow the will of God (2-3), to praise God (4), and to thank God for guiding the Jews in keeping their heritage, reviving their language, and launching their pioneering poems of love for Zion (4-6). It is about a time when the suffering and wandering of Jews will see their redemption arrive (6-7). God saw the afflictions of the Jews and redeemed them (7-8). The land of Israel expects the Jews to speak Hebrew (9). The Torah and Zionism are the substances of the life of the nation (9-10). The Jews have to rise and worship God for their national and individual redemption (10-12). The poetic speaker is God's servant (12). The Jewish people must do everything in their power to build their country and foster their culture (12-14). They should be people of chosen virtues and deeds, peaceful and freedom loving, and concerned for their country, culture, and language (14-15). One poem is God's monologue promising revival and prosperity for the Jewish people (15-16). Two poems wish a groom happiness with the woman he has chosen (16-18). Other poems were inspired by specific events in his community, including blessings for a daughter's birth (18) and for a son's birth (21) and praising an author for his book (20-22).

In one poem, the speaker describes the prominence of the Shabbat (19-20), while in another, he asks God to redeem his people (22).

In these poems, the personal and the national are inseparable. Personal success depends on national success and the revival of the Jewish people and their land. The key concepts in these poems are God, the Jewish people, Israel, Diaspora, revival, unity, the Hebrew language, pioneering, Torah, and good deeds.

Like the Hebrew poetry of the enlightenment period, Aharon Sason viewed himself as an author whose penmanship was drafted for national goals. He did not write poetry for poetry's sake. Rather, he wrote poems with national and Zionist messages and didactic goals. Aharon Sason read Hebrew poetry of his time. He read Hebrew periodicals and viewed his Hebrew creativity only as a vehicle for conveying educational messages. His poetry is not sophisticated esthetically. However, it constitutes another chapter in the emergence of secular Hebrew literature in Babylon. In his use of the written Hebrew word, he struggled more with the conveyance of ideas than with the form of conveying them.

The School Poems of David Hai Abbudi

David Hai Abbudi was a Hebrew teacher in Babylon. In 1942, he taught Hebrew in Basra and later served as the vice principal of Basra's Jewish school "Pardes Ha-Yeladim." In 1945, he was a vice principal in "Midrash Talmud Torah" in Baghdad. He immigrated to Israel in 1951.

In 1930, he published, in Babylon, the first part of *Shireh Bet-Ha-Sefer*. In his introduction, he explains that this publication was in response to a need of Jewish schools in Babylon, that is, Hebrew songs composed to suit pre-existing popular Arabic melodies known by the students. He published seven songs and used Hebrew synonyms and translations to Arabic to explain the Hebrew text. He also pointed out the popular Arabic melodies to which the songs were written. The songs express love for the Iraqi king and for the prince, and Abbudi sang about the spring, compassion, a library, and the scouts.

In his introduction he wrote:

> I have seen the necessity in our schools for Hebrew songs, and one of the hardships is the adaptation of the [Arabic] melodies to the secular social [Hebrew] poems we have from Spain and later from the Ashkenazi Jews. Therefore, I took on me the task of composing these poems and adapting the Arabic melodies that we are most familiar with. At the same time I tried to translate twenty words from each poem by using Hebrew synonyms and Arabic translations, in order to enjoy at the same time the song and the language, because it is better to enjoy both aspects than just one of them, therefore I allocated two pages per song, the first one is for the song itself and the second one is for its explanation.
>
> [...] And I hope that the readers will forgive me for errors in this booklet. Perfection is distinctive to the Lord exclusively.

The song "The Spring" (9) is jolly in its content and rhythm. It urges the young people to enjoy the spring with its radiance, buds and flowers, colors and scents, and sounds of chirping and children's songs. The song "The Compassion" (11) praises compassion as a human virtue that one should emulate. The song "The School" (13) is written as an argument between a studious student and a silly student. The silly student asks the studious student why he is letting go of the pleasures of life and focusing on his studies, and the studious one explains the beauty and illumination he finds in books. The last song is an expression of appreciation for "The Scouts" (17).

The word selections in the dictionary that follow these songs is a testimony to the author's ability to decipher between the more commonly known Hebrew words and the lesser known ones, and for those that find the Hebrew synonyms are insufficient, he translated the selected words into Arabic, too.

One has to keep in mind the goal of the author. He did not think that he published an original volume of poetry but a textbook with educational themes that would contribute to the teaching of Hebrew in Jewish schools. I included the discussion of this booklet in order to portray an aspect of the educational spirit in Babylon at that time (1930) and the sincere desire to expand the knowledge of Hebrew. I did not include the discussion of the booklet in order to portray a significant literary accomplishment.

Shelomo Yitshak Nissim, a Member of the Hebrew Association in Babylon

Shimon Ben Nissim Shimon, Shmuel Shami, Ezra ben Elisha Zikhri, Meir ben Eliahu Zikhri, and Shelomo Yitshak Nissim were a group of Hebrew poets who wrote Hebrew poems individually and collectively. Their poems were included in a poetry volume that was published in 1906 (see Dangour, ed., *Sefer*) and was very well received. The volume included 415 liturgies and poems, many of which were written by Babylonian Jews of that generation as well as in previous generations.

Shimon Ben Nissim Shimon (known as Shimon Mu'alim Nissim, who immigrated to Israel in 1951 and died in 1953) was a teacher and then a principal. He published eight liturgies that were very popular and were sung on various occasions. Shmuel Shami (who died around 1920) was a teacher in Baghdad (in Midrash Talmud Torah) and authored seven liturgies. Ezra ben Elisha Zikhri was his colleague who published four liturgies that were very popular (he died in the 1920s in Baghdad). Another teacher from this group was Meir ben Eliahu Zikhri, who published well-known liturgies.

The most poetically accomplished among them was Shelomo Yitshak Nissim (who died in 1950, refer to Chapter 10 about *Yeshurun*). He was interested in education and law. He published two books in Judeo-Arabic and two books for teaching Hebrew. One of them was the book *Derekh Tovim* (see Nissim), in which he included twenty-one moralistic Hebrew poems. These are didactic poems, written in the meters of medieval Hebrew poems. In *Yeshurun*, he published poems with universal morals, except one, which he specifically addressed to the Babylonian Jewish community.

In his poem "Daughter of Babylon" (*Yeshurun*, no. 1, 5), Shelomo Yitshak Nissim calls on the Jews of Babylon, who formed the Babylonian Talmud, to further contribute to the Jewish culture, to acquire foreign languages and scientific knowledge, and to remain faithful to Judaism. A brief comparison of this poem with the poem of Yehuda Leib Gordon, "Awaken, My People" (1863), may be interesting. Yehuda Leib Gordon (1831-1892) was a prominent nineteenth century Hebrew poet. He was a writer, critic, allegorist, and journalist who was a proponent of the Jewish enlightenment, protested the ills of the Jewish people, and strove for religious and social reform. In his poem "Awaken, My People," he defined the Jewish conduct that he endorsed: "Be a Jew in your home and a man in the street," which became the motto of the enlightened Jews. The message one may conclude from Shelomo Yitshak Nissim's poem is to be a Jew and a man at home and in the street. Shelomo Yitshak Nissim's poem has a pragmatic, educational purpose, and he avoids metaphorical language. Babylonian Jews have to break "the manacles of prejudices" to gather from the homeland "roses and flowers" and to give a hand to Jeshurun (poetic name of Israel) so that it becomes "a blossoming bud."

Both poems are addressed to a present second person. Gordon calls on his people to wake up and to recognize their time and place. Shelomo Yitshak Nissim's call is to Babylonian Jews, who should restore the glory of their past: "Awake, daughter of Babylon, the mother of the Talmud / Return to your old past." Both poets request that their addressees wake up from their sleep. Both of them emphasize the knowledge of foreign languages and science. Shelomo Yitshak Nissim's poem emphasizes more than Gordon the connection between the Jewish people and their history, language, and the values of the prophets: "Daughter of the foreign Babylon / do not desert the language of your forefathers / accustom yourself to Hebrew." Gordon emphasizes the "night," the frozen time, the suffering, and the unfounded hatred for Jewish history. Shelomo Yitshak Nissim emphasizes the glorious chapters in the history of the Babylonian Jewish community, "the mother of the Talmud, is the mother of perspective." Gordon calls the Jews to be closer to the European nations that they live among. Shelomo Yitshak Nissim emphasizes the need for all Jews to participate in their spiritual national renaissance—"help your sister with education and culture." Gordon suggested, "Be an enlightened people and speak their [the Europeans] languages," also "focus on wisdom and knowledge." Shelomo Yitshak Nissim suggests, "Show vigor in the knowledge of languages and science, but do not desert the language of your forefathers / accustom yourself to Hebrew."

The similarities between the poems evidence and illustrate the intellectual, cultural, spiritual, and ideological contact between Baghdad's Jewish intellectuals and those in Europe.

While in Shelomo Yitshak Nissim's poem "Daughter of Babylon," he was influenced by a poet from the Jewish European Enlightenment, his poem "It Kills and Revives" (ibid., 5-6) was influenced by a poem from the medieval Hebrew poet Avrham Ibn Ezra (1092-1167). Ibn Ezra, in his poem "I will Propound a Riddle to Noblemen," described the tongue as a king, "small but very active," the very same words used by Shelomo Yitshak Nissim in his poem about the tongue. Ibn Ezra described the tongue as "sometimes it revives and sometimes it kills" the same words defining the tongue in Shelomo Yitshak Nissim's poem title. Ibn Ezra describes the tongue "as soft as silk and smites / with a hammer" and Shelomo Yitshak Nissim describes the tongue as "soft…and smites, the way the murrain smites." The Babylonian Hebrew authors were familiar with religious and secular Hebrew literature of various generations, and they were influenced by it.

Shelomo Yitshak Nissim's poetic accomplishments are more evident in his moralistic poems that have messages beyond a certain place and time. In these poems, he wrote about themes such as the power of words, the ups and downs in life, the importance of spiritual wealth, the importance of appropriate social conduct, the need to be merciful and hopeful, and the importance of faith and wisdom.

In one of his poems, "The Wise Man," Shelomo Yitshak Nissim writes about those who are going empty handed into the world to come, while they were rich and knowledgeable in this world:

יִדְאַג אִישׁ הַמֵּבִין   וְגַם יִתְעַצֵּב אֶל לִבּוֹ
עַל זֶה הַנּוֹסֵעַ   וְאֵין לוֹ צֵדָה מִטּוּבוֹ
עָשִׁיר אֲשֶׁר יַעְזֹב   אֶת רֹב חֵילוֹ בְּקִרְבּוֹ
וְזֶה בַּעַל דֵּעָה   בְּלִי מַעֲשֶׂה טוֹב יָבֹא

A wistful man is concerned
And also saddened
About a man who is traveling ("plucked")
Without supplies of his goodness
[About] a rich man who leaves
Most of his wealth for himself
And an erudite man
That comes without a good deed.

A wise man is saddened when he sees people—among them rich and erudite—"plucked" from this life, leaving it to "travel" to their death without the "supplies" of the virtuous deeds that they could do in their life. While one hears the echo of the biblical verse "for he seeth that wise men die, the fool and the brutish together perish, and leave their wealth to others" (Psalms 49:11), the poem instructs men on how to prepare themselves for the life to come. Riches and erudition should be used for good deeds.

Another poem by this poet is about the importance of modesty, honoring other people, organized thinking, peaceful speech, understanding that it is hard to change anything, curiosity, and care:

וּבְשִׁבְתְּךָ בְּתוֹךְ חֶבְרָה   אַל תִּתְרָאֶה כַּאֲדוֹנָהּ
וּכְיוֹדֵעַ כָּל שְׁאֵלָה   גַּם מַהוּתָהּ גַּם עִנְיָנָהּ
הָשֵׁב וּשְׁאַל עַל הַסֵּדֶר   לְכָל חֵפֶץ עֵת וְעוֹנָה
דִּבְרֵי חֲכָמִים בְּנַחַת   בִּמְחִילָה וַעֲשֵׂה-נָא
וְהַשִּׁנּוּי לִמְאֹד שָׂנְאוּי   עֵת כָּעוֹרֵב עֵת כַּיּוֹנָה
וּבִפְנֵי הַכֹּל, שְׁאַל הָשֵׁב   מַה נִּתְחַדֵּשׁ מַה נִּשְׁתַּנָּה

And when you are in a social gathering
Do not pretend to be its master
As if you know every query
Its essence and its subject matter
Respond and inquire orderly
And to every purpose there is a season
The words of the wise are heard [spoken] in quiet
With "sorry" and "please do"

And the modification is very reviled
Time as a raven time as a dove
And ask and answer everyone
What is new, what was modified.

We remember that "to everything there is a season, and a time to every purpose under heaven" (Ecclesiastes 3:1) and that "the words of the wise heard in quiet are more acceptable than the cry of the ruler among fools" (Ecclesiastes 9:17). Man hates change because it leads him into the unknown, and he makes contradicting excuses as to why he rejects changes. He may perceive the same change in contradicting ways ("time as a raven time as a dove") only to avoid the change. Addressing the reader as "you" creates an intimate contact between the reader and the speaker, reduces the instructive distance, and may be more persuasive.

In his didactic poem "Be Generous," Shelomo Yitshak Nissim praised generosity, giving honor to people and the ability to learn from every man:

וְהַרְחֵב לֵב עִם נִדְכֵּי לֵב   עִם אַלְמָנָה וַעֲגוּנָה
אַל תְּחָרֵף אִישׁ בַּעַל מוּם   אַל תַּכְלִים צוּרָה מְשֻׁנָּה
כִּי בָז אַתָּה מִי שֶׁבָּרָא   גַּם שֶׁמֶן מוֹר גַּם חֶלְבְּנָה
אֵין לְךָ אָדָם אֵין לוֹ שָׁעָה   טוֹב טַעַם חַכְמֵי הַמִּשְׁנָה
וְאֶבֶן מָאֲסוּ הַבּוֹנִים   הָיֹה תִּהְיֶה לְרֹאשׁ פִּנָּה
לְמַד דַּעַת מִכָּל אָדָם   תַּחְכִּים תִּהְיֶה אִישׁ הֲבָנָה
הֲלֹא הַמַּמְצִיא תּוֹכֵן גָּדוֹל   מִדָּבָר קַל חֹק תְּכוּנָה

And be generous with the downhearted
With a widow and a deserted woman
Do not curse a crippled man
Do not degrade an odd figure
Because it is contemptuous of the Creator
Of oil of myrrh and of resin
Every man has his day
Good is the discernment of the Mishnah sages
And a stone which the builders rejected
Has become the chief corner-stone
Acquire wisdom from every man
Become astute insightful
Indeed an eminent astronomer
Invented the astronomy code from a simple matter.

This is also an instructive poem that guides man on how to treat underprivileged people such as a widow, an Aguna—a woman whose husband deserted her without divorcing her, a disabled person, and a person with a strange appearance. He who degrades these people degrades their creator, who created both a fragrant aromatic plant gum used in perfumes and incense and resin (galbanum) that has a bad smell. The sages of the Mishnah taught us that "every man has his day" (Avot 4:3). The Bible taught us that "the stone which the builders rejected has become the chief corner stone" (Psalms 118:22), and one can and should acquire wisdom from any person and any situation.

The poem "The End of the Matter" has a conclusive idea:

וְסוֹף דָּבָר טוּב הַחַיִּים   אֵין אֱכוֹל רִמּוֹן וּתְאֵנָה
אַךְ הַפְּלָאָה בְּעֹצֶם אֵל   וְשִׂים שֵׂכֶל וּתְבוּנָה
בָּעוֹלָמוֹת - הַיְצוּרִים   בְּיַד יוֹצֵר כַּמְּכוֹנָה
טוּב הַנִּצְחִי כִּי עֵינֵינוּ   נֹעַם ה׳ תֶּחֱזֶינָה

And the end of the matter, the delight of life
Is not eating a pomegranate and a fig
But amazement at the might of God
And astuteness and insightfulness
In the world – the creatures
Are like a machine in the hands
Good is the eternal because our eyes
See the gracefulness of God.

The verse next to the last verse in Ecclesiastes (112:13) concludes that "the end of the matter, all having been heard: Fear God..." The poem's conclusion is that physical delights are not the goal in life but being in awe of God and understanding that "as the clay in the potter's hand, so are ye in my hand" (Jeremiah 18:7). While the verse is addressed to the "house of Israel," in the poem it is a universal truth.

Shelomo Yitshak Nissim employed the medieval Hebrew poetry quantitative meter, with its patterns of short and long syllables. He also employed the basic form of the poem, which is a distich consisting of two lines, ending with a rhyme, which in his poem links it to the whole poem.

I have stated that the Jews of Babylon were people of deep religious faith, and therefore, religious expressions and ideas from prayers played a role in many of their secular works. Some of their poems can be classified as both secular and liturgical poems.

The poems presented here by Shelomo Yitshak Nissim express deep religious faith, yet in their forms and style, objectives, attitude, and tone of the poetic speaker and the disposition, they are not necessarily liturgies. They were not written to be used for prayers and penitential prayers (hymns). Their objective was not to accompany the prayers and make them more vibrant, nor do they allude to a place in the prayers where they should connect. They stand by themselves and do not depend on a permanent pre-existing text.

The poems of this creative and highly accomplished poet demonstrate the familiarity of the Babylonian poets with Hebrew literature from various generations—Bible, Talmud, medieval Hebrew poetry, and poetry from the Jewish European enlightenment.

The Vineyard Poems by Rabbi Shelomo Ben-Salih Shelomo Gabai

On June 1-2, 1941, there was a pogrom against the Jews in Babylon as a result of Nazi incitement, propaganda, and nationalistic and religious instigation (see the introductory chapter in this book).

Some Babylonian Jewish poets wrote poetic responses to this pogrom in Hebrew. Among them were Rabbi Shelomo Ben-Salih Shelomo Gabai (Babylon 1896, immigrated to Israel in 1951, died in Tel-Aviv in 1961), and Rabbi Ezra Nagi Mkammal (born in Baghdad in 1912, died in Israel in 2000). Of the best known poems written in Babylon about the 1941 massacre is the poem by Shelomo Ben-Salih Shelomo.

Israeli poets of Babylonian origin also wrote about this pogrom, among them, Shalom Katav (Basra, 1931 see Katav), Yehezkel Muriel (see Muriel), the twins Herzl and Balfur Hakak (see Hakak, Herzl; and Hakak, Balfur) Yosef Ozer (see Ozer), Ezra Murad (see Murad), and Ratson Mattityahu (see Mattityahu).

The twins, Herzel and Balfur Hakak (born in Baghdad in 1948, immigrated with their family to Israel in 1950), and Yosef Ozer (born in Jerusalem in 1952) went back to the roots of their communities and wrote about the same devastation and the organized massacre of helpless Jews in Babylon in 1941. Yosef Ozer also wrote about the Holocaust in general.

Shmuel Moreh wrote an important article about the way the pogrom was depicted by Babylonian Jews in Arabic songs, Hebrew poems, research, memoirs in Arabic and Hebrew, and in English prose (see Moreh). The Jewish authors in Babylon who wrote in Arabic were afraid to write about the events due to the absence of freedom of speech. The pogrom played a major role in making the Jews of Babylon understand that their peaceful existence in Babylon was only a desire. Additionally, it played a significant role in their mass immigration to Israel.

In order to illustrate the connection between the 1941 pogrom and the Holocaust, I will present the first two stanzas of a poem written by Herzl Hakak. Herzl and Balfur Hakak came to Israel when they were two years old. Their mother's two teenage brothers, Nuri'el and his brother Abraham, were murdered in the pogrom, and their bodies were never found. Each one of the twin poets wrote a poetry volume about it. Herzl (see Hakak, Balfur, ed., 25-28; Hakak, Herzl, *Te'auda,* 61) wrote a cycle of fourteen poems. Herzl wrote a poem entitled "Dear Grandmother, her Torah was Given on a Dreadful Day":

פְּעֻמוֹנִים בּוֹכִים בַּחֲלוֹמוֹתֶיהָ. בְּאוֹתוֹ חַג
שָׁבוּעוֹת, שְׁנַת 1941. זְמַן הָעוֹלָם
נֶחֱרַב. דָּם זָב. חֵילוֹת וַיִּשִׁי מוּבָסִים
בְּלִי קְרָב. הִיטְלֶר לְרוּסְיָה הָלַךְ
וְקָרַב.
מִשְׁפָּחוֹת יְהוּדִיּוֹת שְׁדוּדוֹת וּשְׁכוֹל.
אֲבֵלָה נִבְלָה בָּבֶל, הַכֹּל.

בְּפַעֲמוֹנִים הוֹדִיעוּ הַנָּאצִים בְּעִירָאק:
עוֹד יָבוֹא לָכֶם חַג עָקֹב יוֹתֵר מִדָּם. בְּשַׂרְכֶם
יִתְרוֹנֵן בְּמִשְׂרָפוֹת. אַבּוּ נָאגִ'י (כִּנּוּי לָאַנְגְלִים)
שֶׁלָּכֶם אֵינוֹ. נָדַם. וְרוֹמֶל חַיָּלָיו לִרְבָבוֹת.
יָא רוֹמֶל, רוּץ לְטוּבְּרוּק.
פַּעֲמוֹנֵי שְׁוָקִים. רוֹמֶל כָּבַשׁ אֶת טוּבְּרוּק. וְהַנָּאצִים
מוֹכְרִים בְּבַגְדָּאד כָּל חֵפֶץ בְּשֵׁם טוּבְּרוּק.
לֶחֶם טוּבְּרוּק. שְׁקֵדִים טוּבְּרוּק, יַיִן טוּבְּרוּק.
דִּמְכֶם יָא יָאהוּד טוּבְּרוּק.
עַגִ'ל כַטְוָותָאק יָא רוֹמֶל (הַרְחֵב צְעָדֶיךָ יָא רוֹמֶל).

Bells weep in her dreams. In that Pentecost
Holiday, 1941. The time of the world
Was destroyed. Blood spurted. The Vichy army was subdued
Without a battle. Hitler was getting closer and closer
To Russia.
Jewish families are robbed, and bereaved.
Babylon fainteth and fadeth away, everything was.

With ringing bells the Nazi announced in Iraq:
You are going to have a Holiday more bloody than blood. Your flesh
Will burst into song
In the crematorium. Your Abu Nagi (a nickname for the English)
Is no more here. He is silent.
And Rommel has tens of thousands of soldiers
Hey Rommel, run to Tobruk.
Market bells. Rommel conquered Tobruk. And the Nazi
They call every item sold in Baghdad - Tobruk.
Tobruk bread. Tobruk almonds, Tobruk wine.
Your blood ya Yahood [you Jews] is Tobruk.
Ajil khatwatak ya Rommel (step faster you [hey] Rommel).
Take your sword out of its sheath.
We will celebrate a new holiday and we will throw the Jews of Abu Nagi to the dunghill. They don't have a guard; they do not strive for revenge in their soul. Here is a holiday of bitter news that will touch their person, a holiday for our hot blood. Ajil khatwatak ya Rommel (step faster you [hey] Rommel).

The poem strongly and correctly makes a connection between the Nazis and the pogrom. The poem is written as a nightmare of the grandmother whose two children were murdered in the pogrom. Contrary to the magnitude of the tragic content, the rhythm is of an unhurried, quiet storytelling, and the frequent rhymes cause readrs to pause occasionally: "…Zeman ha-olam / neherav. Dam zav. Helot vichy muvasim, beli kerav. Hitler le-Rusia halakh/ ve-karav" ("....The time of the world / Was destroyed. Blood spurted. The Vichy army was subdued / Without a battle. Hitler was getting closer and closer / to Russia"). Tobruk becomes a word of threat by the Arabs and of dread for the Jews. Interlacing spoken Arabic in a present tense in the Hebrew text adds authenticity to it: "Ajil khatwatak ya Rommel" ("step faster you [hey] Rommel"). The past is present in the nightmare of the grandmother. The Arabs speak to Jews and to Rommel in first person to a second person: "You [hey] Rommel, run to Tobruk... / Your blood ya yahood [you Jews] is Tobruk."

On January 21, 2005, the Los Angeles Holocaust Memorial Museum and California State University's Center for Excellence on the Study of the Holocaust, Genocide, Human Rights, and Tolerance recognized "the Farhud" as a Holocaust pogrom and asked the Holocaust museums and instructors of educational courses to do likewise.

◆ ◆ ◆

Shelomo Ben-Salih Shelomo (who was born in Babylon in 1896, immigrated to Israel in 1951, and died in Tel-Aviv in 1961) wrote, shortly after the time of the massacre, the most famous poem about the 1941 pogrom against the Jews of Babylon. A few years after its publication, he was arrested because of it.

Shelomo Ben-Salih Shelomo studied rabbinical studies (in Yehivat Bet Zilkha), was a promoter of Hebrew in Babylon, and was the founder and the principal of the Jewish school Kerem Ha-Yeladim ("The Children's Vineyard," 1924-1929). In 1914, he published a Hebrew textbook (Ha-Mathil). Among the books he published was his poetry volume Shireh Ha-Kerem (see Shelomo).

The poem begins with a lamentation about the pogrom (1-4), and then it provides detailed illustrations about the pogrom and the harm inflicted on the Jewish people, their holy artifacts, and their property (5-20). The poem concludes with a prayer that expresses wonder as to when God will redeem the Jews (21-24).

אֶשְׁאַג שְׁאָגָה מָרָה כְּלָבִיא
יוֹם חַג תּוֹרָתִי נֶהְפַּךְ לְאֵבֶל
בְּיוֹם הָאוֹרָה חָשְׁכוּ שְׁמֵיהֶם
לִבִּי לִבִּי עַל חַלְלֵיהֶם

אֶקְרַע בְּגָדַי וּסְגוֹר לְבָבִי
בְּאֶרֶץ בָּבֶל חֲבַל עַם חֶבֶל
וְגַם עָזְבוּ מַחֲמַדֵּיהֶם
מֵעַי מֵעַי עַל הֲרוּגֵיהֶם

בְּיַד הָאוֹיֵב אֶקְדָּח וְחֶרֶב
וְהוֹלְכִים לְתֻמָּם לְבֵית אִמָּם
רִטְשׁוּ בִּטְנָם סִמּוּ עֵינֵיהֶם
וְגַם טִמְּאוּ בְּתוּלוֹתֵיהֶן

וּבָא מִתְנַפֵּל כִּזְאֵבֵי עֶרֶב
בַּחוּצוֹת בָּרְחוֹבוֹת נִשְׁפַּךְ דָּמָם
בַּמִּשׁוֹר שָׁחֲטוּ אֶת בַּחוּרֵיהֶם
וְגָזְרוּ לָהֶן גַּם אֶת שְׁדֵיהֶן
לִבִּי לִבִּי

לְתוֹךְ הַבָּתִּים פָּרְצוּ כְּחַיּוֹת
גָּזְלוּ גַּם שָׁדְדוּ בַּיִת וְדִירָה
יָרוּ כַּדּוּרִים בְּלֵב בַּחוּרִים
וּבְנֵי יְשׁוּרוּן נָסוּ לִפְנֵיהֶם

חֲמוּשֵׁי זַיִן חֶרֶב פִּיפִיּוֹת
בְּיוֹם שָׁבוּעוֹת מַתַּן הַתּוֹרָה
גּוּפוֹת קְדוֹשִׁים צָבְרוּ חֳמָרִים
עִמָּם נְשֵׁיהֶם וְגַם טַפֵּיהֶם
לִבִּי לִבִּי

כְּבוֹד יִשְׂרָאֵל סִפְרֵי הַתּוֹרָה
קָרְעוּ יְרִיעוֹת רָמְסוּ בְּמִנְעָל
שָׂרְפוּ תְּפִלִּין וְגַם הַתּוֹרָה
לְזֹאת הִגְדִּילוּ מִסְפֵּד עֲלֵיהֶם

הוֹצִיאוּ זָרִים מִבֵּית אוֹצָרָה
טִמְּאוּ אוֹתָהּ בְּאַף וּבְמַעַל
וּבִרְצוּעוֹת קָשְׁרוּ הַפָּרָה
כִּי בִּידֵי אַכְזָר חֻלַּל קָדְשֵׁיהֶם
לִבִּי לִבִּי

בְּרֹב הַחוּצוֹת דֻּקְּרוּ יְהוּדִים
וּרְכוּשׁ יִשְׂרָאֵל הָיָה לְהֶפְקֵר
קָרְאוּ לִישׁוּעָה וְאֵין מוֹשִׁיעַ
כַּנָּהָר צָרוֹת בָּאוּ עֲלֵיהֶם

מִכָּל עֲבָרִים שָׂמוּ מְצוֹדִים
וְכָל מִתְנַגֵּד בַּלֵּב יְדֻקַּר
רַק אוֹיֵב גּוֹזֵל וְלֵב קוֹרֵעַ
וְצַר מְחָרֵף גַּם אֱלֹהֵיהֶם
לִבִּי לִבִּי

דֶּמַע כַּנָּהָר תִּזַּל כָּל עַיִן
שָׁדוּד פָּצוּעַ נִשְׁאַר הַיְּהוּדִי
אַתָּה ה׳ מָתַי תְּרַחֵם
מָתַי תִּשְׁלַח בֶּן דָּוִד יִפְדֵּהֶם

יַעַן כָּל קִנְיָן הָיָה לְאַיִן
אַיֵּה רְכוּשִׁי אַיֵּה כְּבוֹדִי
בִּנְךָ בְּכוֹרְךָ מָתַי תְּנַחֵם
וּמָתַי תִּבָּנֶה בֵּית מִקְדְּשֵׁיהֶם
לִבִּי לִבִּי

I will roar a bitter roar like a lion
I will rend my clothes and the enclosure of my heart
The day of celebrating my Torah turned into mourning
In Babylon the people of his lot were wounded
My heart my heart for their fallen [people]
My guts my guts for their slain

In the enemy's hand a pistol and a sword
And it came attacking as wolves of the desert
And children innocently walking to their mothers' homes
Outside on the street their blood was spilled
They crushed their tummies blinded their eyes
With a sword they slaughtered their young men
And they defiled their virginity
And also cut off their breast
My heart my heart

Into the homes they broke like beasts
Armed with weapons two-edged swords
They robbed and looted houses and flats

On the Feast of Weeks day of giving the Torah
And they shot bullets into young men's hearts
The corpses of holy people were gathered together in a heap
And the people of Jeshurun fled away from them
With their wives and babies.
My heart my heart

The honor of Israel, the Torah books
Strangers removed from their treasured place
They tore the parchments trampled with shoes
Defiled it with rage and treachery
They burnt down phylacteries and Torah
And tied up cows with the phylacteries straps
Therefore intensely mourn them
Because their sanctity was desecrated by cruel people
My heart my heart

Out on the streets they stabbed Jews
From all sides conducted a comb-out of Jews
And the possessions of the Jews were made ownerless
And every objector was stabbed in his heart
They called for salvation but there was no savior
Only a robbing and heart-tearing enemy
Turbulences like a river they have befallen them
And the enemy vilified their God
My heart my heart

Every eye sheds tears like a brook
Because all the possessions were nullified
The Jew remained robbed and wounded
Where are my honor and my possessions
You God when will you have mercy
When will you comfort your first-born son
When will you send the Messiah to redeem them
When will you build their Temple.
My heart my heart

The images are tragic and dramatic, and the style is highly touching. The poem opens with a dramatic distich. In Isaiah (5:29), the strong enemy will come and punish God's people for their sin: "Their [the enemy's] roaring shall be like a lion." Only the strength of the roar from Isaiah in this simile is alluded to. Similarly, in Hosea (13:8), God illustrates how he will punish his people who forgot him: "...I will rend the enclosure of their heart." Only the force of rending the heart is drawn upon. In "the people of his lot were wounded"—readers hear the echo of biblical verses (Lamentations 5:15; and Deuteronomy 32:9): "Jacob [is] the lot of His inheritance." The Chaldeans are described as a nation whose horses "are more fierce than the wolves of the desert" (Habakkuk 1:8), while in the poem the enemy "came attacking as wolves of the desert."

The internal rhyming contributes to the acceleration of the poetic rhythm. The style becomes informative and restrained outwardly. Thus, the impact on the reader is more powerful: "Veholkhim le-tummam le-vet immam / Ba-hutsot ba-rehovot nishpakh dammam / Ritteshu bitnam..." ("And children innocently walking to their mothers' homes / Outside on the street their blood was spilled / They crushed their tummies"). A similar effect is used in other poetic lines, for example, "Yaru kaddurim be-lev bahurim / gufot kedoshim tsavru homarim" ("And they shot bullets into young men's hearts / The corpses of holy people were gathered together in a heap"). The cry is confined by rhythm and rhymes, and the style is merely informative. Only the caged shriek of the poetic speaker is more touching. The plague of the frogs in Egypt ended up with "they gathered them together in heaps" (Exodus 8:10). Now, the corpses of the murdered Jews "were gathered together in a heap."

The poem follows in its structure a medieval Hebrew lamentation that is attributed to Yitshak Ibn Giat (1089-1039) and is read on the ninth of Ab, a day of fasting and mourning, in which the First and the Second Temples were destroyed. The words that are repeated in the lamentation of Shelomo Ben-Salih Shelomo, "My heart my heart for their fallen [people] / My guts my guts for their slain" are a quotation from Ibn Giat's poem. The poem has similar images to those in the poem by Ibn Giat, such as Torah books rolling on the bloody grounds.

Hayyim Nahman Bialik's "On the Slaughter" was a poem written in reaction to the 1903 pogrom in Kishinev. In his poem, the poetic speaker asks "How long? Until when? How long?" He was alluding to the passages in Psalms that read, "How long shall the wicked, O Lord, how long shall the wicked prosper?" (94:3) and "Until when shall you forget me, forever?" (Psalms 13:2). Shelomo Ben-Salih Shelomo's poem ends with these questions: "You God when will you have mercy / ...When will you comfort / When will you send... / and when will you build." Here, too, there are allusions to Psalms (119:84): "When wilt Thou comfort me?" and "When wilt Thou execute judgment on them that persecuted me?" (119:82).

In his poetry volume *The Vineyard Poems,* Shelomo Salih Shelomo wrote about various themes. He wrote poems praising various generous people and a poem praising the school he founded. He wrote poems of love for Zion and a yearning for Hebrew to become as prominent a language as it used to be.

In one of his poems, the poetic speaker addresses the Hebrew language. The language is personified, as it appears in the figure of a beautiful woman who was chosen to be a queen, with the crown of God, and became a maidservant. It is a poem about love and pride for the Hebrew language, contrasting between the eminence it was meant to have to the status it actually had. The poem ends with breaking the news to the language that the time arrived for its vigor and light and for the end of its degraded condition.

About the Holocaust and the Massacre: Rabbi Menasheh Saliman Shahrabani

Many studies of the Holocaust focus exclusively on European Jewry. Indeed, Jews could have had a common fate no matter where they were (Shtahl, 191-193). The Sephardim in Yugoslavia and Greece suffered as much as the Jews in other European countries. Most of them were annihilated at the time of the Holocaust. The Bulgarians treated the Jews well, and most of the Bulgarian Jews were saved. Turkish Jews suffered many losses. The Jews of Libya, Algeria, and Tunisia went through strife during the time of the Holocaust. Tunisian Jews had to wear a yellow badge, they were terrorized, their property was confiscated, they were taken away from streets and homes and arrested, taken as hostages, worshipers were beaten in synagogues, Jews were executed, deported, and served in forced labor. We have detailed accounts of the suffering of the Sephardim and Near Eastern Jews at the time of the Holocaust (see, for example, Bezalel, Ed). The fate of Near Eastern Jews would have been similar to the fate of their brethren in Europe had the Germans been successful on the North African front.

Hitler insisted that the world Jewry was his enemy. His war against Jewry was global, and his goal was to annihilate Jews wherever they were. Germany had a campaign against Jews in Arab countries, in both the Middle East and North Africa. Already in 1933-1935, the Jews from Near Eastern countries showed solidarity with the German Jews. They responded to Germany by verbal and economic protest, in order to impact Germany so that it would change its attitude toward its Jews (see Eldar). In various countries, Jews boycotted German goods and services, but this boycott did not have critical consequences.

One of the means by which Sephardim and Near Eastern Jews reacted to the tragedy of their brothers in Europe was the writing of folk poetry and poetry (Hakak, "The Holocaust"). Near Eastern Jews expressed deep feelings of brotherhood with the Jewish victims of the Holocaust. In Tunisia, for example, five booklets of folk poetry about the rise of the Nazis in Germany and their conquest of Tunisia were published (see Attal). It is estimated that the first three booklets were published respectively in 1933, 1936, and 1938. They are written in Tunisian Judeo-Arabic in both Hebrew and Latin letters and expressed identification with the sufferings of German Jews. The fourth and fifth booklets expressed the life of Tunisian Jews under the German occupation (1942-1943). The fourth booklet is a 1944 lamentation in French and Tunisian Judeo-Arabic about the concentration camps in Tunisia, the labor and death that took place there. The fifth one (from 1946) is written in Tunisian, Judeo-Arabic, and French. It describes the German occupation of Tunisia, the looting of Jewish property, taking Jews as hostages, and the deportation of young Jews to concentration camps, followed by their liberation.

Near Eastern Jews also wrote in Israel about the Holocaust. One may mention here Shelomo Zamir (who was born in Babylon in 1929 and immigrated to

Israel in 1951, see Hakak, *Im*; and *Pereakim*, 25-26), who wrote a cycle of poems (Zamir, 55-57) about the Holocaust. Sephardic Jews also gave Hebrew poetic expression to their sufferings during the Holocaust. The family roots of the poet Ezra Aruaeti (see Aruaeti) were in Spain. He was born in Bulgaria and immigrated with his family to Israel when he was two years old. Two years later he returned to Bulgaria where he lived as a child during World War II. He returned to Israel in 1949. He witnessed the deportation of the Jews from Salonica and other towns on their way to the concentration camps and wrote poems about the Holocaust. The poet Margalit Mattityahu also wrote poignant poetry about the Holocaust (see Mattityahu).

Rabbi Menasheh Saliman Shahrabani (who was born in Babylon 1881, immigrated to Israel in 1950, and died in 1960) published two volumes of liturgies and poetry in Baghdad (one volume was published without the publication date, the second one in 1928). In addition to his two published books, Rabbi Menasheh Saliman Shahrabani left twenty-two manuscripts, most of them religious. He wrote the poem "I Will Shiver and Quiver" in response to the Holocaust.

"I will Shiver and Quiver" (Hakak, 173-175; Ben-Yaacob, 404) is one of the earliest poetic responses of Near Eastern and Sephardic Jews to the Holocaust. His poem about the Holocaust has twenty-two distiches, and it follows one of the meters of medieval Hebrew poetry. Each distich has four hemistiches, and each hemistich has eight vowels. The first three parts of each quatrain (four-part) distich rhyme with each other, and the rhyme of the first three parts of the quatrain changes from one distich to another, while the fourth parts of all the distiches rhyme with each other.

The poetic speaker shudders because of what the Germans did (distich 1-8). The entire world united against the Jews. Consequently, Jews became sick of life and wanted to die. They were robbed and devoured in the forests (14-16). The poetic speaker prays to God to have mercy on his people (17-20) and bemoans and awakens others to bemoan the Jews who were killed in the Holocaust, even though his hopes were in vain (21-22). The first part (1-8) of the poem will illustrate its style and emotional tone:

אֲנִי אֶרְעַד וְאֶתְחַלְחַל   וּבְקִרְבִּי יִבְעַר אֵשׁ גַּחַל
כִּי הָאַלְמַאן קָם כְּשַׁחַל   וּכְתַנִּין לְבָלְעֵנוּ
בִּשְׁנַת הַתַּ"שׁ תָּשַׁשׁ כֹּחִי   וּמִצָּרוֹת קָצְרָה רוּחִי
כִּי הֵן מִדְּחִי אֶל דֶּחִי   בְּכַף קֶלַע קִלְּעָנוּ
גָּדַע קֶרֶן עַם נֶאֱמָן   וְעָשָׂה בָם כְּשׁוֹד שַׁלְמַן
אַלְמַאן הָרָשָׁע כְּהָמָן   אֲכָלַנוּ הֲמָמָנוּ
דָּת נָתַן הִיתְלֶר צוֹרְרִי   הַכּוֹפֵר וְהָאַכְזָרִי
כָּל הַנִּקְרָא בְּשֵׁם עִבְרִי   אֶת זִכְרוֹ מָחֹה אֶמְחֶנּוּ
הָרַג חֲכָמִים וּנְבוֹנִים   וִישָׁרִים וְנֶאֱמָנִים
וְהִכָּנִי אֵם עַל בָּנִים   שָׁפַךְ כַּמַּיִם דָּמֵינוּ
וְיָצָא הוּא לַמִּלְחָמָה   וְכָבַשׁ מַלְכֵי אֲדָמָה
וְרָדַף בְּאַף וּבְחֵמָה   אוֹתָנוּ לְהַשְׁמִידֵנוּ

זָחַלְתִּי מְאֹד וָאִירָא   וּנְשָׁמָה בִּי לֹא נוֹתְרָה
כִּי חִצֵּי אַפּוֹ בִּי יָרָה   מַטָּרָה לַחֵץ שָׂמָנוּ
חֵרֵף וְגִדֵּף לִבְלִי חֹק   בְּעַמִּי וּנְתָנָם לִצְחֹק
וְיי עָמַד מֵרָחוֹק   נִקְרָא וְלֹא יַעֲנֵנוּ

I will shiver and quiver
And the coal fire will blaze in me
Because the Germans arose as a lion
And as a dragon, to swallow us.

In the year 1940 my vigor was weakened
And due to troubles I became irascible
Because from bad to worse
He slung us out, as from the hollow of the sling.

He cut off the horn of the faithful people
And did with them like Shlaman's spoil did
The Germans who are wicked as Haman
Hath devoured me, hath crushed us hath devoured us

My enemy Hitler enacted a law
Hitler the unbeliever and cruel [:]
["] Whoever has a Hebrew name
I will utterly blot out his remembrance ["]

He killed sages and wise
And honorable and loyal [Jews]
And smote the mother with the children
He spilled our blood as water

And went out to the war
And conquered kings of the earth
And persecuted us with wrath and fury
To annihilate us

I held back (crawled) and durst [dared] not
And my soul died of fear
Because he shot at me the wrath of his arrows
Set us as a mark for the arrow

He taunted and blasphemed my people limitlessly
And put them to mockery

And God stood afar
We pray to him but He does not answer us.

The poem opens with emotional grandeur (1). Then (2) the poet provides readers with realistic information through internally rhyming words. For example, in the year "ha-tash" (1940), his strength "tashash" (was weakened, became feeble). The poem is written in the first person, the poetic speaker fully identifies with the victims, and "I" (synecdoche) represents the people of Israel as a whole. Sound is used to stress meaning: "...tsarot katsra ruhi" (troubles, irascible, 2). Internal rhymes also stress meanings: "Am...bam" ("people...in them," 3), "Alman ke-Haman" ("German like Heman," 3).

Most impressive is the way the poet weaves biblical verses to achieve poetic effects, and a few examples would serve only to demonstrate the use of biblical allusion. The Germans "did with them [the Jews] like Shlaman's spoil did." The Germans did what Shalman (Shalmaneser, king of Assyria) did: "As Shalman spoiled Beth-Arbel... The mother was dashed to the ground in pieces with her children" (Hosea 10:14). Mothers tried to protect their children, but Shalmaneser dashed the mothers together with their children. In the poem, "The Germans... / hath devoured me, hath crushed us hath devoured us." Similarly, "Nebuchadnezzar the king of Babylon hath devoured me, He hath crushed me... hath swallowed me up like a dragon..." (Jeremiah 51:34). The use of language that described past national calamities only contributes to the expression that the speaker—a Jew from the Near East—sees the Holocaust as a disaster inflicted on the Jews no matter where they were located. Abigail wishes for David that "the souls of thine enemies, them shall he [God] sling out, from the hollow of a sling" (First Samuel 25:29). What was wished on David's enemies happens in the poem to the Jews (2): "He slung us out, as from the hollow of the sling." Instead of the biblical, "I will utterly blot out the remembrance of Amalek" (Exodus 17:14), now it is the goal of Hitler to do to the Jews (4): "Whoever has a Hebrew name / I will utterly blot out his remembrance." Elihu (Job 32:6) held back and did not dare express his opinion, because he was young amidst very old people, but then he spoke about God that leads the world with justice. In the poem (7), the poet is frightened; he knows (8) that God stood afar ("why standest Thou afar off, O Lord," Psalms 10:1) and is not answering prayers. In Lamentations (3:5), God bent his bow and set the speaker as a mark for the arrow. The allusion (8) to Lamentations brings with it the notion of destruction, national calamity, persecution, and death.

The poetic speaker fully equates his feelings and troubles with those of the German Jews, because the people of Israel are inseparable, and the catastrophe of the German Jews is the catastrophe of all Jews. The account of what was happening to the German Jews is detailed—pain, persecution, loss of possessions, flee to the forests, thirst and hunger (physically and metaphorically), and death there. The poetic speaker points out that the charges against the Jews are lies. As a religious man, the speaker perceives God as the only one who can bring order and justice.

Rabbi Menasheh Shahrabani wrote a poem of twenty-five stanzas about the 1941 pogrom against the Babylonian Jews. Each one of the first twenty-two stanzas begins with another letter of the Hebrew alphabet and is in the same order as the Hebrew alphabet. The first letters of the line of the last three stanzas create the words: Menasheh Saliman Hazak (the name of the poet and the word "hazak," strong, expressing joy and self-encouragement for the completion of the poem). The first three lines of each stanza rhyme with each other. The fourth lines of all the stanzas rhyme with each other. In the first and the nineteenth stanzas, however, all the lines rhyme with the fourth lines of all the stanzas. The first part of the poem (1-2) defines its subject matter—a lamentation about the tragedy of the Jews of Baghdad. The second part of the poem (3-13) includes images from the pogrom, and the last part (14-25) is a prayer for redemption.

The poem opens with "I will raise my voice and call with my voice"—alluding to "Hear, O Lord, when I call with my voice" (Psalms 27:7) and "give ear unto my voice, when I call unto Thee" (Psalms 141:1). The poetic speaker describes his fright because of the pogrom: "My heart too melted like wax," identifying with Psalms (22:15) and "My heart has become like wax. It is melted in my inmost parts." Psalms describes the conduct of the enemy: "And [they] have aimed their arrow, a poisoned word; that they may shoot in secret places at the blameless" (ibid., 64, 4-5). The poetic speaker of the poem under discussion identifies with this image of the enemy: "And they have aimed their arrow, a poisoned word / to shoot at the covenant keeping people" (see Exodus 31:15, "...the children of Israel shall keep the Sabbath... for a perpetual covenant").

In the poem, the enemies "one called unto another and said: / Pour-out thy wrath on every Jew." The Seraphim (angels) "called unto another, and said: Holy, holy, holy is the Lord of hosts" (Isaiah 6:3). The wrath is being poured on the Jews, instead of "pour out Thy wrath upon the nations that know Thee not" (Psalms 79:6, Jeremiah 10:25). "Their adversaries became the head," complains the poetic speaker, and one cannot avoid remembering the clear allusion to "Her adversaries have become the head; her enemies are at ease" (Lamentations 1:5) that is part of the lamentation for the destruction of Jerusalem.

The enemies "gave me wormwood and poison hemlock to drink"—they caused the Jews affliction and anguish (Lamentations 3:15, 19). The "enemies are strangers and cruel... All their [the Jews] pursuers overtook them within the straight"—and again, Lamentations (1:3) echoes and adds strength to this poetic description.

"The proud have forged a lie against me"—the poetic speaker totally identifies with Psalms (119:69): "And they all are faithless with perverseness [falsification]"—cries the poetic speaker, but the reader remembers: "The perverseness of the faithless shall destroy them" (Proverbs 11:3). The enemies "frame mischief by statute"—inflict suffering on the Jews by wicked laws, and the echo of "shall the seat of wickedness have fellowship with Thee, Which frameth mischief by statute?" (94:20) is inevitable.

The enemies joined those who "violated the statute"—an act in the Bible (Isaiah 24:5) that brings the wrath of God who as a result will empty the Earth. The enemies joined "senseless counsel," and the reader remembers "the wisest counselors of Pharaoh are a senseless counsel" (Isaiah 19:11). The enemy decided to spoil [the property of the Jews] as Shalman spoiled—the language is of Hosea (10:14) describing what Shalmaneser king of Assyria did. The enemies came from all over. They all surrounded the Jews of Baghdad and were "charmers" (see Deuteronomy 18:11)—those who perform magic, witchcraft, sorcery, and cast spells.

After the pogrom's description, the poet is prayerful, asking God to listen to the prayer of the afflicted people. "Regard the prayer of the [tamarisk] destitute" he asks God (Psalms 102:18). The poet represents the people of Israel. The tamarisk is a small plant, but God listened to its prayer in the past: "...He hath regarded the prayer of the [tamarisk] destitute" (Psalms 102:18).

I demonstrated some of the biblical verses, which are included in the poem with extraordinary artistry. Without familiarity with the masterwork of the allusions, one would miss the many effects of the poem, subjective as they may be.

There are other poetic devices used in the poem that draw our attention. One of them is the use of sounds as an element in creating meanings while it receives its interpretation by the other elements that create the meaning (Harshovski). In the twelfth stanza, readers see, "...venashmidem... keshod shalman az nishdedem... nashaira" ("we will annihilate them...we will spoil them like Shalman spoils... we will leave..."). One may hear the sound of a frenzied and evil thinking enemy. In the third stanza, readers see, "...names me'ansheh...hamas... dorsim ketahmas...beshem" ("melted because of people...violence...trampling like a falcon...in a name..."). One may hear in the Hebrew text the sound of rustle, of uproar and aggression. One may hear a sound of determination and forcefulness in the fourth stanza with "...asher...dorsim...Ivri nikra...darko... davar mar lirot...berit shamar kara...ve'amar...Ivri...evra" ("...that...trample... is called a Jew... a poisoned word to shoot...kept the covenant...called...and said...Jewish...wrath"). In other instances, internal rhyme takes part in emphasizing an idea, for example, "Zarim tsarim ha-akhzarim" ("the enemies are strangers and cruel").

"And they Pierced their Heads with Nails": Rabbi Yitshak Nissim Mourned, Rabbi Moshe Ventura Condoled

Rabbi Yitshak Nissim (Baghdad 1896, emigrated to Israel in 1906, returned to Babylon and then emigrated to Israel in 1926, and died in 1981) was born to a family of famous rabbis who emigrated to Erets Yisrael between 1906 and 1908. Rabbi Nissim was highly influential in his Responsa on Jewish law. In 1955, he was appointed as Chief Rabbi of Israel. When he was twenty-one years old, he wrote a lamentation about seventeen honorable Jews who were tortured and then murdered by the Turkish secret police, among them his own brother, Shelomo Zion.

When World War I broke out in 1914, Turkey was part of the central powers that declared war against Britain, France, and Russia (see Introduction). The non-Turkish residents of Iraq were ill treated during World War I. Turkish rulers persecuted the Jews in Babylon. Jewish leaders were arrested, and Jews were accused of causing the Turks' economic hardships by effectuating a decline in Turkish securities. Before the British captured Baghdad in 1917, the persecution against the Jews escalated. Many Jews were arrested and murdered by the Turks, and later they allowed the looting of Jewish stores.

The lamentation of Rabbi Yitshak Nissim has fourteen stanzas. I will present only a few of them describing the cruelty of those who tortured the seventeen Jews and the faith of the tortured man:

מֵהֶם עֵינֵיהֶם עִוְּרוּ וְנִקְּרוּ
וּמַחֲטֵי בַרְזֶל בִּבְשָׂרָם הֶעֱבִירוּ
וּבְמַסְמְרִים אֶת רֹאשָׁם דָּקְרוּ
עַל זֹאת שָׁמַיִם הִתְקַדָּרוּ
לִבִּי לִבִּי

הָאֻמְלָלִים צָעֲקוּ בְּמָרָה
הָאֵל הַגָּדוֹל הַגִּבּוֹר וְהַנּוֹרָא
מִיתָה זוֹ תִּהְיֶה לָנוּ כַּפָּרָה
וּבִמְעֻנֵּינוּ אַפְּךָ יֶחֱרָה
לִבִּי לִבִּי

צָרִים בְּשָׁמְעָם דִּבְרֵיהֶם צָחֲקוּ
וְכָאֲרִי שִׁנֵּיהֶם חָרְקוּ
יְדֵיהֶם וְרַגְלֵיהֶם קָשְׁרוּ וְהִדְּקוּ
וּבְשַׁלְשְׁלוֹת בַּרְזֶל אוֹתָם חָנְקוּ
לִבִּי לִבִּי

יִשְׁמָעֵאל הֵמָּה הַמְּצִיקִים
הִכְבִּידוּם בָּאֲבָנִים תּוֹךְ שַׂקִּים
וְהִשְׁלִיכוּם בִּנְהָרוֹת רְחוֹקִים
מֵעֵינֵי מִשְׁפְּחוֹתָם הַנֶּאֱנָקִים

The eyes of some were blinded and gouged
And iron needles penetrated their flesh
They pierced their heads with nails
Thus the sky gloomed
My heart my heart for their fallen [people]
My guts my guts for their slain

The miserables bitterly cried
To the great God, the mighty, the awful
'May our death be an expiation for us
And your wrath be waxed hot at our torturers'
My heart my heart for their fallen [people]
My guts my guts for their slain

The enemy laughed hearing them
And gnashed their teeth like a lion
They tied and tightened their hands and feet
And choked them with iron shackles
My heart my heart for their fallen [people]
My guts my guts for their slain

The oppressing Ishmaelite
Added stones to the bagged corpses
And threw them into rivers
Faraway from their groaning families
My heart my heart for their fallen [people]
My guts my guts for their slain

In 1917, the value of Turkish securities declined, and the Turkish authorities accused the Jews of causing the decline and profiting from it. The Turkish authorities enacted a new law according to which the merchants had to exchange their silver and gold with Turkish currency. The Turkish authorities looked for but did not find Jews who disregarded the law, yet they accused seventeen innocent Jews of violating the law. They cut their noses and ears, blinded them, pierced their brains with nails, chopped them up, put them in sacks, and threw them into the Tigris River. Among them was the eighty-five-year-old Yehezkel Dangour, a well-known man for his uprightness, and his son. One of the bodies of these people was found in a sealed sack with stones inside it floating on the Tigris River and was the only one who had a burial (Ben-Yaacob, 1979, 148-149).

The lamentation of Rabbi Yitshak Nissim was published several times (in Baghdad in 1917, see Ben-Yaacob, 1970, 414-415; also see Nissim, Yitshak).

Every stanza ends in the same words, taken from the medieval Hebrew lamentation that is attributed to Yitshak Ibn Giat (1089-1039) and is read on the ninth of Ab, a day of fasting and mourning, in which the First and the Second Temples were destroyed. The words of Ibn Giat's lamentation that are repeated in the lamentation of Rabbi Yitshak Nissim are the same ones we found in the lamentations of Shelomo Ben-Salih Shelomo Gabai: "My heart my heart for their fallen [people] / my guts my guts for their slain." Yitshak Nissim's opening lamentation—"violated from their residence home"—reminds readers of the opening from Ibn Giat's lamentation: "Driven out from their pleasures home."

Rabbi Dr. Moshe Ventura sent a poem of condolences to Rabbi Yitshak Nissim, focusing on the death of Nissim's brother.

The First of the Social Protester Poets: David Saliman Tsemah

David Saliman Tsemah (who was born in Babylon in 1902, immigrated to Israel in 1949, and died in 1981) had both a secular and a religious education. He studied in a private religious elementary school ("Heder") in Alliance and in the rabbinical school Midrash Bet Zilkha. At the age of twelve, he had already written Hebrew poems about World War I that his famous teacher Rabbi Yehuda Ptaya wanted to publish, but his father destroyed them because he feared the authorities. At a later stage in his life, he was a trader of manuscripts and books, he interpreted Spanish Hebrew poetry, published Hebrew poetry, fables, proverbs, and articles about medieval Hebrew poetry (Hakak, 2003, 184-199; Ben Yaacob, 1970, 420-435; 1980, 305). About half of his sixty poems follow one of the meters of medieval Hebrew poetry. Tsemah also published an article about the life of Todros ben Yehuda Abulafia (see Bibliography, Vol. 2) based on his poems. In this article, the author displays his thorough knowledge about Todros' works. However, he does not differentiate between the poetic speaker and the biographical poet.

One of his poems is about the hookah (nargilah). He wrote, "One day I was sad. They brought me a nargilah with flowers inside, I smoked it and wrote about it in the following poem":

הֲלֹא אִשֵּׁךְ אֱלֵי רֹאשֵׁךְ   אֲבָל אִשִּׁי מְסֻתֶּרֶת
אַךְ דְּמָעַי מְפֻרְסָמוֹת   וּדְמָעַיִךְ בְּמַחְתֶּרֶת
וַאֲנִי כָלוּא לִזְמָן   וְאָכֵן אַתְּ מְשֻׁחְרֶרֶת
קוֹלֵךְ תִּבְכִּי, וְאָכֵן אַתְּ   לְמוּל בִּכְיִי מְשׁוֹרֶרֶת
מִמְּעַיִךְ אִינַק עָשָׁן בּוֹ   גַּחַלְתִּי מִתְקָרֶרֶת
פְּרָחִים יְרַקְּדוּ בָךְ   מַרְאֵיהֶם דַּר וְסוֹחֶרֶת
וּבְלִבִּי יִרְקֹד דְּאָגוֹת   גַּם נַפְשִׁי מְאֹד נֶעְכֶּרֶת
אַף כִּי כַחְשִׁי בַּעֲבוּרֵךְ   לֹא אֲמִירֵךְ בְּאַחֶרֶת
יֹאהֲבוּךְ כִּי אֲדַמֵּךְ   בַּעֲלַת אוֹב וְחוֹבֶרֶת

Surely your fire is at your head
But my fire is concealed
My tears however are in the open
While your tears are surreptitious
And I am a prisoner of time
While you are indeed unbound
Your voice cries and indeed you
Chant facing my cry
From your guts I will suckle smoke by which
My burning coal cools down
Flowers will dance inside you
They look like pearls and onyx marble
And in my heart dance qualms

And my soul becomes melancholic
Albeit I became skinny because of you
I will not trade you for another
They love you because I liken you with
A woman that divineth by a ghost and a Charmer

The poem's basic form is a distich consisting of two lines. The second lines end with the same rhyme, with a consistent meter of eight cords in each line.

The poem emphasizes the opposite analogies between the poetic speaker and his hookah; the fire of the hookah is visible at the top of the pipe, while the speaker's fire is concealed. His cry is visible by everyone while the "tears" of the (personified) hookah are covert. He is imprisoned by his fate, "time," while the hookah is free.

Medieval Hebrew poets described "time" as perpetually flowing and inflicting death on people; it is the fate that smites man blindly and suddenly in order to embarrass him and torture him (Levin, 68-79).

The hookah spews smoke, while he suckles it in order to cool down his burning coal. Flowers dance in the hookah while worries dance in his heart. The hookah charms him (Deuteronomy 18:11). In these comparative analogies, one condition is "real" and the other one is figurative. The fire of the hookah is real, but his fire is figurative; his tears are real, but the tears of the hookah are figurative; his cry is real, but the hookah's cry is figurative; the hookah's smoke is real, but his "coal" is figurative; the hookah's flowers that were placed in it for beauty and scent dance, but his worries only figuratively dance.

The description of the hookah begins with the grandeur of the first line rhyming ("ishekh," your fire, with "roshekh," your head) and includes the use of all senses in order to depict its beauty and impact. It has fire (touching); it cries and sings (hearing); it has the beauty and the smell of flowers (vision, smell); and its smoke is suckled (taste). The poem fuses the sensual with the abstract and the emotional. The use of forms in Spanish Hebrew poetry in distiches and meter does not hinder the poem from being innovative in its topic and images and rich in its style.

The basic form of another poem of Tsemah, the complaint poem "Is There Any Grieving Man Like a Father Who Sent His Children Away," is a distich consisting of two lines. All of the second lines end with the same rhyme, and the poem is written in one of the Spanish Hebrew poetry meters (a peg and three cords).

The poet introduces his poems by the following words: "I have composed this poem in October 1945. I traveled with my family to Damascus and from there I arranged for their illegal immigration to Israel. At the same time, I received a letter from Israel, from my son Yosef, who asked me to come to Israel even if it would be for only one month (a honeymoon). I wrote him this poem."

הֲיֵשׁ כּוֹאֵב כְּאָב הִרְחִיק יְלָדָיו   וְיֵשׁ עָשׁוּק כְּגוֹלֶה מִידִידָיו ?
וְיֵשׁ גֵּר נֶחְשָׁב תּוֹךְ מִשְׁכְּנוֹתָיו   וְאֵין מֵבִין צְפוּן לִבּוֹ וְסוֹדָיו
וּבָדָד הוּא וְדוֹמֶה אֶל אֲחֵי רָשׁ   שְׂנֵאוּהוּ וּבָגְדוּ בוֹ בְּגָדָיו
וְהוּא נִמְצָא רְאוּת עַיִן לְבוֹזְזָיו   וְהוּא נִתַּן כְּמַטָּרָה לְשׁוֹדְדָיו
וְהַזְּמַן כְּצַר נֶגְדּוֹ, וְתֶבֶל   כְּמַאְסָר לוֹ, וְהָרְחוֹבוֹת צְמִידָיו
וְצָרוֹתָיו וְאַנְחוֹתָיו עֲנָקָיו   יְגוֹנוֹתָיו וְתוּגוֹתָיו רְבִידָיו
וּמִתְאוֹנֵן עֲלֵי זְמַן עֲבָרוֹ   וּמִתְבּוֹנֵן וְצוֹפֶה אֶל עֲתִידָיו
וְנָע וָנָד בְּכֹל יָמָיו כְּקַיִן   וְלֹא הָרַג לְאָח יָנַק בְּדַדָיו
וְהוּא רוֹדֵף וְהוּא נִרְדָּף כְּדָוִד   וְלֹא הָרַג לְאוּרִיָּה בְּחֶמְדָּיו
וּמִתְאוֹנֵן לְגוֹרָלוֹ כְּיַעֲקֹב   וְלֹא צָדָה כְּתַחְבּוּלוֹת נְקֻדָּיו
אֲבָל נִשְׁעַן בְּחַיָּיו עַל תְּבוּנוֹת   כְּמוֹ יוֹסֵף לְמוּל פַּרְעֹה בְּעָמְדָיו
בְּעֵת רָחַק בְּנוֹ יוֹסֵף אֲהוּבוֹ   כְּאוֹר עֵינָיו וְיֹתֶרֶת כְּבֵדָיו
וְהוּא צוֹפֶה לְיוֹם בֹּא הַתְּשׁוּעָה   יְחַכֶּה עֵת אֲשֶׁר יִכְלוּ נְדוּדָיו
וְיוֹם קָרֵב אֱלֵי נְוֵה יְדִידִים   מְנָעוּהוּ בְּלִי לִרְאוֹת גְּדוּדָיו
כְּמוֹ רָעֵב וְיֵשׁ לוֹ פַּת בְּסַלּוֹ   וְכַצָּמֵא וְהַמַּיִם בְּכַדָּיו
וְלֹא אֵדַע הַאִם שָׁכַח חֲנוֹת אֵל   וְהוּא צִוָּה לְהָרַע לוֹ פְּקִידָיו
אֲשֶׁר הָיוּ לְפָנִים הַזְּמַנִּים   יְשָׁרְתוּהוּ וְהַיָּמִים עֲבָדָיו
וּפָנָיו כַּפְּרָחִים אָדְמוּ אָז   וְכַיַּסְמִין הֲכִי יָרֵק בְּבַדָּיו
קְרָאָהוּ בְּנוֹ אֶצְלוֹ לְחֹדֶשׁ   הֲיֵשׁ נַחַת לְחוֹתֶה אֵשׁ בְּיָדָיו
וְיֵשׁ דְּבַשׁ אֱלֵי דְּבַ"שׁ בְּחָדְשׁוֹ   אֱמֶת מָתוֹק וְאָכֵן רוֹשׁ צְדָדָיו
וְאֵיךְ יוּכַל דְּפֹק שַׁעַר חֲצֵרוֹ   וְאֵיךְ יוּכַל לְחַבֵּק אֶת עַמּוּדָיו
וּמִי יִתֵּן לְחוֹנֵן אֶת עֲפָרָיו   וְלוּ יוּכַל לְנַשֵּׁק אֶת יְתֵדָיו
יְחִיד אָב שָׁב בְּאֶפֶס כֹּל וְנִפְרָד   מְאוֹהֲבָיו הֲכִי רַבּוּ יְחוּדָיו
וְאֵין לוֹ בַּיְּקוּם מִשְׁעָן וּמִבְטָח   וְאֵין לוֹ מִי יְכַבֶּה אֶת יְקוֹדָיו
לְבַד תִּקְוָה אֲשֶׁר תָּבֹא בְּאַחֲרִית   וְאוּלַי אָז יְאֻשַּׁר עִם יְלָדָיו
יְהוֹסֵף אַל תְּהִי נִכְאָב עֲלֵי אָב   שְׁמֹר אָמְךָ הֲכִי הִיא מַחֲמַדָּיו
יְחָנֵּךְ אֵל וְיִשְׁמַע לִי תְּפִלָּה   אֲשֶׁר יִשְׁמַע תְּפִלַּת כָּל חֲסִידָיו

The splendor of the opening distich is reflected in the following question: "Is there any grieving man like a father who sent his children far away / And is there anyone browbeaten like the one who was exiled from his friends?" These questions express the poem's essence. They are clear and present a complete idea. The first and second lines are rhetorical questions. The second line completes the first one and does not present another idea. All four lines of the first two distiches have the same rhyme. Another sound effect is reflected in the homonyms "koa'ev" ("grieving") and "keav" ("like a father").

In the next distiches (2-7) we find a description of the grieved father:

And there is one, considered a stranger at his own home
And nobody understands his heart-hidden secrets
And he is alone and resembles a poor man whose brethren
Do hate him and deal with him treacherously
And he is in plan view of his plunderers
And he is a target of his rubbers

And time is like an enemy opposing him, and the world
Like a jail for him, and the streets are his bracelets [cuffs]

The speaker feels he is like a poor man whose brethren hate him and deal with him treacherously. Two biblical verses echo this idea: "All the brethren of the poor do hate him. How much more do his friends go far from him" (Proverbs 19:7)—because he chases them in order to ask for support—and "Wherefore are all they secure that deal very treacherously" (Jeremiah 12:1)—why do the wrong people prosper?

The poetic speaker complains against "time" and the "world," which offend the poetic speaker:

And time is like an enemy opposing him, and the world
Is like a jail for him, and the streets are his handcuffs.

Characteristics of "time" in this poem were presented above. I will now present characteristics of the "world" ("Tevel") in medieval Hebrew poetry. The "world" is personified as a wicked living entity that strives to inflict trouble and death on mankind. It is in contradiction to worshiping God and of the life-to-be. It is a prison for the good people and a paradise for the evil ones. It is an illusion and a dream, at the end awaits a bitter awakening. If it conferred good things, one should not trust it, because it will soon hurt him. The world is described as a whore who seduces, deceives, and is disloyal. She murders and denies her act. She resembles a bad mother who kills her children. People dishonor her, yet are seduced by her beauty. Only by treating her indifferently can one find peace in this world (Levin, ibid.). The poetic speaker lives in pain:

And his quandaries and sighs are his choker
His agony and woe his chains
And he complains about his past
And awaits and observes his future

He conducted himself wisely and did not sin; yet he is suffering like biblical characters that sinned (distiches 8-11) such as Cain, David, and Jacob. Here are two of their sins:

A fugitive and a wanderer like Cain
But did not kill the brother who suckled from the same breasts
And he is pursued and persecuted like David
And he did not kill Uriah because he is covetous

In the Bible, it reads, "And the Lord said unto Cain: A fugitive and a wanderer shalt thou be in the earth" (Genesis 4:11). Unlike Cain, David, and Jacob, the poetic speaker relied on his wisdom, as Joseph did in front of Pharaoh. He expresses pain, because despite the fact that he is geographically close to his beloved son, he cannot see him (13-24). He wishes for the end of his wandering and separation from his family, otherwise, the poetic speaker feels that "he does not have in the world support and security / and he does not have someone who would extinguish his blazes." If he accepts his son's invitation, the consequences would be harsh. He is hoping for a better future. He prays and blesses his family (25-27).

Tsemah's style is intense, and his devices are used as an integral part of the content. For example, he addresses his son: "Yehosef do not ache about a father / guard your mother because she is his beloved." The Hebrew "ache" ("nikh'av") and "father" ("av") rhyme with "his beloved" ("mahmudav"). His tragedy is expressed in these three words—he is in pain as a father and a husband for separating from his beloved family.

One may detect the playfulness in the distich "and there is honey for honey for a month / it is truly sweet but indeed has a poisonous end" (20). The word honey in Hebrew has the initials of the poem's poet David Ben Shelomo—if he, the honey (dbsh), visits his son, they will have honey like in a honeymoon, but the consequences will be fatal.

Tsemah uses images from nature in order to depict his situation. For example, in the past he had a good life "and his face like flowers was reddened / and like the jasmine with the darkest green branches" (18), but now he has a bitter fate. Some of his images illustrate the emotional pain with physical instances; he is "like a hungry man who has a meal in his basket / and a thirsty man who has water in his jars" (15). He has a family ("meal" and "water"), but he is lonely ("hungry," "thirsty"), because he had to be separated from it. The poem does not even entertain the question if the illegal immigration to Israel is worth all the family troubles, because the love for Israel is a matter of course. Tsemah wrote other poems about separation from his family (these and some other poems were published for the first time in Hakak, 2003, 194-195).

Tsemah visited Israel earlier in 1932. He developed friendly relations with Hayyim Nahaman Bialik (1873-1934), the Hebrew poet, storywriter, essayist, translator, and editor, who is considered the greatest Hebrew poet of modern times and strongly influenced modern Hebrew culture. In 1935, Tsemah visited Israel again and developed similar relations with H. Brody (1868-1942), who was an important scholar of medieval Hebrew poetry and Sephardic liturgies.

In honor of Bialik's sixtieth birthday, Tsemah wrote a poem in 1932 called *Yeshurun* (poetic biblical name of Israel, Jeshurun). He describes the beauty of medieval Hebrew poetry (1-6) and wonders about the origin of this unique poetry (7-9). Hebrew poetry identifies itself as a daughter of strong, highly gifted forefathers. The poetic speaker points out some of these forefathers (15-19)—Shelomo ibn Gabirol and Moshe ibn Ezra—whose poetry (that was republished by Bialik and Yehoshua Hana Ravnitski) excites many readers. He ends with praising Bialik for his works in the Hebrew language and literature (20-26).

The description of medieval Hebrew poetry in the poem expresses the admiration Hebrew authors in Babylon had for medieval Hebrew poetry. Here is an example of the description of medieval Hebrew poetry in this poem by Tsemah:

יְשִׁירוּן עֵת יְשׁוּרוּן בּוֹ יְשׁוּרוּן   עֲדִינַת הַיֳּפִי בִּימֵי עֲלוּמִים
מְנַגֶּנֶת וְכִנּוֹרָהּ בְּחֵיקָהּ   וְזִמְרָתָהּ תְּשַׂמַּח לֵב עֲגוּמִים
וְיַעֲלַת חֵן בְּלֹא כֹּחַל וְשָׂרֹק   מְעֻטֶּרֶת בְּכֹל מִינֵי בְשָׂמִים
וְטֻפְּחָה בְּתוֹךְ עֲרָב וּמֵהֶם   מְקֻשֶּׁטֶת וְעַל אַפָּהּ נְזָמִים
וְאַרְבַּעַת צְמִידִים עַל יָדֶיהָ   וְחָרוּז דַּר מְיַפֶּה הַגְּלָמִים
וְעַל שׁוּלֵי מְעִילָהּ פַּעֲמוֹנִים   מְצַלְצְלִים עֲלֵי שֵׁם הַחֲכָמִים
יְתוֹמָה הִיא וְאָבִיהָ הֲכִי חַי   וְנוֹלְדָה לוֹ בְּלִי צִירִים וְדָמִים?
אֲנִי מֵאָז שְׁמַעְתִּיהָ תְּרַנֵּן   וְאָבִינָה נְגִינַת הַיְתוֹמִים

Jeshurun sings when they see him
Tender beauty in her youth
She plays and her violin is on her bosom
And its singing brings gladness to the heart of the gloomy
An unadorned graceful gazelle
Embellished with a variety of fragrances
And it was nourished among the Arabs and from them
With nose-rings
And four bracelets on her arms
And a string of pearls beautifies her corpse
And bells are upon the skirts of her fur
Ring the name of the sages

The first Hebrew line challenges the reader, who wants to know who will sing, when, why, and in honor of whom. This is the transliteration of the line: "Yeshirun 'aet Yeshurun bo yeshurun." The people of Israel (Yeshurun, poetic biblical name of Israel, Jeshurun) will sing ("Yeshirun") when they will see ("yeshurun") him, Bialik. The poem's introduction states that the poem was written for Bialik's sixtieth birthday, and the poem praises him.

The poem opens in grandeur with three perplexing homonyms in a short line. The medieval Hebrew poetry that was ornamented by figurative language and forms is personified as a beautiful, young, ornamented woman. The ornaments influence various senses—auditory (she plays the violin, sings, and has bells), visual (a graceful gazelle, beautiful, has ornaments including bracelets, nose rings, and pearls), and smell (fragrances). The bells remind us of the biblical holy garments (Exodus 28:34).

The forefathers of this poetry were almighty in their literary works. The poetry identifies itself this way: "I am the daughter that the hand / of my forefathers turned the rock into pool of water" (10). It is the Lord "who turned the rock into a pool of water, the flint into a fountain of waters" (Psalms 114:8). However, when it came to writing poetry, the poets were almighty. The forefathers of Hebrew poetry are "Gabirol with his son Ezra" (16). Bialik interpreted their poems and significantly contributed to understanding them, and he is highly praised in this poem.

Tsemah also wrote two lamentations about Bialik's death (published for the first time and discussed in Hakak, 2003, 195-199) and poems praising David Yellin, the well-known scholar of medieval Hebrew poetry.

Tsemah was the first poet of Near Eastern origin that protested the treatment of Near Eastern Jews in Israel (see Hakak, *Yerudim*; Hakak, *Perakim*). Tsemah wrote this poem after he immigrated to Israel in 1949. His poetry profoundly and repeatedly expresses his love for Israel and the Jewish people. He wrote this poem about the way his community was treated:

וְהָעֵדָה וְעֵדָהּ בַּשְּׁחָקִים   אֲנָשֶׁיהָ עֲלֵי יֹשֶׁר אֱמוּנִים
בְּנֵי בָבֶל אֲשֶׁר גָּלוּ וְעָלוּ   וְעָזְבוּ שָׁם לְבִנְיָנִים וְהוֹנִים
בְּדוּקִים הֵם בְּשֶׁפֶר הַיִּחֲסִים   חֲקוּקִים הֵם בְּסֵפֶר תַּחְכְּמוֹנִים
וְהַתַּלְמוּד הֲלֹא חֻבַּר בְּבָבֶל   וְכַמָּה יֵשׁ בְּדוֹרוֹתָם גְּאוֹנִים
וְהִתְפַּזְּרוּ פְּנִינֵיהֶם יְקַוּוּ   לְהַצְמִיד כָּאן חֲרוּזֵי הָאֲבָנִים
וְהִנֵּה נָבְקָה רוּחָם בְּקִרְבָּם   וְלִבּוֹתָם בְּלִבּוֹתָם סְאוֹנִים
וְלֵב אִישִׁים בְּיַיִן לֹא יְנֻחַם   רָצוּף מַחַל וְלֹא יַעֲלֶה עֲשָׁנִים
לְיִשְׂרָאֵל אֲשֶׁר הִפְלָה בְּבָנָיו   כְּתֹנֶת פַּס לְבַד אֶל בֵּן זְקוּנִים
בְּמַצָּב זֶה הֶתָנוּחַ מְדִינָה   וְאֵיךְ יוּכְלוּ שְׂאֵת זֹאת הַמְּדִינִים
הֲלֹא הִתְרוֹצְצוּ בָנִים בְּקִרְבָּהּ   וְהוֹי פּוֹתִים! וְהוֹי הַשַּׁאֲנַנִּים!
וַיָּקָם חַד בְּתוֹכְמוֹ וְנָאַם   לְהַרְגִּיעַ לְבָבוֹת מְיֻגּוֹנִים
הֲלֹא צָרִיךְ לְשַׁגְשֵׁג הַמְּדִינָה   אֱלֵי שֶׂכֶל אֱלֵי אוֹתָהּ מְבִינִים
הֲלֹא הֶפְסֵד בְּהִפָּרֵד חֲזָקִים   וְנִצָּחוֹן בְּהִתְאַחֵד רְזוֹנִים
הֲלֹא רַעַל כְּמוֹ חֹמֶץ וּמֵימָן   בְּהִתְאַחֲדָם יְהוּ מֵימֵי עֲיָנִים
וְאַל תִּהְיוּ בְּפֵרוּדְכֶם בְּנֵי עָשׁ   הֱיוּ כִּימָה וְכוֹכָבֶיהָ רְצִינִים
וְתִהְיוּ אָז כְּאִישׁ נוֹאָשׁ בְּעֶרֶב   יָלִין בֶּכִי וְלַבֹּקֶר רְנָנִים

And the community and its witness in heaven
Is of people faithful to frankness
The Jews of Babylon who were exiled and immigrated
And left behind edifices and riches
The grace of their relationships is proven
They are engraved in the book of astuteness
And the Talmud was authored in Babylon
And there are many geniuses [Gaonits]
And their pearls scattered and they hoped
To string here the precious stones
But here their spirit was emptied within them

And their hearts are agitated
And the hearts of men will not be comforted with wine
To be filled with exculpation and not with wrath
For Israel that discriminated its people
Has a coat of many colors only for the youngest son
Under these circumstances would the state be peaceful
And how can its leaders endure it
Her children struggle together within her
And woe to the fools! And woe to the indifferent!

The spirit of the Babylonian Jews was made empty within it, just as it is written in the Bible "the spirit of Egypt shall be made empty within it" (Isaiah 19:3). Rebecca conceived, "and the children struggled together within her" (Genesis 25:22); they were Esau and Jacob. Only fools and uncaring leaders can ignore the struggle between Jews of different origins, and it cannot be ignored in Israel. "Intoxicating" the Babylonian Jews, giving them illusions rather than action will not prevent wrath in a country that had "a coat of many colors" only for part of its population. In a later part of this poem, President Yitshak ben-Zvi explained the importance of unity in Israel, and everything was resolved.

The poem's form is still influenced by medieval Hebrew poetry—a distich consisting of two lines. The entire second line ends with the same rhyme, and the poem is written in one of the Spanish Hebrew poetry meters (a peg and three cords). The content is, however, new in terms of its theme and the characters in it. The style is concise, rich and restrained, yet clearly emotional, using questions and exclamation marks while admonishing.

I will illustrate the esthetic accomplishments in this poem by its first two distiches:

כְּנַף דֶּגֶל אֲשֶׁר הֵפֵאה עֲנָנִים
וְאִם דֶּגֶל יְנוֹפֵף בִּמְעוֹנִים
לְקַבֵּץ עַם אֲשֶׁר נִזְעָם וְנִרְעַם
וְרַב פְּצָעִים כְּרֹב יָמִים וְשָׁנִים

[Is it] a sun wing that scattered clouds
Or a flag that flutters in the dwellings
To assemble a wrathful and enraged nation
With as many wounds as the many days and years

As in the case of the other poems presented here, the unavoidable injustice that the translation provides in contrast to the original makes it difficult to appreciate the poetic abilities of Tsemah. Some of the poetic devices reflected in these two distiches will be briefly pointed out.

The poem opens with two curious questions. Both questions relate to a positive change in Jewish history. The metaphor of "sun wing" augments the status of the national flag, because the flag has analogous powers to those of the sun. The fluttering of the flag may remind us of a fluttering wing ("sun wing"). The first two lines rhyme with each other ("ananim," "clouds," with "meonim," "dwellings"). Both lines of the second distich are highly melodious: in the first line, "'am" (a nation), "niz'am" ("wrathful"), and "nir'am" ("enraged," thundered). The Hebrew word for "scattered" ("hif'ah") was chosen carefully, ending with the same sound that precedes the word next to it, "Ananim" (clouds). Similarly, the Hebrew words for wounds ("pets'aim"), days ("yamim"), and years ("shanim") rhyme by their grammatical suffixes. The form of questions and the intense rhyming draw special attention to the opening distiches. The national tragedy is presented in somewhat of an understated way, and its wounds are not detailed.

The Hebrew of David Tsemah, as reflected in this poem, is the product of Hebrew education and his love for Hebrew in Babylon. It is not the product of his life in Israel. He wrote the poem shortly after he arrived in Israel. His artistic use of the language demonstrates a meticulous and creative knowledge of the language.

Part 2: Folktales, Reportage, Epistles, Research of Literature, and a Story

Chapter 4: The Folktales of Rabbi Yosef Hayyim

The folktales of Rabbi Yosef Hayyim are aimed at benefitting the listeners, to teach them something that would improve their lives and characters. These are educational, didactic stories, dominated by their moralistic message. The characters and plot are illustrations to a message. The tale is only a sweet wrapper for a plot with a bitter pill.

These folktales illustrate significant aesthetic achievement. They employ many literary devices such as intriguing plots, illustrative episodes, dialogues and monologues, direct and indirect speech, imagery, heroes and anti-heroes, allegories, humor, passive and active voicing, flashbacks, flash-forwards, symbols, and parallelism.

The folk literature of Babylonian Jews was written in Hebrew, Aramaic, and Judeo-Arabic, depending on the period in which they were written. There is substantial literature about the folktales of Babylonian Jews (Noy; Avishur, "Hassifrut," *Hassippur*; Jason, "Hassipur" and *Sippureh*; Hasan-Rokem, "Iyyun"; Shennhar, "Hassifrut"; Agasi; Ben-Yaacob, *Haotsar*). We find folk literature of Babylonian Jews in the Babylonian Talmud and in the homiletic interpretations of the Scriptures ("midrashim"). We also find folk literature in the work of the Gaonites (highly learned geniuses), who headed the Babylonian Yeshivot.

From the twelfth century to the seventeenth century (a difficult period), we have almost no folk literature from the Babylonian Jews. However, from the eighteenth century forward we have substantial folk literature.

Hebrew folktales of Babylonian Jews from the first millennium are rich. In later times, Hebrew folktales were given a special place in the works of Rabbi Yosef Hayyim, Rabbi Shelomo Bekhor Hutsin, and Rabbi Shelomo Twena. Rabbi Shelomo Bekhor Hutsin (Hakak, *Iggerot*) published three volumes of folk literature. Today, folktales of Babylonian Jews are found in print or are recorded in manuscripts. Yitzhak Avishur did important work in the field of Babylonian Jewish folk literature (Avishir, *Hassippur*, Vol. 1, 7-25). In 1988, Jason published a book in which she presented an index that draws a profile of folktales of Arabic-speaking Jews who emigrated from Babylon to Israel. The first part of the book lists the folktales by the tale-type scheme of Aarne and Thompson. The folktales were told in Judeo Arabic.

Rabbi Yosef Hayyim (1834-1909) was born into a family of notable Rabbis. He was also known as Ben Ish Hai, which is the title of his major work on Jewish law published in Jerusalem in 1898. Yosef Hayyim was considered the most prominent Rabbi of the Babylonian Jews in the latest generations. At the age of thirteen, he was admitted into the famous Midrash Bet Zilkha, where the great Rabbi Abdallah Somekh taught him. A few years later, he retreated to his attic to study alone. At age twenty-one, he was already well known for his vast knowledge and brilliance. At age twenty-five, his father died, whereupon he took his father's place as a Jewish preacher ("darshan") in Baghdad for fifty years. He preached every Saturday in a synagogue known as "Slat Alzariri" ("The Small Synagogue"), except for four Saturdays a year in which he preached at "Slat Alkabbiri" ("The Big Synagogue"). On these four Saturdays, he was the only Jewish preacher preaching in the synagogues of Baghdad.

Yosef Hayyim was renowned in the Jewish world, particularly in all Middle Eastern countries, as a mystic (Kabbalist) and as a decisor (a Rabbinical authority who presides over Jewish law). He responded to questions from many countries about Jewish law. He was also known as a highly gifted preacher, who instituted Rabbinical and communal enactments. He authored about two hundred liturgies—seventy of which came into our hands—that were used and sung in various countries, including Iraq, Israel, and India. He published sixty books concerning a variety of topics, including Jewish law, liturgies, sermons, biblical interpretations, and mysticism.

Rabbi Yosef Hayyim (who read secular Hebrew literature of his time) was considered a supreme decisor. His book *Ben Ish Hai* (Jerusalem, 1898) was the authoritative code of Jewish law for Babylonian Jews. Even today many Sephardi Jews consider it to be their concise book of Jewish law.

Rabbi Yosef Hayyim loved Israel and was active in supporting the Jews who settled in it. In 1869, he went to visit Israel. On the way to Israel one Saturday, pirates attacked his convoy in the desert. Seeing Rabbi Yosef Hayyim continuing his studies with serenity, the pirates, confused and astonished, decided to move on.

The Rabbis of Jerusalem welcomed him with love and admiration. He went to visit the Rabbi of Hebron, Eliahu Mani (see in this book the chapters about Mani's two sons), who was an old friend of Rabbi Yosef Hayyim. When he tried to visit the graves of the forefathers, he was attacked and burst into tears. He explained that it was not the danger that caused him to cry, but the status of the graves of the forefathers.

Rabbi Yosef Hayyim was a scholar who kept away from the business world. However, his four brothers were interested in both business and religious studies. They named their business after their famous brother. At one time, they had business difficulties, and their embittered creditors sued them. The brothers were acquitted of any wrongdoing, and they later paid all their debts. But, Rabbi Yosef Hayyim was so embarrassed by this incident that for several years he would not leave his home.

While Rabbi Yosef Hayyim was a decisor, the Alliance strove to implement changes in Jewish education in Baghdad (see Hakak, *Iggerot*). Rabbi Yosef Hayyim was in favor of various kinds of changes, but when he felt that they were going too far, he stopped supporting them. Jacob Obermayer, who came from Vienna in 1876 to teach in Baghdad, supported the easing of some religious requirements. He published a harsh criticism in a Hebrew periodical in Europe against Rabbi Yosef Hayyim. When the Rabbis in Baghdad read it, they excommunicated Obermayer and protested the publication of the article. They forgave Obermayer only after he publicly asked forgiveness from Rabbi Yosef Hayyim.

Ben-Yaacob published the first twenty of Rabbi Yosef Hayyim's poems (1970, 317-119), a chapter in a book (1980, 190-200), a monograph (see Bibliography), and then a collection of Rabbi Yosef Hayyim's liturgies and poems (see Bibliography). Zvi Yehuda edited an important collection of articles about Rabbi Yosef Hayyim (see Yehuda).

The Babylonian Rabbis wrote poetry as part of their intellectual creativity, and most of their motifs were religious and national. The poems and liturgies of Rabbi Yosef Hayyim have a strong religious-moralistic slant. Rabbi Yosef Hayyim did not achieve the same recognition and status with his poetry that he enjoyed with his rabbinical writing (Hakak, 2003, 74-76).

Rabbi Yosef Hayyim, a gifted speaker, used folktales in his sermons that deeply touched the hearts of his listeners. Every tale had a clear lesson. These tales were collected by his disciple, Rabbi Ben-Zion Hazan, and published in a book called *Nifl'aim Ma'asekha* ("Splendid are Your Deeds"). The book was published in 1912 in Jerusalem, and another book of folk literature was gathered from Rabbi Yosef Hayyim's works in 1913 (Hayyim, 1912, and Hayyim, 1913). These books appeared in numerous editions. Hazan's collection is incomplete. In 1988, a five volume edition appeared that included additional folktales of Rabbi Yosef Hayyim (Hayyim, 1988).

Rabbi Yosef Hayyim did not author all the folktales that he told. Some of them he heard and some he read and adapted. By these didactic stories, Rabbi Yosef Hayyim captured the attention of his listeners. The stories demonstrate how deeply he understood his people's hearts.

In her introduction to the book *Chacham Yosef Chayim: Parables from Baghdad* (see Bibliography), Nehama Conuelo Nahmoud wrote that Rabbi Yosef Hayyim's place "in the lives and the hearts of Sephardim throughout the world is analogous to that of the Vilna Gaon of the Ba'al Shem Tov in the hearts of Ashkenazi Jews—and the number of his followers is continually increasing" (9). She published English adaptations of these stories.

Included in this chapter are several folktales that I translated for this book and some brief introductory remarks to each one of them. These folktales were told by one man, and therefore, his choices, his values, his style, and his use of various literary devices, such as suspense, humor, and frequent dialogues, are common to them. Some of these stories are about the relationship between two people rather than God and man.

◈ ◈ ◈

In the following folktale, a rich man throws a party. A smart and courageous guest encounters him and illustrates and dramatizes to him how he, the rich man, exalted the ignorant guests and demeaned the knowledgeable ones. The guest demonstrates his opinion by using a balance, in which the empty scale is up and the full scale is down. At the end of the tale, Rabbi Yosef Hayyim expresses a pessimistic view of the quality of leaders and rich people. The tale promotes faith, because in such a world we can depend on God. At the climax of the story, a face-to-face encounter between the rich host and his smart guest is dramatized by a direct speech. Like other folktales of Rabbi Yosef Hayyim, it is an emotional story with a short plot and a climactic ending.

There once was ("ma'seh") a smart man who came to a party of his friend, and there were some people who were invited to the feast. When the smart man entered the party hall, he saw that the seating was upside down, topsy-turvy. The host had placed the rich people who were unknowledgeable and ignorant at the top, and the sages that were full of wisdom and knowledge at the bottom, under the rich men. The smart man became furious because of it, and he left the house and returned with one balance and a heavy stone. He hung the balance free of weight by a rope that came out of the middle of the ceiling of the party hall, and when the two scales of the balance were empty, they stood equally side by side. Then he put the big heavy stone on one of the scales, and the empty scale jumped immediately and came up and the full, heavy one went down. The host asked, "What did you accomplish by this?" The smart man answered, "I did the same as you did, that you placed the empty people on the top and the ones full of wisdom down below."

The moral is that in this world the broken part is larger than the sound portion, "the wisdom of the learned will degenerate and the sin-fearing will be despised" [Sota, 49b], "go away impure" they will be shouted at, and all the wicked and the robbers and the swindlers take part as the heads of the speakers. All the affairs of the countries and the communities are decided by them, and there is no one wise [among them who walks in] an honest way and "it is for us to rely upon our father who is in heaven" [Ibid].

◈ ◈ ◈

In this tale, Rabbi Yosef Hayyim illustrates how people are prejudiced concerning the poor and the rich. People tend to believe that anything worn by a poor man has to be cheap, no matter how expensive. The same is true about their perception of the rich, that anything they are wearing must be expensive. The Rabbis of Babylon were moderate. Even though they highly valued learning, they were very practical and encouraged success in business. Many of them preferred relying on their work and businesses for a living. They neither encouraged poverty nor supported ignoring the economic needs of people. However, other people's gullibility is illustrated by the following dialogue showing how flamboyant embellishments win their admiration. During Rabbi Yosef Hayyim's time, conversational Hebrew was uncommon. Hebrew was mainly a written language. Nevertheless, he creates a style of dialogue that can be differentiated from the style of a narrator. For example, in one sentence, the predicate is missing: "This [is worth]—at least about eighty gold Dinars." In another sentence, the style is slang: "What are you talking about?" ("What are you saying?"). Of course, the contemporary Hebrew reader feels the absence of the rich colloquial Hebrew at that period. For example, for the term "most," Rabbi Yosef Hayyim uses the rabbinical language of "limrubbeh," while the spoken Hebrew today would be "hakhi harbeh."

There once were two bridegrooms that entered a synagogue.. One was rich, and one was poor. First entered the rich, and he was wearing a belt [sash] made of simple cotton, which he bought for seven silver Dinars. He wore on his finger a ring with a simple stone that he bought for two silver Dinars that looked like a precious stone.

People started looking at him, in their usual way, and one of them said to his friend,

"Look how expensive this belt is, certainly its value is fifty gold Dinars."

And his friend responded, "This [is worth]—at least about eighty gold Dinars."

And his friend asked about the ring, if one can find a ring like it for two hundred Dinars, and his friend said to him, "What are you talking about? A ring such as this would not be sold even for four hundred gold Dinars!"

Afterward entered the poor bridegroom to the synagogue, and he was wearing an expensive belt that was worth one hundred gold Dinars that he borrowed from a rich man for one day only. On his finger there was a ring with a precious stone that he also borrowed, and it was worth five hundred Dinars.

One of the people in the congregation said to his friend, "What do you think, how much did this poor man pay for his belt?"

"Ten Dinars at most, because it is made of cotton," his friend responded.

And he asked him about the ring, and he responded, "It is worth two silver Dinars at most."

Readers find that when the poor man wears the clothing and the jewelry, they are ugly in the eyes of the world, and he will be [considered] also ugly as to his deeds and his virtues. However, the opposite is true about the rich man, as it was said, "money will even legitimize bastards." The folktale illustrates how poverty inflicts ugliness on a person in all aspects, and therefore, the poverty is called "ugly afflictions" that troubles a man.

◈ ◈ ◈

In the following tale, Rabbi Yosef Hayyim illustrates the importance of "honour thy father and thy mother." The younger generation, represented by the grandson, is the one who reprimands his father. He has compassion for his grandfather, and he stirs proper thoughts and feelings in his father's heart. It is important to note that Baghdad's rabbis at that time acknowledged people should be honored and recognized on the basis of their wisdom, not their age (see, for example, Bibliography, Hutsin, *Hamaggid*; Hakak, *Iggerot*, Introduction).

Direct speech is used in this tale in important stages of the story. The grandfather's touching request is expressed in a direct speech, which is juxtaposed with the father's unfeeling reaction. Rabbi Yosef Hayyim attempted (like other Hebrew authors of his time) to create a Hebrew dialogue with a style distinguished and lower than the one of the narrator. However, in the short father-son dialogue, the son uses the wisdom and style of the sages ("the parents are a good omen for their children").

The story has suspense—the listeners knew before the fathers what the son did in the attic, but they do not know why he did what he did, and the question of the father represents their curiosity, too. As to the father, he cannot see what happens in the attic, and his son does not respond to his questions, which prolongs the suspense. The story advances within time; the suspense increases when the son ignores the father. The son explains his own enigmatic actions. The reader identifies with the compassion, wisdom, and courage of the son, and then is relieved when the reader knows that the father changed his ways. As he did in other folktales, Rabbi Yosef Hayyim spelled out the moral of the story through a mosaic style of allusions that together close the story with a positive tenor.

There once was a man who had an elderly father but did not have compassion for his father to bring him to his home to feed him and to cloth him. This elderly man lived with the poor man of that town.

And it came to pass during one of the cold days that the old man was sitting with the poor man of his town, and the grandson of the elderly man passed by. The old man begged his grandson and said, "See how the cold is great and mighty, and I am naked [thin clothed] at the peak of the cold? Therefore, tell your father to send me a raiment to cover myself with and put on during this cold time."

And the grandson went and told his father what his grandfather told him, and his father said to him, "Go to the attic and find a raiment hanging on a hook, take it, and bring it to your grandfather."

And the grandson went up to the attic, found well-worn raiment that was torn in several places, and he became infuriated. He took scissors and cut the raiment through its length to two equal halves, and thus he was delayed in the attic.

And his father shouted, "What's holding you up? And what are doing there?"

After his father called him several times, the son came down from the attic, and he had half a raiment in his hand.

He told his father, "The second half—I placed for you, because when you become old I will take you out of this house, and you will sit among the poor against your will. During the cold days—when you will ask me for a raiment to dress with—I will send you the half that is left here, because like fathers like sons. The deeds of the parents are a good omen for their children, and I will treat you in the same way you are treating your father!"

And the father was ashamed and confounded, and he knew that he had sinned terribly by dishonoring his father. Concerned that one day he would experience this same humiliation, he went to his father and asked his forgiveness and brought him home.

Let him that glorieth glory [Jeremiah 9, 23]. He who is wise knows that there is a judging God up above in heaven for every matter of transgression and sin—although that will by no means clear the guilty. All the measures came to an end—but measure for measure [tit for tat, punishment fitting the crime] did not come to an end.

Therefore, only men who are strong and of good courage do good deeds, "and thou shalt do that which is right and good in the sight of the Lord" (Deuteronomy 6, 18). And if man does so, then "thy children like olive plants, round about thy table" (Psalms 128, 3) that is laden, "thy wife shall be as a fruitful vine, in the innermost parts of the house" (ibid), and richness and honor shall not depart out of your home "besides the still waters" (Psalms 23, 2) "in thy presence is fullness of joy" (Psalms 16, 11).

◆ ◆ ◆

In this tale, Rabbi Yosef Hayyim prompts his listeners to accept a small transgression in order for God to save them from a larger transgression. The emotions of the man in the story shift from "he began wailing and screaming" to "he began to sing and be joyful." First he cried "about his bad luck," but once he understood that his insignificant injury and monetary loss saved his life, "he began to sing and be joyful about his good fortune." The opposing feelings in this concise and rhythmic story stir excitement in the hearts of the listeners. It is a story that encourages acceptance of troubles in human life. It provides comfort and encouragement and inspires faith.

There once was a man who saw a big boat sailing overseas. He ran to his home in order to retrieve his merchandise and sail overseas, but before he reached the boat a nail penetrated his foot, and he could not move. Meanwhile, the boat left the dock and embarked.

He began wailing and screaming about his bad luck, because there would not be another boat going overseas for a year, and his merchandise would remain with him.

Three days later, he learned that the boat had sunk. He began to sing and be joyful about his good fortune, and he began kissing the nail that had pinned his foot, because it had spared his life and his property.

It is deducible from the context that no matter what trouble a man encounters he has to be generous-spirited and open-minded and to accept harship with love and appreciation, for heaven's mandate is never ill willed. If a man encounters a loss of money or illnesses, he should absolutely recognize that the Creator was merciful with him, because the merciful One does not take life, but with the rod of his wrath he would strike man with torture or monetary loss, in order to bring him and his family back to good conduct.

The following tale contrasts the lifestyle between two male characters. Both men are neighbors, living in close proximity to one another (geographically). One "had sheep and oxen;" the other one "did not have the means to buy meat everyday—but only once a week, enough for Saturdays." One had "fields and vineyards," while the other one "did not have furniture and utensils." One had a house that "was fine-looking and spacious;" the other one had a house that "was small and narrow." In short, one was "very rich" and "his table was a king's table," while the other one "was a craftsman." The difference between the two men is puzzling and surprising (and pleasing to the hard working, low-income audience). The "very rich" man "was very thin and grew weak" while the craftsman was "very healthy physically and powerful [big, fat] and his face always looked rosy." The main part of the tale is a monologue of the craftsman, who first dwells on the rich man's character, followed by an explanation of his own character.

The explanation also juxtaposes the characters. The craftsman tells the rich man that he (the wealthy man) is by nature "angry and full of rage" while the craftsman is by his "nature and temper, very congenial, and not angry nor furious even when the issue justifies anger." The rich man is "desirous and covetous, and very envious" while the craftsman describes himself as a man with the "virtue of frugality and contentment" who is "not envious of other people."

The craftsman's character is illustrated by his positive self-image and by the way he addresses the rich man. He is confident and direct. He recognizes his self-worth and does not feel inferior to the confused rich man.

The story provides a comforting message to its readers. The proud craftsman instills confidence in his audience by his manner of speaking to the confused and needy-of-advice rich man. The story cautions its listeners not to equate having wealth to having a fulfilling life.

There once were two men who were neighbors. One of them was very rich and had sheep and oxen, fields and vineyards. His table was a king's table, and his house was fine-looking and spacious, but he was very thin and grew weak.

His neighbor was a craftsman—a silversmith who did not have the means to buy meat every day, rather, only once a week, enough for Saturdays—and his house did not have furniture, utensils, or a fine mattress. His house was undersized, small and narrow, but he was as fit as a fiddle, very healthy physically and powerful [big, fat], and his face always looked rosy.

The rich neighbor asked him, "Why do I look the way I do, and you look the way you do?"

The craftsman responded, "The reason is that by your nature you are angry and full of rage, and therefore, at least ten times a day you will encounter anger and rage with your servants and your family. The anger causes a person to be skinny and weakens him and strongly harms him. Moreover, your nature is that you are desirous and covetous and very envious, and thus, all your life is painful, because you became confused and troubled, a money chaser. It is impossible for you to fulfill all your cravings, and therefore, sighs and sorrow always consume your flesh and strength. How can you become healthy by the food that you eat while all these vices of yours consume your strength and flesh!"

The craftsman continued, "Whereas me, as to my nature and temper, I am very congenial. I am not angry and not furious, even when the issue justifies anger. I also have the virtue of frugality and contentment, and I rejoice in my portion and see the little that I have as plentiful. I am not envious of other people about everything, therefore, I am always very healthy physically, thanks to the comfort that I have!"

It is deducible from the tale that jealousy, lust, and ambition were obstacles and stumbling blocks for the children of Israel in all their good pathways. If the world was cautious about these three essentials, then people would be healthy and well in their body and soul, they would be happy in this world, and they would have it good in the world to come.

◆◆◆

In the following tale, Rabbi Yosef Hayyim illustrates the importance of setting an example for the younger generation. A parent's proper conduct is not only important for himself, it sets an example for his children. The tale is didactic, and justice is on the side of the son, not the father. One's transgressions do not end there; they continue for generations. Physical punishment illustrates this point.

There once was a man who came to hit his son, because the son ate without washing his hands. The father held the two legs of his son with one hand and a stick with the other hand. When the father raised the stick to hit his son's feet, the stick instead landed on the father's hand that was holding the son's legs. The father's hand was hit forcefully and gravely, and the son said to his father, "Your hand was justly and rightfully hit, because you are hitting my legs for not washing my hands, while you yourself always eat without washing your hands. By having your own hands hit, they spoke to you from heaven, saying, 'Why are you hitting his legs for not washing his hands? Hit your own hands for not washing them.' Don't you know that like father like son, that if I saw that you would not eat without washing your hands, than I, too, would not eat without washing my hands?"

◆◆◆

Baghdad rabbis were far from being fanatics; they were moderate. In the following tale (1988 edition), Rabbi Yosef Hayyim acknowledges the value of telling a "white lie." Goel ("redeemer") and a creature called Lie (sheker) hold opposite positions as to the use, need, impact, and nature of lying. The story is structured as a trip that begins in the morning while Goel is still in bed. It also ends in his bed after various encounters with the people who are important in his life, while he is determined not to lie. At the opening of the first scene, Goel is still in his bed, and he is vigorous and sure of himself during his encounter with his maid. However, after various encounters, he understands that because he rejected Lie and everything Lie represents, he loses everything. The order in which the tragedies occur go from bad to worse. First, his finances collapse. Then, he loses his cook and his inheritance. Next, his creditor sues him, and finally, he loses his fiancée's love.

The tragic events are obvious; however, the tale contains humor, too. Goel says to his uncle, "...if your death day were earlier, you would truly perform an act of kindness." "He wanted to hit his head against the wall," but instead he hit it "against the head of a passerby," who happened to be his creditor. His fiancée and her aunt were upset because Goel, upon the aunt's request, correctly estimated her age. "She gets upset if one tells her that she is of an old age," explains the fiancée.

Nevertheless, since the folktales of Rabbi Yosef Hayyim are aimed at providing comfort and encouragement, the closure of the tale is happy. This closure is in the form of a direct speech from Goel, who changed his view of lying based on the lesson that Lie taught him.

There once was a young man whose name was Goel. On the evening of the New Year, while he was sitting on his bed, he took his clothes off in order to go to bed and fall asleep, and he thought, "Woe, the world is full of scoundrels and wicked, that speak insincerely. Lies have slain many people and the number of victims is high! This world would have been a paradise, had lying not been so deeply rooted in our hearts; may the curse of God come upon those who follow the path of lying."

And with a heart full of fury because of the ways of the world and its deceitfulness, he went to bed and pulled up the blanket to cover his face. After closing his eyes, he saw in his sleep a little Creature [little being] standing across from him and looking at him with a mocking smile in its shiny eyes. Goel stared at him and called, "Who are you?"

And the small Creature answered, "I am Lie."

Goel sat on his bed, and called out with rage and fury and wrath, "Come here, closer, and I will speak firmly to you. I will shatter your head and cut you into pieces, and this act will be considered an act of piety, for it saves tens of thousands of people from your evil!"

When Goel said that, he wanted to extend his arms to catch the Creature, but the Creature backed up. Goel stretched his hands out twice, but to his sorrow, his efforts were in vain, and he utterly failed, because the Creature slipped away and hid time and again and escaped, until Goel became tired and stopped running after it.

The Creature said to Goel mockingly, "Lie will not be caught easily! And now, what use do you have for my blood, so that you maliciously want to kill me? And be it known, that you will harm the world, you will gravely damage it if you harm its benefactor and charitable person."

Goel called out laughingly and angrily, "You, the despicable, are the 'benefactor and charitable person' of the world?"

And the Creature responded, "Indeed I am. You and all the people of the world together could not exist without me. I am telling you the truth now, even though I am the Lie, and I firmly promise you that you could not get through one day peacefully if I did not walk beside you."

Goel responded, "Were you called Lie so that you will tell the truth? I will live all my life peacefully and happily without ever seeing your face."

And the Creature said, "All right, let's try that. I surely have justification to leave you for a long time, because you are a man with a quick temper, and you maliciously raised your hand to hit me. However, I will not take revenge and will not bear a grudge. I do not want to disgrace my name and be called Cruel, because I will be considered Cruel if I leave you for a long time. But in order to try you and to educate you, I will leave you tomorrow, and we will see what happens and how will you spend that day. Do not call me, and do not ask for my help during moments of troubles, because I will not listen to you even if it is a matter of risking of [costing the price of] your life. I will not rescue you so that the trial will be comprehensive. Tomorrow will be a holy day for your brethren, and you will remember it. In the evening, I will return and ask you whether or not you have use for me."

The eyes of the Creature seemed odd to Goel, because his look changed time and again. One time they were greenish, one time reddish, and one time azure. Then there was a miracle, and the Creature all of a sudden became an old woman, and its face was full of wrinkles. Next, within a moment, he changed and became a tender boy whose face emitted beauty and grace.

And Goel thought, "Since this Creature is the Lie itself, it is not odd that he changes himself, because it is the way of Lie to be changeable and alter his colors as the wind blows."

Again Goel quickly stretched out his hand to strike the Creature, but this time, too, he missed the target, because the Creature moved aside. Goel could not hurt him, and the following words came to Goel's ears: "Be well, and tomorrow at this time I will come back to see you in person, and we will see how this matter ends."

Goel replied, "We will see," and then his eyes closed and he fell asleep.

Goel did not have a wife and children, and at his home there was only one old woman who cooked for him every day. That day—New Year's Day—while he was still lying in his bed, the cook served him a glass of water. When he opened his eyes, she said to him, "I wish you, dear Sir, for the coming good New Year, that you will have life and tranquility, riches and honor, and I will pray to God with all my heart that you will be successful in everything you do, and that whithersoever direction you turn you will be wise and successful, and we will live a long life together forever."

Goel said when he opened his eyes, "If only the day will quickly come that I will be freed from you, relieved of you, so that I don't have to see your wrinkled, appalling face anymore."

The old woman said, "Woe to the ears that hear this! I will not let this man violate my honor, to speak evil to me, because I am a well respected woman."

Goel responded, "It is the truth indeed, you deceived me!" and she said to him, "If I deceived you, take another woman in my place that would know how to appreciate a man like you, that instead of giving his maid presents for the New Year—which is the proper thing to do—he speaks haughtily to her and humiliates her!"

Goel did not answer her at all. He only brandished one of his shoes to throw at her. The cook understood his intent, and she forestalled the evil and left the room. Goel heard her voice behind the door, as she was talking to herself, saying, "May he do as he pleases. Who could ever have thought that one would hear such words coming out of his mouth on this holy day? It must be that he has gone mad!"

Goel felt remorse in his heart, and thought, "Why did I have to quarrel today with this old woman? True, deep in my heart I am dissatisfied with her, and I don't want her if I find someone better than her. Nevertheless, I should not have made her bitterly outraged on this holiday, and I did not have to reveal the truth that was in my heart."

With shattered strength [weakly] and a frightened heart, he got dressed, and he remembered the holiness of the day. He closed his heart to grief and went to the synagogue. When he came back home, he ate a little bit and went to look for his friends and the people who loved him.

"I will go first to my uncle's home," thought Goel, "because he is sick and going to die, and I will inherit his property, because he does not have a son."

So he went to his uncle's home. When he approached the bed of his sick uncle who sat at that time on an ivory bed, instead of saying to him, "I am happy to see that you are doing well," he said, "I am happy to see you sick, lying on your sick-bed, and that you will never get off the bed that you lay on; I am waiting impatiently to inherit your wealth."

He told his uncle the truth that was in his heart, lest he would utter any lie. The uncle, hearing a hard curse instead of a blessing, said to him, "Your words let you down, dear. Are you truly waiting impatiently for your uncle's death, the uncle that profoundly loves you?"

Goel replied, "If you would only find a shelter under the aegis of death, dear uncle!"

Goel sighed and continued, "Do you know, uncle, my situation? I need money, and only your property would redeem me from my poverty. Truly, uncle, I love you, but is a man immortal? Even if you would live one or two more years, it is the same for you. If your death day would come earlier, you will truly perform an act of kindness."

This is how Goel spoke to his uncle, wanting to atone for his first words, but in fact he just continued to heap coals of fire upon his uncle's head, and his uncle shouted loudly, "Get out of my home, vile! Do not come to see me again! You have neither part nor lot in my house, and you will not inherit one cent! You, hurry up and get out, before I order my servants to chase you and throw you out like an abhorred offshoot!"

And Goel stood up astonished and confused and went out. He bit his lips with his teeth, his face was pale, his knees shaking, and his heart was likely broken, and he thought, "Woe, what got into me and why on earth did I say these words to my uncle? Because of my fickle-mindedness, I destroyed all the buildings that I have built with my thoughts! Many years I worked hard to attract his heart to love me, and in one moment, I mercilessly destroyed the entire building that for years I worked to build! I acted foolishly!"

This is how Goel thought in his heart bitterly, and he wanted to hit his head against the wall, because of his immense remorse. However, to his regret or to his tragedy, he did not hit his head against the wall but against the head of a passer-by that he did not see because he was immersed in his thoughts and stuck in their sad abyss.

The passerby felt the impact of Goel's strike, and he said, "Pay attention to the road!"

And Goel responded, "To hell with you!"

However, when Goel raised his eyes and looked at the man, he saw that it was one of his lenders, a lender to whom Goel owed a lot of money. Instead of telling him properly, "I am happy to see you today and to wish you a Happy New Year," Goel said to him, to the contrary, "I am seized by horror and rage when I see you. You chase me and disturb my rest even on a holiday!"

The lender thought that Goel was kidding and made efforts to show a joyful face. He said to Goel, "I am glad to hear you kidding and teasing on this holy day. It must be that you feel fine because you heard good news, and thus your spirit is very joyful. Apparently you are coming out of the house of your honorable uncle, so what did you hear about your inheritance, how much does he intend to bequeath to you?"

Goel replied, "He will not bequeath to me even one cent!"

Goel said that because he was angry and out of control; he told the passerby his secret, against his own will. The lender said, "If so, listen to what I am telling you. Even though it is improper to discuss business and money issues today, my guts compel me to tell you that if you don't pay me back my money within a week from now, I will submit your promissory notes to the court and file a lawsuit against you! How long will I wait for you? It is hard to bear anymore!"

Goel said, "This, too, God stored up for me," and he turned around and went away sullen and displeased.

From there, he went to his boss to fulfill his obligation to wish him a Happy New Year, but he did not find him at his home. He was very happy about it, because undoubtedly, he would have quarreled with him, too, because the truth was his guiding light, and the Lie was the darkness on his road. Therefore, he left his boss's home joyfully. Next, he went to the home of his fiancée to wish her a Happy New Year.

His fiancée was an orphan, deprived by death of both parents, and she grew up in the home of her aunt. Goel decided to weigh his words with a scale and to put a rein on his mouth and to bridle it. However, his bad luck once again did not leave him alone because there were issues between him and the fiancée's aunt, and he pained her with his words, too, when she asked him, "Guess how old I am?"

Goel replied, "Over fifty."

His fiancée's aunt became furious over his response, and the fiancée was on her side, and she said to Goel, "What prompted you to shame and disgrace my dear aunt on this holy day?"

And he said, "What did I do? Did I lie? Isn't she fifty years old?"

Goel's fiancée said, "Indeed it is the truth, but she fumes if one tells her that she is of an old age."

And he replied, "My beloved, may I find grace in your eyes and you will not consider me as guilty of a sin."

From one issue to another that he discussed with his matched fiancée, he told her that she was his fourth woman that he had married three women before, but he despised them and divorced them. Goel's fiancée became enraged, and she said, "Get out of here, vile, and don't ever come again to see me! After you have divorced three women, how can I trust you and be your wife?"

By now Goel was frightened by his bad luck, how in one moment he destroyed his future and the towers that he had built with his imagination, and he went out of his fiancée's home sullen and displeased.

He went back to his home at the end of the day and thought about the incidents he had that day. He fell face down and cried bitterly about the incident he had with the old cook, his uncle, the lender, and his fiancée. He wanted to tell his heart's truth, but there was no cure for any of these incidents but by telling lies and not expressing the truth which was shut up in his bosom.

Goel began praising Lie, and he confirmed and justified the words that the creature told him, and he blessed the creature.

At the end of this, Goel woke up from his sleep, opened his eyes, and saw that he was sleeping on his bed and the sun was shining. He also saw that the old cook was standing near his bed above his head, and in her hand she held a glass of water. She said to him, "I wish you, dear Sir, for the coming good New Year, that you will have life and tranquility, riches and honor, and I will pray to God with all my heart that you will be successful in everything you do, and that whithersoever direction you turn you will be wise and successful, and we will live a long life together forever."

And Goel answered her, "What are you talking about? Is today the New Year holiday, and it is now the first morning of the New Year?"

The cook replied, "You still don't you know, Sir, that today is the first day of the New Year? It appears that you slept well, and therefore, I could not wake you up from your sleep. I stayed standing above the headboard of your bed for some time until you woke up by yourself, and they have already begun praying at the synagogue!"

Goel looked at his watch and saw that it was morning already. At that time, he clearly knew that everything he experienced—seeing the Creature, conversing and quarreling with him, quarreling with the cook, and visiting his uncle, and the conversation he had with his uncle and the lender and his fiancée and her aunt—everything took place in his dream, in his vision of the night. He was horrified by the terrible dream, and his reins rejoiced, and he was happy that he did not lose the riches of his uncle and did not lose his fiancée. He said, "You, angel of dreams, are a faithful messenger. True, you have pained my heart, and you filled me with anger and pain. But you did not inflict any evil upon me, because you taught me how to behave. And you showed me that a man does not have the strength to walk down the road of truth in this life, but he will encounter times when he would have to decline the truth and bond with a lie. And if he does not do so, he is committing suicide. I thank you, angel of dreams, for this teaching!"

◆ ◆ ◆

The dichotomy between a righteous man and a wicked man is central to the following story. The righteous man is different from the wicked in life and in death. In life, the righteous man is strong and can endure the predicaments (storms) of life because of his deep roots (like those of a palm tree), while the wicked man is weak and cannot endure any problem (wind) because his roots are shallow (like those of a weed). After life in this world, the righteous man is not considered dead because of his deeds and the people he left behind. Determining the stability of the righteous versus the wicked man's character is delayed until their character traits (and depth of their roots) emerge. This folktale exposes the depth of these roots and the implications of their differences. The differences between the righteous and the wicked are dramatized by a bet that has a winner and a loser, a contrast that is further expounded upon and detailed in describing a palm tree and the weeds that grow around it.

There once were two men that stood near a mulberry tree or a palm tree, and one of them said, "I estimate with my mind that this tree is about twenty cubits [an ancient form of measurement from elbow to fingertip] tall." The second man answered him, and he said, "It is incorrect; the tree is more than twenty-five cubits tall." The first man rushed to climb to the top of the tree, took a rope with him, measured the tree, and found out that the height of the tree from its top to the ground was twenty cubits exactly. And he said to his friend, "My estimate was correct. I have just measured the tree, and it was as I said." And the second one answered, "You are wrong, and I am right. Let's bet, and I will show you how this tree is more than twenty-five cubits tall." His friend replied, "Fine," and his heart was glad because he was sure that he would win, because he just measured the tree to be just twenty cubits long. After they deposited the bet with a referee, the second man took a spade and dug five feet deep around the tree. The tree was still standing in the soil because it is the nature of a tree to go deep into the thick ground. And he said, "Here are five cubits in addition to the twenty that you measured from the top of the tree to the ground. Altogether, including the five cubits that were hidden in the soil, the tree exceeded twenty-five cubits, as I have estimated." And he took the Dinars that were deposited by the first man with the referee.

It came to pass a few days later that the first man, the man who lost the bet, went to walk in the fields with another man. They found long weeds in the field, and the first man who lost asked his friend, "How tall are the weeds?" His friend said, "I estimate with my mind that the weeds are only five cubits tall." The first man said, "It is not so, I say that the weeds are over seven cubits tall." So, his friend measured the weeds from top to bottom and found that he well estimated that they were five cubits tall, and he said, "Behold I have measured and I found that the weeds are, as I estimated, only five cubits tall." And the first man was glad in his heart, and he thought, "Now I will recover what I lost that day regarding the tree measurement, because what happened to me that day when it did not occur to me to calculate the estimated part that was hidden beneath the ground is now happening to this man. Therefore, I will now bet with this man who is innocently calculating how tall the weeds are, and I will recapture the loss I incurred in measuring the tree." He said to his friend, "You are wrong in measuring the weeds and saying that they are five cubits tall. I am right; the weeds are taller than seven cubits. Let's bet in writing ten Dinars each, and if I show you that it is as I say, that the weeds are indeed taller than seven cubits, I will win the bet. If not, you will win." And his friend said, "Fine," and each one of them deposited ten Dinars with a referee. The man who lost the first bet started digging around the weeds, and the weeds fell when he dug one finger deep, because there were no roots inside the soil, and the roots do not penetrate the soil more than half a finger deep.

The same is true about righteous and wicked people, because the wicked person has no foundation and no deep roots that enable him to exist mightily and courageously, and he resembles a weed. The success of the wicked extends only as far the eye can see, and this is why it was said about the wicked, "and when all the workers of inequity do flourish; it is that they may be destroyed for ever" [Psalms 92, 8], because a soft wind uproots them, but "the righteous shall flourish like the palm-tree" [Psalms, 92, 13]. In addition to what one can see, the righteous person has deep roots, and all the wind of the world cannot uproot him.

I am saying that the resemblance of the tree to a righteous man and the weed to a wicked man is as follows: For the wicked man, his days on Earth are the only days to be considered as his life. When he dies he does not have any more life in this world at all, and this resembles a weed, because it does not have any other dimension except the one that is readily seen above the ground. After he falls and is uprooted, one can see the dimensions of the weed on the ground, and he will not have any hidden existence beneath the soil. However, the righteous man, in addition to his visible life span on Earth, has another existence in this world even after he dies, because by having children that he guided to walk in the path of uprightness and disciples whom he taught to maintain good customs and to perform virtuous and good deeds. These substitute for him and reflect his good ways and good virtues that are named after him; death does not apply to him. He is still alive and not dead. As our sages of blessed memory wrote, "Why does scripture use 'sleep' with regard to David and 'death' with regard to Joab? 'Sleep' is used for David because he left a son; 'death' is used for Joab because he left no son" [Babylonian Talmud, Bava Batra, 116a].

The righteous man resembles a tree, that in addition to its overt part, which is above ground and visible to everyone, it has a part that is hidden beneath the ground. This exists but is not visible, yet is known and recognized through observing and by estimating through the mind's eye. Therefore, the righteous man resembles a palm tree whose major roots lie hidden beneath the soil.

Chapter 5: Rabbi Shelomo Bekhor Hutsin (Rashbah): The Words of an Enlightened Jew

Rabbi Shelomo Bekhor Hutsin (Rashbah, 1843-1892) was one of the disciples of Rabbi Abdallah Somekh (1813-1904) in Baghdad. Rabbi Abdallah Somekh was one of the key religious figures of his time (Hakak, *Iggerot*; and Hakak, "Shlomo"). He did not find personal fulfillment in business. Rather, he had spiritual and intellectual aspirations. As a result, he selected a small number of students and began an education enterprise that lasted forty years. In 1854, he established a rabbinical school. The graduates of this school (Yeshivat Bet Zilkha) became top community leaders, authors of religious books, poets and founders of a Hebrew press, rabbis, and ritual slaughterers (*shohatim*) for Iraq, Israel, Kurdistan, Persia, India, and other countries (Ben-Yaacob, *Toledot*; and 1979, 150-156). Rabbi Somekh was interested in Hebrew periodicals and in news pertaining to the Jewish world. He raised funds for Jewish causes and responded to questions that were addressed to him from various countries about Jewish law. The site of Baghdad's Jewish court (also the site for Kurdistan and Iraq's Jewish court of appeals) was located in Zilkha's rabbinical school, Yeshivat Bet Zilkha.

Rashbah was a graduate of this school. He admired his teacher (Rashbah, *Ha-Levanon*, March 18, 1869; and *Ha-Tsefira*, 16th year, no. 217, 891) who was thirty years his senior. The traveler Efrayim Neimark praised Rabbi Abdallah Somekh and mentioned Rashbah as one of Somekh's greatest disciples. He also noted a dispute in Baghdad's Jewish community over who should be the community leader. Rashbah was viewed as one of the few who was at peace with two major groups, the rich men's party and the sages' party (see Neimark, 45-47).

A. The Various Pursuits of Rashbah

Rashbah was active in various fields, all of which expressed and illustrated his spiritual and intellectual priorities and abilities. In all his endeavors, he was, as he frequently concluded at the end of his articles, the person seeking to do good for his people ("ha-dotl," abbreviations of "ha-doresh tov le-'ammo").

Rashbah wrote liturgies, rabbinical articles, and journalistic articles about the Jewish communities in Babylon, Kurdistan, and Persia. Additionally, he wrote educational articles that guided young people in the correct way of living, including tenets on proper behavior and virtuous conduct. Rashbah's articles were published in Hebrew periodicals that appeared in Baghdad (*Ha-Dover*), India (*Ha-Perah, Ha-Mevasser*), Jerusalem (*Ha-Havatselet, Ha-Levanon*), and in European cities (*Ha-Maggid, Ha-Tsefira, Ha-Melits).*

Rashbah published articles in Hebrew periodicals that captured the attention of different audiences and had different or even conflicting orientations. For example, he published in both *Ha-Maggid* and *Ha-Levanon* in the years 1867-1877 when the *Ha-Levanon*'s editor published articles against the editor of *Ha-Maggid*. Rashbah made this possible by expressing moderate positions and Jewish values in his articles that were common to Jewish ideological streams. His articles expressed support for Jewish Enlightenment ideologies, and he concurrently believed in the centrality of Jewish faith and religion.

In addition, Rashbah was an important source of information for the countries about which he wrote. The Hebrew periodicals needed this information in order to provide a more complete picture about Jewish communities in the world. Rashbah's articles are an important historical source chronicling events, characters, and Jewish life. For example, one of his articles provided the names of Hebrew authors in Iraq and the titles of their books (*Ha-Tsefira,* 16th year, no. 278, 1145). Another article (*Ha-Maggid*, 7th year, no. 11 (12 March 1863) 84) provided descriptions of Baghdad's Jewish community institutes, synagogues, day schools, and charitable organizations, including charitable organizations for the Jews in the land of Israel.

Rashbah also translated from Hebrew to Judeo Arabic part of the prayer book and the Passover *Haggadah.* He was the principal of a Jewish day school (*Midrash Talmud Torah*) and a teacher of the Talmud in Alliance in Baghdad. He promoted Hebrew periodicals of his time (*Ha-Maggid, Ha-Levanon, Ha-Tsefira, Ha-Melits, Perah and Ha-Mevsasser*). He was Baghdad's branch manager and Vice President of a Society for the Preservation of Religious Duties ("Hevrat Shomreh Mitsva", see *Ha-Levanon*, 6th year, no. 12 (18 March 1969) 95-96). The organization focused on the education and support of Jewish children, the promotion of Jewish studies, charitable activities, and promotion of good deeds.

Rashbah published the Hebrew speech he made in front of the Jewish community leaders in Baghdad when the Society was inaugurated (*Ha-Maggid*, 12th year, no. 49 (16 December 1868) 387). He owned a bookstore, selling old and new manuscripts (see *Ha-Maggid*, 6th year, no. 48 (December 1862) 377). In 1867, he founded a Hebrew printing house in Baghdad that his son continued to operate following Rashbah's demise.

B. The Hebrew Printing House and the Antiquarianism of Rashbah

By the beginning of the sixteenth century, the Jews were already pioneers in establishing printing houses in the Muslim world. In the middle of the nineteenth century, there were Hebrew printing houses in some Middle Eastern countries. However, until World War I, the only significant Hebrew printing houses were in Babylon.

In the eighteenth century and during the first half of the nineteenth century, the rabbis of Babylon printed their books in Constantinople. During the second half of the nineteenth century, book printing took place in Livorno. When he was twenty years-old, Rashbah asked (in an article) that Sir Moses Montefiore assist in founding a Hebrew printing house in Baghdad (*Ha-Maggid*, no. 34 (26 August 1863) 268). In 1888, after a break of six years in the chain of Hebrew printing houses in Baghdad, Rashbah established his printing house. In the absence of a Hebrew printing license during the first three years of operation, Rashbah did not admit to being the publisher—he merely hinted at it. However, once the license was granted, he printed his name and the city of the publication—Baghdad. An illustration of how Rashbah hinted at his name in the first three years he operated his Hebrew printing house may be found in the title page of the book *Sefer Ma'aseh Nissim* (*A Book of Miraculous Deeds*): "Vetaron leshon illem divreh sheva"h," meaning, "and the tongue of the mute will sing words of praise." The word "praise" in Hebrew is "shevah" ("sheba"h"), which is the short form of the name of the publisher.

Rashbah published original manuscripts as well as reprinted books. After Rashbah's death, one of his sons continued his activities at the publishing house. (For books published by Rashbah, see Ye'ari 117-131. See also Zamir; Hakak, *Iggerot*, 272-274.) Rashbah and his son printed seventy Hebrew books about Jewish law and religion, Jewish customs and holidays, Jewish prayer and poetry, and Jewish folktales and homiletic interpretations (including the biblical Song of Songs.) Rashbah edited all these books and added decorative illustrations to them such as a bird on a branch, a sailboat, and a vine tree. He collected folktales and published them, added separate chapters into books that he republished, corrected errors in books that were published elsewhere and printed a new, corrected edition, and he divided books into various parts. Rashbah knew and selected for publication Hebrew manuscripts of rabbis from Baghdad who lived before his time. He also knew of some Hebrew books that were published in Berlin, Vilna, Amsterdam, India, Constantinople, and elsewhere. He published books that were necessary and important (instructive books, rare books, and books that readers wanted in a new, corrected edition). He proofread the books he published and improved their formats and presentations. One concludes that in his printing house, Rashbah was the publisher, editor, style editor, and design director.

In addition to his activity as a publisher, Rashbah sold Hebrew books to buyers in Middle Eastern and European countries, including the British Museum.

C. The Periodicals in which Rashbah Published

Most of the short articles of Rashbah were published between 1862 and 1891 in *Ha-Maggid* and *Ha-Tsefira*. More than ten of Rashbah's articles were published in *Ha-Levanon,* and one-quarter of his articles were published in other Hebrew periodicals of his time. Hebrew periodicals in those days connected Jews from other lands, expressed their desires, shaped their opinions, offered information and interpretations about various events, and paved new ways for Jewish life (see Guthalf, 7-12).

Rashbah published his first article in 1862 when he was nineteen years old and continued publishing until 1891, the year prior to his death. From 1862 until 1881, Rashbah published articles in *Ha-Maggid. Ha-Maggid* was founded in Lyck, East Prussia, in 1856, and continued until 1903 (see *Ha-Maggid* in Kressel and Gilbowa). It was the first Modern Hebrew weekly. Within a few years, *Ha-Maggid* became the only Hebrew periodical for Hibbat Tsion. *Ha-Maggid* is an important source for Hebrew language, literature, and Jewish history. *Ha-Maggid* represented moderate positions regarding Jewish matters; its predictable readers were both religious and secular Jews. When Rashbah began publishing in this periodical, *Ha-Maggid* expanded to eight pages. Rashbah's short articles appeared in the first part of each issue, which included news about Jewish life in Europe, America, Northern Africa, Israel, Babylon, Turkey, and Persia. Most of Rashbah's publications appeared in letter format under the caption "Asia." The openings and closures of the letters were written eloquently.

Rashbah's articles provided information about the Jews of Babylon, Kurdistan, and Persia. Rashbah, however, did not limit himself to mere reporting. He expressed his opinions about educational issues, such as the importance of teaching young people crafts and foreign languages so that they could integrate with the general population of their home country. In 1861, when *Ha-Maggid*'s editor founded a publishing organization ("Hevrat Mekitseh Nirdamim") for rare Hebrew books and manuscripts, Rashbah enthusiastically supported this venture by eliciting subscribers from Baghdad for the publication of this organization (see *Ha-Maggid,* no. 48 (December 1862) 377).

Select publications of Rashbah were those that he published in response to specific requests from the editor or in response to readers' questions. Some of these questions related to information rooted in Babylon, such as the question as to whether anything survived from the great Babylonian Yeshivot (*Ha-Maggid,* no. 28 (16 July 1873) 258-259) or from a certain river that is mentioned in the Talmud (*Ha-Maggid,* no. 23 (9 June 1874) 204-205). Rashbah also responded to readers' inquiries, among them inquiries about Jewish law (Hutsin, *Perah,* no. 45 (4 May 1883) 271; *Perah,* no. 8 (3 August 1883) 44).

Approximately a year after he began publishing some of his articles in *Ha-Maggid,* Rashbah began publishing in a second Hebrew paper in Palestine, *Havatselet,* that appeared in Jerusalem in 1863-1864, and 1870-1911. *Havatselet* supported the position of the Hasidic minority regarding the way the money donated for the Jews in Palestine was distributed. *Havatselet* published news, poetry, prose, and articles. Rashbah also published in the first Hebrew paper in Palestine, *Ha-Levanon* (1863-1886, Jerusalem-Paris-Mainz-London). *Ha-Levanon* is an important source about Jewish life in Palestine. Its editor was pro religious reform. It had a literary supplement.

In 1874, Rashbah began publishing in the first Polish Jewish newspaper, *Ha-Tsefira* (Warsaw 1862-1931, Berlin 1874-1875), known for its contribution to Modern Hebrew literature and support of Zionism. Rashbah published more than forty articles in *Ha-Tsefira*. The editor at the time Rashbah published was Hayyim Zelig Slanimski, who, like Rashbah, did not view religion and enlightenment as conflicting viewpoints. Rashbah wanted to educate, teach, and inculcate good habits and appreciation for crafts. He supported the pursuit of science and innovations at the same time that he supported the traditionalist way of life around him.

Rashbah published a few articles in *Ha-Ivri, Ha-Melits, Ha-Dover, Ha-Mevasser*, and *Perah*. *Ha-Mevasser* and *Perah* were among the periodicals that were published in India in the years 1855-1902 by Jews who immigrated to India from Babylon. These periodicals were mostly written in Judeo-Arabic and published by Jews from Babylonia. The periodicals were *Doresh Tov Le'ammo, Ha-Mevasser, Perah, Maggid Mesharim*, and *Shoshanna*. The founding of periodicals by Jews in Iraq, Calcutta, and Bombay was influenced by several factors, including the Jewish European Enlightenment Movement and the exposure to Hebrew periodicals from Europe and Israel. These periodicals spread the ideas of enlightenment and Zionism. There were more readers in Judeo-Arabic than in Hebrew, English, or Arabic. The Hebrew component in some of these periodicals was mainly highlighted in the names and captions.

In 1863, the first printing house was established in Baghdad, and Moshe Barukh Mizrahi published the first Hebrew periodical, *Ha-Dover* or *Dover Mesharim*. By the time publication reached its finale in 1871, seventeen issues were completed.

In *Ha-Perah* and *Aleh Ha-Perah*, Rashbah published in Hebrew informative pieces or requests for help on behalf of other people who were in search of a job or a family member who disappeared. In *Ha-Dover*, 1868 (see *Ha-Dover*), Rashbah published an article reflecting his admiration for Sir Moses Montefiore by describing an event in Baghdad in honor of Montefiore.

D. Rashbah's Reflections and Thoughts on the Jewish Enlightenment Movement

Analyzing the intellectual-spiritual activity of Rashbah helps us not only learn about historical events that occurred in Iraq, Kurdistan, and Persia during his time, but also enables us to follow up on Hebrew culture in Baghdad. Rashbah was influenced by the Jewish spiritual and social Enlightenment movement that began in Germany at the end of the eighteenth century and spread into Eastern Europe during the nineteenth century. In Rashbah's thoughts, however, there is no evidence of any religious, intellectual, or spiritual crisis known to us from Hebrew literature written by his contemporaries in Europe. Furthermore, Rashbah's writings reflected his steadfast and unconditional faith. He recognized the need for changes in his community, but at the same time, he strove to deepen its traditional religious roots by promoting further commitment to religious studies and religious duties. Rashbah's desire for modernization and adaptation of Jewish Enlightenment ideas did not conflict with faith and tradition. Rather, it paralleled them. His articles were written in Hebrew, which was an expression of his commitment to the language.

In his reports, Rashbah did not limit himself to facts. He also expressed his opinions about education and ways to improve oneself. Rashbah praised knowledge and science, ethics and virtues, education and human relations. He touted the importance of general education and foreign languages as critical to life within the Jewish community and as necessary to qualify for public employment. He highlighted the importance of love, of honoring one another, of handicrafts, and awareness of world news. As an enlightened Jew, he portrayed the ways a Jew should behave at home, in the house of study, in business, in matters of hygiene, for his emotional well being, in matters of human relationships, and in matters between God and self.

The importance of etiquette is central to Rashbah's "Sefer Hanokh la-Noar" (his introduction to the book, *Sefer Talmud Katan*). This book resulted in three editions, all of which present Jewish law for daily life. In the book's introduction, Rashbah promotes honoring parents and educators, showing respect in school, in the synagogue, and when invited as a guest. Rashbah promotes dignity and self respect, showing respect to all fellow human beings, wearing clean and neat clothes, maintaining bodily cleanliness, and paying attention to personal grooming and hygiene. Rashbah wrote about the value of having good table manners, hand washing, the use of utensils when eating, and refraining from overeating. He described the advantages of practicing proper behavior in a group setting. In his writings, he counsels readers on how to walk properly, how to be the first to greet people, and underscores the importance of being a soft-spoken person. In building character, it is most essential that a person be good hearted, shy away from haste and fickle-mindedness, respectful of fellow human beings, and sustain good relationships with the people of his community.

Rashbah explains to his young readers the importance of confidentiality, respect of the needy, ethics in business, and rejection of greed and avariciousness. The foundation of business ethics must be built upon honesty, wisdom, and good sense. For honor's sake, he deplored jealousy, lust, and ambition. He advocated moderation and the application of the Golden Rule when managing finances, planning a future, avoiding wicked people, maintaining lasting friendships, showing compassion for invalids or the impaired, and not judging others harshly. He reprimanded arrogance and dishonesty, cherished love, and emphasized the need to stay healthy. Rashbah advocated the preservation of the Jewish religion and tradition at the same time that he supported modernization and recognized the importance of science. He did not consider his position to be a conflicting viewpoint. He treated superstitions with mockery and preferred West to East. Rashbah's positions were far from fanatical.

Rashbah paid great respect to women. For example, in his introduction to *Sefer Talmud Katan,* Rashbah details (in an emotional style) and enumerates the acts of love and dedication of a mother toward her baby. He illustrates her pain (and joy) of pregnancy, childbirth, infant care, breast-feeding, rocking the cradle, carrying the baby, and jumping out of bed in the middle of winter (when everyone is asleep) in order to feed (or sing a lullaby) to calm a baby who has awakened during the night. When the baby is weaned, the mother still works hard to provide tasty food for her baby. As her baby grows, she closely follows her child so that the child does not stumble and get hurt. Even when she retains a nanny she stays vigilant to ensure her child's happiness.

Unlike some community leaders in Baghdad, Rashbah proudly announced the establishment of an Alliance school in Baghdad and its success (Yehuda, *Bateh*). He noted that its goal was "to teach the young Jewish people foreign languages also, and to inculcate knowledge that is necessary to a person of this generation" (Hutsin, *Ha-Levanon*, no. 13 (25 June 1869) 102-103). Rashbah embraced a school curriculum that included secular studies. However, he made it clear that Babylonian Jews were interested in enlightenment, and they were people of faith, believers before anything else:

> ...And from this may our brethren in Europe judge that their brethren in Arab lands have eyes to see what is good and beneficial for them. Only [the Jews in Arab lands] want the good and beneficial to be bound by God-fearing-ness, because the fear of the Lord is the beginning of wisdom [Psalms 111:1]. It is not [as] they think that no one among us knows anything, as to the value of sciences, and that we are incapable of receiving abundance of conferred benefits, and from this [from the success of Alliance in Baghdad] you can see and have the proof that such an opinion is incorrect. We aspire, however, to go in the way of the Torah and wisdom and faith (see Hutsin, *Ha-Levanon*, no 13 (25 June 1869) 102-103).

Rashbah's denunciation of superstitions is also part of his enlightenment ideology. For example, he describes a non-Jewish widespread custom in his land that was related to a lunar eclipse:

> At a time of a lunar eclipse, men and woman hit with their fist or with a stone various utensils, such as pots, they shoot at the moon with guns and arrows and shout and demand that the big dragon takes out of his mouth the moon that fell prey to him, because they believe that the big dragon went up from the ocean to swallow the moon.
>
> ...The light of knowledge and enlightenment chased away all the shadows of ignorance and folly... Nevertheless the people that we [the Jews] live among are still delirious and sleep in the lap of folly and ignorance. They still believe [in this and] the West did not impact them at all to uproot their superstitions that are surround them (*Ha-Maggid*, no. 39 (10 October 1877) 356).

Rashbah did not differentiate between Jews and non-Jews when it came to his condemnation of superstitions. He writes about a superstition among his people regarding a person who has been seriously frightened and, thus, emotionally harmed. Superstitious people attribute this condition to the anger of genies and the subsequent need to appease them. He viewed this as "a matter of abominable foolishness" (Hutsin, *Ha-Tsefira,* 28 Shevat, no. 12 (1887)).

Rashbah believed that education was the catalyst for enlightenment. As the head of Midrash Talmud Tora 'im Derekh 'Erets, he decided on the curriculum for the school (see Hutsin, *Ha-Levanon*, no. 7 (11 February 1870) 54-55), which included teaching skills that were not directly connected to religious life but would enable integration within the society as a whole. These skills included the knowledge of foreign languages and etiquette, both necessary for public service positions and business and had the potential of generating income and job security. Like enlightened Jews in East Europe, he, too, believed in the importance of acquiring a skill, which can explain the pride he took in his community that started a program for poor children to become apprentices to tailors, shoemakers, and carpenters (*Ha-Maggid*, no. 34 (26 August 1863) 208). Rashbah urged young people to learn from the success of craftsmen in Europe (*Sefer Talmud Katan*, 6).

Rashbah felt that it would be best for a sick person who needed a physician to seek the help of one who had studied in Europe (see *Sefer Talmud Katan*, pp. 8-9). He also published on matters of Jewish law.

Of special interest in this context is an article (*Ha-Maggid*, no. 41 (21 October 1868) 325) in which he interpreted a paragraph from the Talmud that had a vision for a millennial setting. The Talmudic paragraph reads as follows:

> In the footsteps of the Messiah, insolence will increase and honour will dwindle. The vine will yield its fruit [abundantly] but wine will be dear. The

> government will turn to heresy and there will be none [to offer them] reproof. The meeting place [of scholars] will be used for immorality. Galilee will be destroyed, Gablan desolated, and dwellers on the frontier will go about [begging] from place to place without anyone to take pity on them. The wisdom of the learned will degenerate, the righteous will be despised, and the truth will be lacking. The young will put old men to shame, the old will stand up in the presence of the young, a son will revile his father, a daughter will rise up against her mother-in-law, and a man's enemies will be the members of his household. The face of a generation will be like the face of a dog. A son will not feel ashamed before his father. So upon whom may we rely? Upon our Father who is in heaven. (The Babylonian Talmud, Sotah, 49b, Tr. By I. Epstein, London, The Soncini Press 1936, 266-267).

Rashbah's interpretation emphasizes the importance of education. He envisioned the rising power of technology and its impact and imagined a world with electronics and cables, train tracks, and ships that could cross borders between countries. He envisioned a world with freedom of speech, where one's status is determined not by age but by wisdom and knowledge, a world in which Jews incorporate into their education religious studies, science, faith, and knowledge. Rashbah's interpretation is optimistic and reflects his profound open-mindedness.

The quotation, "In the footsteps of the Messiah insolence will increase," Rashbah interpreted as: at the footsteps of the Messiah many people, including the Jews, will pursue wisdom and knowledge in spite of the fact that their pursuit will be obstructed. Rashbah interpreted the sentence "the vine will yield its fruit [abundantly] but wine will be dear" as meaning that due to a highly developed technology, products such as wine will be transported from one place to another and, consequently, will be expensive. "There will be none [to offer them] reproof," because everyone will be wise and enlightened in the future. "The meeting-place [of scholars] will be used for immortality," because not only religious, but also secular studies will be discussed in it. The "Galilee will be destroyed," because wisdom will be available in every place in the world, not only in the Galilee. "Gablan desolated," because the Kurdistani people will go to seek wisdom elsewhere. Wisdom will bring peace in the world, "and dwellers on the frontier will go about [begging] from place to place without anyone to take pity on them," because these dwellers are quarrelsome people. "The wisdom of the learned will degenerate," that is, in its status, because everyone will be highly knowledgeable. "Fearers of sin will be despised" is directed at those who have no knowledge and wisdom. "And the truth will be lacking" are the people who will be highly educated and innovative. Therefore, they will have various opinions that will be hard to understand. "The young will put old men to shame, " as in young, unwise people will put old, wise people to shame. "The old will stand up in the presence of the young," Because there will be young people who are wiser than the old, and the old will give them due respect. "A son will revile his father, a daughter will rise up against her mother-in-law" because of the conflict between the young and the old generations. "And a man's enemies will be the members of his household," because the wife will be like an enemy to her husband when she protects her children from their father's wrath. "The face of the generation will be like the face of a dog," because young people will not be inhibited in front of the old, and they will rebuke the statements of the old when they disagree with them.

Rashbah dedicated an extensive explanation to the words, "So upon whom shall we rely? Upon our Father who is in heaven." He emphasized the importance of trusting God and following the path of the Torah. He attacked those young people who disregarded Jewish law and rituals and arrogantly put down the institutes of the Jewish community.

Rashbah's interpretation of this article, with its respectful treatment of young people, does not leave room for young people to claim that he is biased about their abilities or character merely because they are young. Thus, his protest in this article against the conduct of some young people who acquired general education remains sound.

Rashbah addressed the rest of this article to the leaders of the Alliance. He writes about graduate students who acquired cursory knowledge and skills in a foreign language and began treating their community with pompousness and contempt. Rashbah expressed (in many other articles) a great appreciation for the work of the Alliance (see *Ha-Maggid*, no. 32 (31 August 31) 1866 252; *Ha-Maggid*, no. 46 (28 November 1866) 363-364; *Ha-Tsefira*, no. 11 (16 September 1874) 83-84; *Ha-Levanon*, no. 13 (25 June 1869) 102-103). In 1864, the Alliance attempted to affect cultural changes in the life of the Jewish community in Baghdad through education.

The Alliance banned, for example, wearing a hat popular with Jewish students and attempted to use French as the teaching language. The Jewish community in Baghdad was interested in modern education but viewed the acculturation attempts of the Alliance as detrimental to their religious tradition. After a long clash between the Alliance and the community, the Babylonian Jews decided to forgo any support by the Alliance and developed their own educational system (see Yehuda, 1996).

Rashbah used the above-referenced article about interpreting a Talmudic paragraph to attack those graduate students of the Alliance who treated the community with pompousness and contempt. He called these youngsters "little foxes that spoil the vineyards" (The Song of Songs, 2:15), They "do not know how to read books of wisdom and science" but "chatter like a swallow or a crane" (Asiah 38:14). Rashbah asks the Alliance leaders to appoint school principals who will nurture both Jewish studies and general studies, "real enlightenment" with faith. He portrayed Europe as a place of freedom and good education (medicine and handicrafts). The Hebrew authors of the Jewish enlightenment movement depicted similarly the cultural and political progress of Europe.

Rashbah wrote about the people from the Near Eastern countries as people who "were not accustomed to European languages and periodicals in foreign languages that stored up treasuries of science and enlightenment" (*Ha-Tsefira,* no. 11 (16 September 1874) 83-84). He imagined the European Jews as living safe and calm lives with freedom and liberty, contrary to the Jews in Babylon who had troublesome and oppressed lives (*Ha-Maggid,* no. 11 (12 March 1863) 84). On the one hand, he wrote about "European illuminated brethren," and on the other hand, he wrote about Babylonian Jews who still believed in "fiddlesticks and vanity" (*Ha-Tsefira,* no. 16 (25 April 1866) 124). He asked the Jewish leaders in Europe to support various causes, such as maintaining the shrine of the Scribe Ezra (*Ha-Maggid,* no. 16 (25 April 1866) 124), saving the Jews of Persia from persecution (*Ha-Maggid,* no. 34 (29 August 1866) 268), and supporting the efforts of the Babylonian Jewish community in absorbing numerous Jews who went to Babylon from Persia and needed medicine, food, and clothing (*Ha-Maggid,* no. 50 (26 December 1866) 396), supporting the improvement of the political status of the Babylonian Jews (*Ha-Tsefira,* no. 9 (1877) 67), and helping them in a time of famine (*Ha-Levanon,* no. 20 (24 January 1872) 158). He also asked the Jewish European leaders to defend the Jews of Kurdistan from malicious oppression (*Ha-Tsefira,* no. 42 (1879) 331).

Rashbah viewed the life of European Jews as economically and politically different from the life of Babylonian Jews, many of whom were poor. He wrote, "Unlike our brethren in Europe that live peacefully and serenely, each one of them sitting under his own vine and fig tree with freedom and liberty in their countries, we Babylonian Jews live in stress and quandaries, under enemies and troubles" (*Ha-Maggid,* no. 11 (12 March 1863) 84).

E. Is Rashbah's Reportage Reliable?

Rashbah, a Rabbi who promoted truth in human relations and communication, reported actual events and conditions in the community. In two instances, he reported something that was questionable, and in both cases, he did so as a religious man. In one instance, he reported that a woman saw a pig after she took a ritual bath and then she gave birth to a creature that resembled a pig (*Ha-Levanon*, no. 15 (30 August 1876) 134). This incident proved, according to Rashbah, "that Jewish sages were right in instructing women to avoid seeing anything impure after they took a bath as a religious duty." In another instance, Rashbah announced that a Jewish man was found in Baghdad who had breasts like a woman, and his breasts dripped milk (*Ha-Maggid*, no. 15 (14 April 1875) 34). This incident proved, according to Rashbah, the credibility of the Talmudic story (in Shabbat Tractate) about a poor widower that experienced a miracle when he developed breasts like a woman and he nursed his baby.

In Rashbah's articles there is information that Rashbah's article served as its exclusive source. In other cases, Rashbah's information contradicts other sources or verifies and validates them. For example, he wrote about Rabbi Eliahu Mani's visit to Baghdad from Hebron and about the squabble the Rabbi had with his opponents in Hebron (*Ha-Havatselet,* no. 25 (1880)). The visit and the squabble are facts known to us from various sources (Ben-Yaacob, 1980, 73-82). Similarly, other events in the life of the Jewish community reported by Rashbah are corroborated by other authorities.

F. Rashbah's Style

The majority of Rashbah's articles are informative texts, and a few are articles about Jewish law. Another subject he wrote about was ethics of young people. One might expect Rashbah's reporting style to be unemotional. However, Rashbah was emotionally, religiously, ethically, and sometimes personally involved in what he wrote. He did not merely report facts—he also responded to them. The contemporary Hebrew reader does not expect coverage of events to be conveyed in Rashbah's biblical and rabbinical style.

Rashbah's style is emotional and inspiring, because he wrote about matters that were close to the heart, many of which were gut-wrenching and tragic. Occasionally, Rashbah used Judeo-Arabic words, specifically when a mere translation to Hebrew could not provide its full meaning. For example, he used the word "ziara" to describe visiting, particularly during Shavuot (Feast of Weeks, Pentecost), the holy tombs in Babylon of the prophet Ezekiel, the Scribe Ezra, and Joshua Cohen Gadol.

Rashbah wrote with pathos and passion when he described community calamities. Here is an example of how he reported the consequences of a plague on the Jewish community:

> All the people from different populations walk and sob and wander in the markets and on the streets from morning until evening, they earn wages for a bag of holes [they make no profit in business, Haggai 1:6] to make a little money for buying them a little food to refresh their family's souls and their soul [Lamentations 1:11, 1:19] lest they will get sick with an illness that results from hunger, but they cannot [earn the wages]...woe to the day in which Babylon tumbled and tumbled and all its joys ceased and everyone that passeth by it shall be astonished and shall hiss at all the plagues [Jeremiah 49, 17] that God inflicted on it. Cut off the sower from Babylon, and him that handleth the sickle in the time of harvest [Jeremiah 50, 16], for the hurt of the daughter of our people we are seized with anguish, we are black, astonishment hath taken hold of us [Jeremiah 8, 21] and by the rivers of Babylon there we sat down, yea, we wept [Psalms 137, 1] about our poor brethren that faint for hunger at the head of every street [Lamentations 2,19] (*Ha-Maggid*, no. 37 (20 September 1871) 292).

The above example illustrates the way Rashbah wove and inserted biblical expressions into his articles. The main punctuation mark used by Rashbah is a period at the end of a sentence, but most of his sentences end without one. Sometimes, he wove fragments from several biblical verses. For example, in the above-referenced article, Rashbah writes about Sir Moses Montefiore as "the famous lord in all the ends of the earth and of the far distant sea" [Psalms 65, 6]. "He who heareth the cry of his people" [Job 34, 28] and "he who rose up and saved them" [Judges 3, 9]. In his description of Montefiore, Rashbah used an eloquent style, typical of his time, and its effect on the reader by the use of the biblical verse should be carefully considered. For example, the expressions taken from Psalms and Job describe God. Rashbah, as a religious man, did not intend to elevate Montefiore to God's level.

While the Bible was the main source for Rashbah's allusions, it was not the exclusive one. Rashbah had a far-reaching knowledge of the Talmud (see Yosef Hayyim, *Sefer Rav Pe'alim*).

In another article (*Ha-Maggid*, no. 34 (26 August 1863) 268), Rashbah wrote about a plague of locusts in Babylon and he reminds his readers, "Whoever saves a single soul of Israel, Scriptures ascribe to him as though he had saved a whole world," based on Sanhedrin (4, 5). The rich Jews of Baghdad could not take care of all the hungry Jews, as there was not enough to satisfy so great a need. Rashbah expressed this reality by quoting another Jewish source (Berakhot 3): "A scrap will not satisfy the lion." He also employed the language of the sages, reminding his readers in the same context that "the cistern is not filled by the rain-water entering through its hole" (or "the pit cannot be filled from its own digging"), meaning that the Jews of Baghdad could not subsist at the time of the plague without help from Jews of other countries. Rashbah asked Montefiore to help establish a school in Baghdad to teach various occupations, including the "Study of the Torah with good manners" (based on Avot 2, 2). He reminded his readers that deeds count and not words alone. He wrote, "Fine words butter no parsnips; actions speak louder than words" (Avot 1, 17).

In all of Rashbah's articles, the reader will find references to major Jewish literary sources. Rashbah made respectful use of Jewish sources by avoiding sarcasm and humor. His use of well-known Jewish texts had a purpose and was not merely decorative. Rashbah found the exact language in the old Jewish sources to describe characters, events, conditions, and feelings specific to his location and era. In his published debates, Rashbah used respectful rhetoric (*Ha-Maggid,* no. 49 (16 December 1873) 448), and in his responses to questions about Jewish law, he used unassuming language (*Perah,* no. 45 (4 May 1883) 271).

Chapter 6: An Epistle as a Literary Work: Rabbi Ya'acov Hayyim's Letter to Farha Sason

Until the advent of modern technology, Jews corresponded long distance through Hebrew letter writing. Despite living in different countries, Hebrew remained the common written language for Jews rather than their respective mother tongue. For example, Rashbah, who could not speak Polish, could correspond in Hebrew with a Jew in Warsaw who could not speak Arabic. Epistles provide examples of how Hebrew culture was active in many countries. In this chapter, I will illustrate how this letter can be considered a creative piece of literature.

Rabbi Ya'acov Hayyim (1854-1920), the son of Rabbi Yosef Hayyim (1834-1909), published two books and authored unpublished religious manuscripts. His primary teacher was his father (ibid., Chapter 4)

In 1888, Rabbi Ya'acov Hayyim wrote a rhyming epistle (see the entire epistle in Ben-Yaacob, Perakim, 452-456) discussed in this chapter. This epistle was addressed to Farha (1856-1936), the wife of the renowned Saliman Sason (1841-1894). Rabbi Yosef Hayyim reviewed the epistle prior to sending it to Farha.

Saliman Sason was born in Bombay. A member of the Sason dynasty, Sason spoke Hebrew and studied Judaism. He was a successful businessman, a philanthropist, and a beloved public figure. He also held a managerial post for the Central Bank in Bombay.

Farha was born in Bombay into a wealthy religious Jewish family of noble Baghdadi lineage. Farha studied with five Rabbis and attended a Catholic school. She was well versed in the Bible, the Talmud, Jewish law, Hebrew, Arabic, English, French, and Latin. She gained recognition for her knowledge, wisdom, and good character. In 1894, she became administrator for the family business. In 1911, she relocated to London where she continued her philanthropic work. Farha became a leader for Iraqi Jews in England and befriended the royal family.

Rabbi Ya'acov Hayyim's epistle included a narrative, a riddle, a fable, and a wish. He introduced the epistle with the following comment: "Here is my fable and riddle / henceforth my statement / and a discussion about the phrases of my ornate speech." In his epistle, Rabbi Ya'acov Hayyim indicated that he wrote the letter in deference to his father's request to write a "delicacy" to his father's beloved friends.

Upon leaving the city, Hayyim imagined a story about a ram that left his ewe behind to find work in the city. The ram headed toward the house of Ahinoam, an influential woman whom he perceived would help him. As he approached her home, twilight arrived:

> It was dusk; the sun peeked through magenta colored clouds and haze, and cast onto the earth its last golden rays, and the crescent moon slowly and steadily glowed as the sun set, and made rays for the crescent moon, and the moon walked amidst the splendor of the stars in the sky, the same way that one of the small town young clerks would behave in a conceited and haughty manner after his supervisor walks away, as if the young clerk was saying, "I will rule."

During the night, the ram became restless and could not sleep. Yet he was hopeful that Ahinoam would help him find employment. The ram imagined that he met Ahinoam. When he praised her, she did not remain indifferent. Rather, she initially asked him what he wanted, then proceeded to offer him money. The ram rejected her monetary gift. Instead, he requested that she use her influence with a powerful man named Yedidyah (Jedidia) to secure a position for him so he could earn a living. The ram and Ahinoam exchanged devotional gifts (Ben-Yaacob, 453).Then, the author digresses to describe hope and imagination as powerful forces:

> Imagination transforms time and space, arranging everything according to its will, especially when accompanied by hope. Hopes born to the imagination portray earth as a paradise, as a smoothly paved road without obstacles. Indeed, hope is powerful and with the sweetness of its lips, it will seduce the wise and sagacious to aspire to greater things. Hope will revive the soul of the gloomy and the poor-spirited; it will console the poor in his poverty and will promise him thousands of gold and silver [coins]. Hope will sweeten that which is sour and will persuade the miserable through loving and comforting words. It will promise the poor who embrace a dunghill, that it will lift him from the dust and enable him to sit with princes [First Samuel 2:8] in adorned palaces and spacious, expensive properties (ibid.).

This short essay about the power of hope diverges from the epistle's focal point. The author slows down the rhythm of the plot, enabling him to bring forth and illustrate his language skills and his creativity.

Continuing the story, the morning for which the ram waited impatiently finally arrived:

> When he awakened the sun had already risen and he rejoiced like a strong man ready to run his race [Psalms 19:6] under a clear sky whose clouds lifted the previous night, clouds with magenta red rims like that of a silkworm. A choir of birds sang a new song following their long silence throughout the night and beneath the sky's galaxy was heard the shriek of crows and the sounds of birds. The light is sweet. How good it is for the eyes to get a glimpse of the sun. In the backyard a beautiful rooster walks with grandeur. Haughtily and generously he stretches his exquisite feathers like a bow while he strikes the earth with his wings. His head is red like blood mixed with azure and his nose sets high above his beak, he walks round and round with an air of grandeur and turns his stretched tail towards his audience so they will gaze at him, and from time to time he will sound his call that is melodious to the ears. And here the turtledove makes love to his dove, and they kiss one another lovingly (ibid., 454).

In this paragraph, the author moderates the rhythm of the plot and illustrates his descriptive poetic abilities. This paragraph also interrupts his story. It is an illustration intended to demonstrate the literary skills and Hebrew knowledge of its author. Whereas the discussion about the power of human imagination is expected to be analytical, the description is not. Rather, the description is detailed and colorful. It shifts its focus from one object in nature to another, including from the sky to the Earth. The language employed is not meant to convey any particular message.

When the ram arrived at the house of Ahinoam, he was driven away by the guard. Ahinoam overheard the guard and proceeded to scold him. Then, she invited the ram (man) into her home, where she received and acknowledged him respectfully.

The epistle was written during the spring and it included a poetic description of the season. Specifically, it included a quotation from the Medieval Hebrew poet Immanuel Haromi (Immanuel of Rome), who characterized the beauty of springtime (*Mahbarot Immanuel*). The epistle concludes in praise of patience, hope, and hard work, portraying a diligent poor man as being nobler than a foolish rich man.

The "ram" in the "fable" was the author, who was prepared to leave his ewe behind. Ahinoam was Farha, and Yedidyah (Jedidia) was her husband. Ahinoam was described as a "lovable ewe." When she hosted the ram in her room and they became better acquainted, she realized her heart felt love for him. The ram then took hold of his violin and played a love song to her.

Nevertheless, the epistle was not a love letter written by a second generation rabbi to a married woman. Farha loved her husband. When he died at fifty-three years of age she wrote, "Not a person but an angel was taken from me… there has never been nor will there ever be anyone like him…" (ibid., Vol. I, 96).

Rabbi Yosef Hayyim, the father of Rabbi Ya'acov Hayyim, reviewed the epistle prior to its delivery. He was a righteous, religious man, who had great appreciation for Farha's knowledge and righteous behavior. She was the only woman with whom he corresponded.

In a letter he sent to Farha (ibid., Vol. II, 426-427), he wrote that finding work for his son was a matter of necessity, even if it meant his son would have to depart from his relatives, which would undoubtedly cause them pain.

Rabbi Yosef Hayyim described his son as a man who wrote beautifully, had extensive knowledge, and was a reliable person. Rabbi Yosef Hayyim asked his son to write the letter to illustrate his Hebrew writing skills. His son composed his epistle in two days. This epistle was merely meant to demonstrate his son's abilities and to amuse Farha and her family. Therefore, Rabbi Yosef Hayyim also wanted Farha's husband to familiarize himself with this epistle.

In another letter (ibid., 428), Rabbi Yosef Hayyim mentioned that this epistle was written to be an amusing fable, and he, too, found it humorous. Rabbi Yosef Hayyim noted that this Hebrew style was used in Eastern European Jewish journals and books. All of this information, of course, prevented the reader from regarding the epistle as an act of a suitor trying to seduce a religious, married woman.

Indeed, the epistle demonstrated the proficiency of its author to write in Hebrew. The author alluded to biblical verses, wove Medieval Hebrew literature into his text, and wrote some paragraphs with rhymes and rhythm. He incorporated poetic language and imagery. He built suspense by interrupting the plot to digress with dialogues, descriptions about nature, and short essays. He quoted from Medieval Hebrew poetry and demonstrated his awareness of different literary genres. Even this epistle that was meant to amuse and illustrate literary skills was evidence of a rich Hebrew culture thriving in Iraq and of the ongoing cultural contact between Iraqi and European Hebrew culture.

If one insists on reading the text independently, disregarding the intent of the author and the circumstances under which it was written, one might conclude the author lost control of his text and interpret the text to describe a very daring attempt to court a married woman whom he never met.

Chapter 7: Shaul Abdullah Yosef: A Scholar of Medieval Hebrew Poetry

> I found it necessary to comment that this is the rule, that any time our European brethren wanted to interpret some matters that concern us, the Near Eastern Jews, our brethren did not plunge into the depth of the matter and they only judged and discussed it from their point of view.
>
> Shaul Yosef, in a letter dated Jan. 27, 1896

A. Shaul Yosef's Literary Activities

In a previous chapter, I presented Shaul Yosef's world of poetry. Baghdadi-born Shaul Yosef (1849-1906) settled in Hong Kong. He was a poet, a scholar of Medieval Hebrew poetics and its poetry, and could skillfully interpret its texts.

Shaul Yosef felt that he understood the Arabic way of life similar to Medieval Hebrew poets who lived among Arabs and were familiar with their poets, their poetry, their style, motifs, their "ornamental speech," metaphorical language, conventional images, and phrases. Shaul Yosef's colleagues often behaved arrogantly toward him.

Dan Pagis wrote the following excerpt about Shaul Yosef's contribution to understanding Medieval Hebrew poetry:

> At the beginning of our century [20th] only two scholars rose to systematically engage in studying the foundations of Hebrew poetry's literary expression or distinctive features. Both scholars were familiar with this poetry from childhood and remained attentive towards it until they could write similar style poetry. One of these scholars was Shaul Abdullah Yosef, a resident of Hong Kong whose birthplace was Babylon. David Yellin dedicated his book

to the memory of Shaul Yosef. The second scholar was David Yellin. Yellin was more familiar than Shaul Yosef with his current readership, who were already familiar with other poetic systems and styles (see Yellin, Torat, G).

Yellin praised Shaul Yosef for dedicating his life to Medieval Hebrew poetry and for making major contributions to its textual criticism. Shaul Yosef was the first person to announce finding the Divan of Todros Abulafia. He earnestly tried to "clean it and correct it with his sophisticated remarks and corrections" (see Abulafia, *Gan*, Vol. II, c-c1). Moses ibn Ezra (1055-1135) wrote *Kitab al-Muhadara wa—al-Mudhakara*, a compilation of his poetry. Herein, he presented his views about the essence of poetry and its theory of ornamentation, its sources and functions. One hundred years following Shaul Yosef, Yellin was the first to reiterate that one must understand this theory to interpret Medieval Hebrew poetry of Spain (ibid., LVII).

Shaul Yosef was involved in a number of intellectual areas. I will summarize his works in these areas.

Shaul Yosef wrote poetry employing Medieval Hebrew poetry, its style of "ornamental speech," metaphorical language, conventional images and phrases, and motifs. He published a variety of articles, particularly about the poetics of Medieval Hebrew poetry, its interpretations, and errors made by its interpreters. As of 1887, Shaul Yosef's articles were published in *Ha-Tsefira*, *Perah*, and *Maggid Mesharim*. Some of his articles appeared in periodicals, while some of them remained unpublished. He also wrote an article about the influence of Arabic poetry on Medieval Hebrew poetry.

Shaul Yosef discovered and interpreted the Diwan of Todros Joseph Halevi Abulafia (Abulafia, 1220-1298), *Gan Ha-Meshalim Ve-Ha-Hidot*. It was published in Shaul Yosef's handwriting and later by Yellin, who also contrasted it with similar manuscripts. Yellin reiterated numerous comments made by Shaul Yosef in writing his textbook (Yosef, *Gan*).

Yellin left behind interpretations to poems of Rabbi Yehuda Ha-Levi and to *Sefer Ha-Tarshish* of Rabbi Moses ibn Ezra, which were published in two books by Samuel Krauss (Yosef, *Giv'at*; Yosef, *Mishbetset*).

Shaul Yosef also left biblical commentaries, including comments about sections of the Psalms. He helped increase the number of subscribers to the periodical *Ha-Tsefira* and to *Mekitseh Nirdamim*.

Shaul Yosef's literary estate included a dictionary of Arabic poetry and poetics. He was familiar with the Badi'a ("marvellows," "'ilm al-badi'a," which means the art of beautiful style, a branch of Arabic rhetoric). Yosef's dictionary included poetic terminology, their interpretations, and illustrations from Arabic poetry. In addition, he left a manuscript about Arabic poetics and explicated images from Medieval Hebrew poetry by pointing out their Arabic source. He also left clarifications to biblical words and works in Hebrew, Arabic, and English about Arabic and Hebrew prosody.

Yosef Shaul also corresponded with many scholars and editors. His letters conveyed personal sentiments and explained his opinions about a number of literary subjects. In addition, his letters reflected suggestions for developing new words in Hebrew (See Yosef, *Gan*, LXV).

B. The Articles of Shaul Yosef

From 1887 on, Shaul Yosef contributed seven articles to *Ha-Tesfira*, some of which were continued and published section by section over several issues. In addition, he published articles in the weekly *Perah* that appeared in Calcutta, India, and in *Maggid Mesharim* that appeared after *Perah*. He also left an article that was published after his death about Arabic influence on Medieval Hebrew poetry.

Shaul Yosef was appreciative of Medieval Hebrew poetry's high achievements. After the expulsion of the Jews from Spain (in 1492), this poetry was neglected. In the nineteenth century, there were scholars who were interested in restoring its eminence, interpreting it, and publishing updated editions of it. In his articles, Shaul Yosef criticized the work of some of these scholars and their interpretations.

Shaul Yosef's criticism of Medieval Hebrew poetry publications focused on two aspects. One was the major errors he found in vocalizing the poems, choosing incorrect versions and applying incorrect divisions between two lines of the distich. The second aspect related to the extensive errors found in the annotations and interpretations of these poems. Shaul Yosef illustrated his arguments with numerous examples.

His article "Kol Ha-Sirim tahat Ha-Shir" ("the sound of thorns instead of the poem," alluding to Ecclesiastes 7:6) was published in three sections (see Bibliography). In the first section, Shaul Yosef expressed his discomfort with the errors found in Medieval Hebrew poetry publications. He regarded the accomplishments of leading scholars in this field to be insignificant.

Republications of Medieval Hebrew poems included numerous errors. Shaul Yosef made it a personal mission to communicate with Medieval Hebrew scholars about the numerous errors found in these publications. In the second section of Shaul Yosef's article, which was published in *Ha-Tsefira*, he pointed out errors he found in vocalizing Medieval Hebrew poems and incorrectly dividing two lines of the distich. He then referred to Medieval Hebrew poetry books published during this era, enumerating the multitude of errors made in these books. Shaul Yosef also referenced a prominent scholar in this field whose innovations, interpretations, and remarks he referred to as "humorous." He continued his arguments in the third section of his article. This time he points to a particular poem, noting that the poet was not the one the poem was ascribed to, but a different poet.

In another article written under the same title (see Yosef, Bibliography, 1889) he expressed reservation about poems translated by Shmuel Ben Adayah from Arabic to Hebrew. He wrote:

> I read with joy the third booklet about the history of Hebrew literature that was just published, [I read] everything that was said about Arabic Jews and

> their poets that were mentioned according to their names... However, if the reader is from the Middle East, one that the Arabic language is not foreign to, he would wonder who are these descendants of Judah, because the copyist [translator] did not copy most of their names meticulously... The face of this precious poetry was covered with thorns... *(Ha-Tsefira,* No. 214, 2).

In these few sentences, the reader observes Shaul Yosef's passion for Medieval Hebrew poetry ("precious"), the importance of Arabic knowledge ("if the reader is from the Middle East"), and the damage that the translators inflicted on this poetry (thorns covered its face). Shaul Yosef felt that he could do more justice to this poetry by offering his translation of the poems from Arabic to Hebrew, based on his knowledge of Shmuel ben Adaya's biography and his knowledge of Arabic history and culture. He illustrated the problematic treatment of Medieval Hebrew poetry by presenting errors found in major works of prominent scholars of his time in the field of Medieval Hebrew poetry (see Yosef, *Ha-Tesifira,* No. 215). In another article (see Yosef, "Kol Ha-Shirim"), he systematically presents his opinion, suggesting that a major scholar of Medieval Hebrew poetry (during his era) erred about the life, time, and works of the Medieval Hebrew poet, Rabbi Ya'acov ben Ela'azar Hameshorer.

In Shaul Yosef's last and longest article in *Ha-Tesifira* (see Yosef, 1901), he expressed his disappointment over being marginalized for pointing out numerous errors in Medieval Hebrew poetry publications. These errors were identified in the vocalization, translations, and interpretations of Medieval Hebrew poetry, including the poems of Rabbi Yehuda Halevi and Rabbi Moses ibn Ezra. Shaul Yosef expressed his frustration after observing the discrepancy between the great reputations of scholars of his time and their actual achievements in the field of Medieval Hebrew poetry. These scholars were prepared to deal with European languages, while the research of Medieval Hebrew poetry required comprehension of the Arabic language, style, and philosophy. The absence of cultural knowledge and linguistic background of Medieval Hebrew poets prevented scholars from being able to choose the correct versions and interpretations of the highly successful Medieval Hebrew poetry. These scholars were not equipped to see the strong links between Medieval Hebrew poetry and the Arabic language and literature.

Shaul Yosef also published articles that were not related to the field of literary criticism. One of them was about the Jews in Hong Kong and in China (see Yosef, "Ha-Yehudim"). Another article was about a Torah scroll that was brought from China to his town in Hong Kong (see Shaul, "Rea'eh").

C. The Books of Shaul Yosef

Shaul Yosef left behind interpretations to poems of Rabbi Yehuda Ha-Levi and to *Sefer Ha-Tarshish* of Rabbi Moses ibn Ezra, which were published in two books by Samuel Krauss (Yosef, *Giv'at*; Yosef, *Mishbetset*). *Giva't Shaul,* written by Shaul Yosef, was published in Vienna in 1923. It was a book of interpretations of Rabbi Yehuda Halevi's poetry. The poetry of Yehuda Halevi was published by Hayyim Brody (1868-1942) who was a scholar in the field of Medieval Hebrew poetry and Sephardi liturgies. Shaul Yosef argued that Brody made hundreds of errors in this publication (see Hakak, 2003, 250-251). Another book of Shaul Yosef that was published after his death was *Mishbetset Ha-Tarshish,* in which he interpreted Moses ibn Ezra's book. Shaul Yosef argued that this edition, which appeared in 1886, was replete with errors. Samuel Krauss also prepared Shaul Yosef's book for print.

Shaul Yosef discovered the Diwan of Todros Joseph Halevi Abulafia (Abulafia, 1220-1298), *Gan Ha-Meshalim Ve-Ha-Hidot,* and interpreted it. It was published in Shaul Yosef's handwriting and later by Yellin, who also compared it to other manuscripts of similar works and used hundreds of Shaul Yosef's comments in the text of this book (Yosef, *Gan*).

Shaul Yosef was correct in sensing that he had much to offer by interpreting Medieval Hebrew poetry and by presenting the correct version of its texts. He had a passion for this poetry and dedicated himself to it. He published articles and wrote letters to voice his discomfort in seeing many errors made in its interpretation and voiced his interest in selecting the correct versions. Many of his corrections were accepted and entered into later editions without acknowledging him. He was a knowledgeable man, well versed in the cultural background of Medieval Hebrew poetry and its poetics. However, it appears he only gained recognition following his demise.

Chapter 8: Rabbi Saliman Mani: Hebron, Gaza, and the Demons

While a young man in his thirties, Rabbi Saliman Mani (see Chapter 2) published in Eliezer Ben Yehuda's *Ha-Tsevi*. He wrote two exposés about Hebron and Gaza and a short story.

His short story, "The Valley of the Demons" (*Ha-Tsevi*, 1885, No. 31-34) is a didactic story (about two thousand words) written in the first person. The narrator informs readers that since his youth he was a skeptic—he vacillated in his belief about demons. He could not substantiate their existence, yet he did not reject their existence. A Dervish rekindled his belief in demonic existence. He studied demonism extensively until he ultimately perceived himself as superior to human beings and able to dominate demons. In vain he attempted to rule demons in the desert and in graveyards.

While in the graveyard, he thought he saw Asmodeus (the king of demons). However, when he approached the creature, he realized that what he observed in the dark graveyard was just a black dog that was bound. The dog bit him. Then he returned home and described his encounter. Old women prepared his home to rebuke the demons ("Indulko") while he went to seek medical attention for his bite. Upon his return home, he learned that a woman who divined by a familiar spirit (a soothsayer, wizard) was brought to his home to ward off the demons. Angered by this occurrence, he went to seek help from his friend to learn more about this superstition.

When he went to sleep that night he had a nightmare. In the nightmare, he dreamed he was rebuked for believing in the existence of demons. So, he killed the soothsayer. When he awakened, he ceased believing in demonic existence.

Rabbi Saliman Mani's short story was viewed by Galia Hayardeni as "picturesque and highly humorous." His story detailed a strange custom of his time. When someone had a serious illness, such as blindness, madness, or fright, or when a woman was barren, it was customary to clean and paint the house and remove all religious books. The ill person was instructed to desist from prayer and not to mention God. Rather, a soothsayer was summoned. She prepared a medley of wheat, malt, water, salt, and honey. At midnight she sprinkled this mixture around the bed of the sick person and in other areas of the house while muttering incantations.

Eliezer Ben Yehuda, the pioneer of Hebrew speech in Palestine and the editor of *Ha-Tsevi*, viewed this as an abominable custom, as one can observe from his remark at the end of the story. Rabbi Saliman Mani's story paralleled Eliezer Ben Yehuda's beliefs. Secular and educated Jews viewed this custom as an annoyance.

In a previous issue of *Ha-Tsevi* (No. 30, 1885), an article surfaced about a school for girls that was closed for two weeks in order to implement this custom. Eliezer Ben-Yehuda wrote that Rabbi Saliman Mani's beautiful piece was produced after that publication. Moshe David Gaon (see Bibliography) enumerated thirteen different procedures of this custom. One of them was to protect a home that came under demonic attack. It was a home designated for a couple planning to marry. The demons chose a house near the couple to be and threw stones and burning torches at their house to drive the inhabitants away. The house was vacated, and its dwellers prepared tasty food for the demons and beautiful candles, enough to last them for at least a week.

Eliezer Ben-Yehuda liked the Sephardic Jews. He observed unity among them and viewed them as the future Jewish leaders. However, he wanted to fight against superstitions such as the one described in the story that was also adopted by Ashkenazi Jews. Eliezer Ben-Yehuda based the writing style he used in *Ha-Tsevi* on modern European journalism of his era. The periodical exemplifies the evolution of Hebrew from a sacred language to a secular language that expressed all the requirements needed to fulfill one's life. *Ha-Tsevi* encouraged local young authors and strove to encourage modifications in Jewish life to reflect the spirit of the Jewish Enlightenment.

Rabbi Saliman Mani was one of the first authors in Palestine to write a didactic Hebrew story. His intent was to utilize literature to renew, modify, delineate accordingly, and enable life to progress. The author's desire to contribute to a progression of Jewish life in Palestine in the story far outweighed his concern to highlight its flaws.

The story is written in biblical style. It begins with an exposition that provides readers with the necessary information and background to set the stage for the story. The story is told in the first person, and the narrator is also the main character. He is a witness and a participant in the events that take place. He tells his story in chronological order. He is a dynamic character, whose beliefs change in the process of writing about the events that occur.

Years after the events in the story took place, the narrator reiterates the story, at which time he no longer believes in demons. Even though he writes about the events years after they happened, he reacts to them in the story as if he is going through the experiences he describes. As a result, he appears to be a reliable character, often emotional as he relives the events, intimately involved with all the details that take place.

The narrator expresses his opinion about various issues in the story (such as the influence of the Dervish's vanity on innocent people). Actions that took a very long time are presented briefly, such as the ones he took in order to try to find demons. His preparation for meeting with the demons and his encounter with the dog in the graveyard, however, took a short time but are described in detail and with strong emotions.

One of the devices used to build up to the emotional experience is the use of the present tense in depicting an event that took place years before the reader is told about it. The event becomes vivid and present: "I am seized by trembling and quaking: Indeed, what is this? Why is it that the closer I get to it the sadder I become?"

Rabbi Saliman Mani also created a dialogue between the narrator and the old women who told him about what they are doing in order to protect him from the demons, the demons' children, and their slaves. The dialogue moderates the plot and illustrates the gap between the narrator and the old women. It also demonstrates the hardships in presenting the spoken Hebrew language at that time. Moderating the rhythm of the plot through dialogues or detailed descriptions contributes to the reader's anticipation and suspense.

The story ends with a transformation in the narrator, who stopped believing in demons. This didactic story presents an appealing plot, a "sweet shell," whose primary bitter, spiritual, esthetical, and educational message is found. The author uses various devices, including humor, irony, satire, exaggerations, overstatements and fantastic distortions, in order to shame and mock the phenomenon he is writing about. For example, he describes in detail the old woman who came to his home to drive away the demons: "Her face is like a face of a monkey, her eyes are like the eyes of an owl, and upon her eyelashes sits the shadow of death. Her body is like a vine crouched under its clusters, her belly swollen..."

At times, the narrator melodramatizes, like the time he experienced great excitement when he thought he finally encountered the demon in the graveyard, only to realize it was merely a dog. At the time the narrator told the story, he knew it was only a dog. However, he kept the reader in suspense just like he was in suspense at the time the event occurred. He uses puns as a device for injecting humor. For example, he spent a lot of money in order to research and encounter demons, which brought him no results: "Ha-shedim…hayu shoddedeh caspi" ("shedim"-demons, while "shodedim" are robbers, "The demons became the robbers of my money").

The style of the story is informative in some parts and highly emotional in other parts. The style is highly emotional and poetic in some of the descriptions about his belief in the existence of demons, where the author employs exclamation words and marks and emotional images. This style only deepens the effect of his disbelief in demons later in the story. The short, exclamatory sentences are in contrast to the long, informative sentences that are less demonstrative.

While the story begins with a question about the existence of demons, its finale is clear;: the narrator came to the conclusion that they do not exist.

Professor Yosef Halevi (see Bibliography) writes that it is possible that Rabbi Saliman Mani was the first author in the Middle East to write modern Hebrew prose. This is because this story was the first Hebrew story in which a religious Jewish author from Middle Eastern origin addressed a sore spot in his community, using literary devices, descriptions of nature for its own sake, irony, and imagination, in the customary style of rabbinic reproof.

In his 1885 depiction about Hebron (see Rabbi Saliman Mani, "Hebron"), Rabbi Saliman Mani briefly discusses Hebron's biblical history. He then discusses the bravery of Hebron's residents. Hebron is a small town; it "dwells in the ridges of the mountains, as a dove in the clefts of a rock." The town extends across a wide area, surrounded by mountains covered with olive and vine tress. On its eastern side there is an old, tall palace made of expensive stones that serves as a mosque. In the palace, one can find the access opening to the Cave of Makhpelah. From the top of that mountain, one can see a beautiful valley, covered in green and woven with roses and vines. Fountains flow through the valley and water the fruit trees of the holy land. At the end of the valley there is a very tall tree that resembles a king of a regiment to whom all the fruit trees bow. The water of Hebron is so pure that it is considered medicinal.

The residents of Hebron are both brave and virtuous. The women are beautiful and modest. The residents used to make their living by producing glasswork. Later, however, they made a living by working their vineyards. Non-Jewish residents in Hebron lived contentedly in the vineyards four months out of the year.

Historically, the Sephardic and Ashkenazi Jews of Hebron were impoverished and persecuted. Ashkenazi Jews left Hebron at one point in time. However, they later returned. Gradually, the Sephardic and Ashkenazi communities split from one another. Some Jews of Hebron were shoemakers and merchants, while others depended on charity for their survival. There were also those who accepted an impoverished lifestyle in order to dedicate themselves to religious studies.

Rabbi Saliman Mani's portrayal of Hebron is both informative and poetic. He even wove a short poem into his description of the vineyards in addition to his poetic prose. In his poem, he describes in poetic detail Hebron and its residents, highlighting the sense of joy these people exuded.

◆ ◆ ◆

In his "Massa' le-Aza" ("A Trip to Gaza," *Ha-Tsevi*, 1886, No. 7), Rabbi Saliman Mani wrote about a quandary over the distribution ("halukkah") of charitable funds that were received in Palestine from Jews abroad. The funds were to be distributed among the needy. At that time there were about fifteen thousand Jews, most of whom lived in Jerusalem, Hebron, Safed, and Tiberia. In Gaza, there was no such charitable fund. Hence, there were fewer disputes in Gaza's Jewish community.

Rabbi Saliman Mani describes his travels in a camels' caravan that transported grapes from Hebron to Gaza. On their way they passed a Bedouin (Arabic Nomad) camp, with shepherds and shepherdesses. The shepherdesses were singing songs of love and heroism. They also wove and embroidered. Gaza had an abundance of olive trees and palm trees. From a distance, he thought that Gaza was a beautiful town because of the fields and the trees surrounding it. When he entered Gaza, however, he found a village with narrow roads laden with garbage. Most of the houses were flat, simply designed, and aesthetically ugly. There were, however, luxurious homes. Yet, they were also unattractive. A Jewish family hosted him. The following day he went and toured the rest of Gaza.

Gaza had clear air. Its residents looked healthy. They were tall, kindhearted, and economically successful. Gaza had a population of 19,700, including two hundred Christians and sixteen Jewish families. The Jews had their own synagogue, but there was no Jewish graveyard and no ritual bath. Most of the people were farmers. However, there were also pottery workers, weavers, and basket makers.

Part 3: Hebrew Periodicals in Babylon

Chapter 9: *Ha-Dover:* The First Hebrew Journal in Babylon

Hebrew authors in Iraq published books. They also published poems in prayer books and participated in Hebrew publications that circulated in Babylon, Israel, India, and other countries in Europe.

The efforts and difficulties in establishing and maintaining a Hebrew periodical in Iraq are not surprising when we observe how Hebrew journals struggled economically (including in prosperous times) in order to survive, even in places where there was a large Jewish population.

In 1863, Barukh Moshe Mizrahi established the first printing house in Baghdad (see Introduction, "The Hebrew Press in Babylon"). During that year, Hebrew books were written and published in Baghdad. Barukh Moshe Mizrahi published Hebrew books and a Hebrew journal, *Ha-Dover* or *Dover Mesharim* (1863-1871). He also published short articles in *Ha-Maggid.* In 1871, he assumed the role of agent who represented *Ha-Havatselet* in Iraq and Iran (see *Ha-Havatselet,* No. 25, 1841).

Barukh Moshe Mizrahi's reports in *Ha-Maggid* were short and informative. He advocated teaching foreign languages and crafts (*Ha-Maggid,* No. 15, 1869). In a short brief, he reported an incident about a woman whose husband disappeared before divorcing her (ibid., No. 13). In another article, he elaborated on the activities conducted by the Alliance in Baghdad (ibid., No. 33, under the name Brakhia Ben Yedidya).

In 1863, the monthly publication *Ha-Levanon* surfaced in Jerusalem. It was the first Hebrew newspaper in Palestine. It appears that the publication of *Ha-Levanon* inspired the Jewish communities in Baghdad and Syria to establish their own Hebrew printing houses. It is noteworthy that *Ha-Dover* and *Ha-Levanon* appeared during the same year.

Ha-Dover was not published in regular intervals. Rather, seventeen issues surfaced sporadically between 1863-1868, followed by additional issues during 1870-1871. Apparently, from the description on the cover page of the publication, the original plan was to publish *Ha-Dover* biweekly (see *Ha-Maggid,* 1869, No. 22).

On the cover page of the publication was a frame that was divided into three sections. In the right hand section, a Hebrew date and a thank you note to a donor appeared. In the middle section, the Hebrew abbreviation *Shilt* ("I have set the Lord always before me," Psalms 16, 8) was written. Beneath this abbreviation was a message to inform its readership that this publication focused on news and events. Over time the editor changed his message to indicate that his publication was also "for the advancement of the Hebrew language."

The journal prices for Iraq, Persia, India, and Europe were printed on the left side of the frame. The price for an annual subscription, however, was not specified. Rather, it was understood (as stated on the cover page) that an impoverished reader would not overpay and a wealthy reader would pay generously. Readers were invited to advertise, and agents were promised one sixth of the advertising revenue as their commission.

Presently, there are only a few copies of *Ha-Dover* found worldwide. I will try to capture the spirit of this periodical by illustrating some of its contents.

Most issues of *Ha-Dover* began by addressing their readers about some concern. This followed with news about other countries. Some of the news was drawn from other Hebrew periodicals, in which case credit was given to the source (such as *Ha-Levanon* or *Ha-Maggid*). The publication included announcements, notes of gratitude to donors, and solicitations for new membership. News reports generally focused on Jews worldwide, specifically on Middle Eastern Jews.

Special focus was placed on news from the Jewish community in Iraq. For example, *Ha-Dover* described the activities conducted by the Alliance in Baghdad (1870, No. 2) and provided news about Jewish schools and community life in Baghdad. Examples included reporting on a burglary (1870, No. 3). Another report detailed an accident that occurred at the Alliance school (1870, No. 20) where a child had a major fall. *Ha-Dover* reported to its readers about a new, exquisite Torah book that was donated to a synagogue. It reported on transportation and holiday travels, such as the paving of a new railroad and the annual Babylonian pilgrimage to the holy tombs of the prophet Ezekiel, the Scribe Ezra, and Joshua Cohen Gadol (1870, No. 4) during the Feast of Weeks (Shavuot, Pentecost).

Speaking of the pilgrimage to the holy tombs, the author pointed out that it was customary to make this journey specifically during the holiday. He mentioned that in earlier times it was very challenging and demanding to make this voyage. However, at the time he reported about this journey, there were numerous steamboats operating that simplified making such a pilgrimage. Jews came from other countries, such as Persia, to Baghdad in order to visit the holy tombs. The government provided reduced rates to enable more people to make this pilgrimage by steamboat.

In another issue of *Ha-Dover*, a report detailed the difficulties that beset the visitors on their journey back and forth (ibid., 1870, No. 5) after they paid for their round trip ticket to visit the holy tombs. In a successive issue, the reader is presented with details about a captivating, delightful sermon delivered by Rabbi Yosef Hayyim one Saturday. This took place when many people went to visit the holy Jewish tombs. Rabbi Yosef Hayyim sermonized for three hours to a congregation that filled the synagogue (ibid.).

Ha-Dover related general information about the population of Baghdad. For example, Baghdad is described as a place with many import shops and export businesses (1870, No. 10).

Ha-Dover praised (ibid., No. 20) and blessed Madhat Pasha, the presiding ruler in Baghdad from 1869-1872. In one issue of *Ha-Dover* (1869, No. 4), readers are advised about Madhat Pasha's visit to the Alliance school. He is noted to have played a role in the modernization of Turkish law. The students showed their respect to him with a welcome reception. They demonstrated fine etiquette; they were well dressed and well mannered. Community leaders also attended this event. Communication took place in French, including greeting the guests and the Sultan.

Ha-Dover described the honorable send-off the community gave Rabbi Yosef Hayyim upon his departure to and return from Israel (1870, No. 12). *Ha-Dover* also republished literature, such as an historical story about fifteenth century Spain.

Ha-Dover provided evidence of the rich Hebrew culture that flourished in Babylon during this era. It was expected that there was an interested readership available that could understand and read this periodical. *Ha-Dover* illustrated the connection between Hebrew culture in Babylon and Hebrew culture in Israel and in Europe (certain pieces in *Ha-Dover* were a republication from Hebrew periodicals that appeared in Israel or in Europe).

The economic struggle for *Ha-Dover's* survival was commonplace for many Hebrew publications during this era.

Chapter 10: *Yeshurun*: "The Newspaper is the Heart of the People"

Between 1909 and 1948, eight Jewish newspapers circulated in Iraq. *Yeshurun* (the poetic biblical name for Israel, Jeshurun) was one of these newspapers. Published in 1921, it was the only newspaper that included a Hebrew section. The publication of this periodical was part of the Zionist activity that flourished in Iraq from 1918 until 1935. Some of their activities included fund raising, establishing a youth movement, and circulating Zionist publications.

In 1920, an association was established—Agguddat Tsea'ireh Yehudah, ("Youth Association of Judah"), or Aguddah Ivrit Sifrutit ("Hebrew Literary Association"). The Association obtained a permit from the government to conduct its activities. It endeavored to promote Hebrew language and Hebrew literature. It established clubs to conduct lectures about Jewish matters and to publish Hebrew newspapers. The Association established a Hebrew public library and provided free Hebrew evening classes. Within a few months, this Association grew to seven hundred members (*Yeshurun*, No. 1, 1921). The Association's founder, Shelomo Reuven Hiyya, was a police officer. The publication of *Yeshurun* was part of this Hebrew literary society's activity.

The director in charge of *Yeshurun* was Aharon Sason Ben-Eliahu Nahum, a veteran teacher who taught Hebrew in Jewish schools. He taught Jewish studies and was one of the leaders of Zionist activities in Baghdad. In 1921, Aharon Sason Ben-Eliahu Nahum was elected president of the Zionist Association of Mesopotamia. Together with his deputy, Yosef Eliahu Gabai, they endeavored with conviction on behalf of the Zionist movement. In Jewish schools, they circulated Hebrew literature and newspapers and organized lectures.

The specific active role Aharon Sason assumed in *Yeshurun* was well suited to his ideology and public activity in general. *Yeshurun* emerged from a Zionist background that included promoting and fostering Hebrew language and literature. The editors of *Yeshurun* were Zion Adar'ai, a teacher, and Ya'acov Tsion Mu'alim Nissim, a vice principal.

Only five issues of *Yeshurun* were published, all in 1921. This periodical was defined as a literary, social, and historical publication. The "Table of Contents" reflected its bilingual nature. On the right hand side of "The Table of Contents" appeared the titles of the Hebrew articles in the issue. On the left hand side of the same page appeared the Judeo-Arabic titles written in Hebrew. All sixteen pages were divided equally between two languages, Hebrew and Judeo-Arabic. My focus is directed toward the Hebrew publications only.

The First Issue

The first issue begins with a manifesto, an essay that emphasizes the importance of publications in general. "The newspaper is the heart of the people, their tongue and their weapons"—the press reflects its people; it influences them and is influenced by them. Due to the significant impact of the press, Babylonian Jews decided to publish their own medium of expression, reflecting their two languages—Hebrew and Judeo-Arabic—in order to report the world news in general and news from the Jewish world in particular. The editors expressed their hope that the Jewish community would support this publication spiritually and financially. This editorial is written in a celebratory style and with emotional rhythm. Herein I present this manifesto:

> **The Voice of *Yeshurun* to the Hebrews**
>
> Brothers, the great necessity and the significant need for the publication of newspapers in [any] state are well known in all countries. It is common knowledge. And you will not find one opposing opinion in the state wherein you find newspapers published, through which you value the culture of the people, their progress, knowledge and talents, thoughts and feelings. In a few words, the nation's character is embodied in its newspapers.
>
> The newspaper expresses the desires of the people, their will and their spirit. The newspaper is the heart of the people, their tongue and their weapons. Through the newspaper one party can triumph over another party. The newspaper is a general public creation and not a private one. The newspaper is like a mirror that reflects the position, appearance, and configuration of everything that faces it; the newspaper shows us the status of a nation, its level of education, and its various ideologies.
>
> The general counselor of a state is the newspaper. The newspaper gives the people what a trainer gives a trainee, it paves for the people the road for life, it is masculine and feminine, it influences and is influenced at the same time. So why should our share, we the Hebrews of the world, be missing?
>
> Therefore, we felt obliged to edit a weekly called Yeshurun, half of which is in our forefathers' language while the other is in spoken Arabic. Let our brothers who live in Babylon hear the news of the world in general and the news of the Hebrew world in particular and understand the obligations of every Jew to act for his people and community.
>
> Brothers, we know and realize the heavy responsibility that is more than we can take. We trust you and we are sure of your support. And because you know this enormous venture, you know this holy responsibility that applies

> to you too; and that we are your delegates, and you will encourage us and help us financially and spiritually. Make efforts to expand the newspaper, its circulation among the Jews, so that Jacob [the Jews] will not be ashamed among the nations. And we will not further tire the dear reader and will end with these words: You will love your community.
>
> You are Israel, run to the *Yeshurun*.

The first issue included articles about a variety of subjects. One of the articles (2-3) reported about the elections of the "Executive Board" ("Material Board," Va'ad Gashmi) of Baghdadi Jews. For twelve years the Jews of Baghdad did not hold elections for this board. World War I had an impact, and board members resigned. Young people demanded new elections for a new board that would take an interest in the community's needs and manage its affairs. The article reflected the initial struggle of the young educated man's desire for community reforms. This struggle continued throughout the 1920s and culminated with the younger generation participating in the management of the community.

The day of the election was announced and voters arrived. Voting rules and regulations, as well as the necessity, duties, and advantage of having such a board, were explained. There were sixty delegates. Many arguments, disputes, and criticisms were heard, and the elections were postponed.

Who are these boards mentioned in these articles? At the time of the Turkish Empire, the Jews of Iraq had autonomy in organizational, religious, educational, and charitable matters. There was a board of wealthy people that managed the community business, supervised the community income and expenses, and their community tax payments (the "Executive Board," "Material Board," Va'ad Gashmi). The community taxpayers, who elected that board, also elected a "spiritual board" that was composed of rabbis who focused on religious and domestic matters. The leader of the Jewish community was Hakham Bashi, who was also elected by the General Board. The election law was enacted in 1864 and was applied to the Jewish community until 1931. In 1931, the Iraqi government enacted the "Law for the Jewish Community No. 77 until 1931" that replaced Turkish law and made it possible for someone who was not a rabbi to be the head of the Jewish community.

Included in this first issue of *Yeshurun* was news about the establishment of a Hebrew Literary Association in Baghdad, the meeting of a congress for the establishment of a world organization for Sephardic Jews, a forthcoming conference for the protection of Catholic interests in Israel, the death of Rabbi Ya'acov Hayyim, and the visit of Hakham Bashi to The High Commissioner. The High Commissioner promised the Hakham Bashi that the Jews will have equal rights and that he will visit the Jewish schools. In addition, this issue included the first section of an article about "The Losses in Jewish Thought" (3), four poems (5-6), and the first part of a feuilleton (7-8).

The author of the four poems was Salim Yitshak (ShelomoYitshak Nissim), who was one of the progressive educated members of the Jewish community. He was affiliated with education and law and promoted Hebrew culture in Iraq. He published two textbooks (1912, 1938). In his 1912 book (*Lekah Tov*, "A Good Lesson"), he published more than twenty castigating poems.

The Second Issue

The second issue begins with the first section (1-2) of an article about "The Jews of Babylon." The second section is the second part of the essay, entitled "The Losses in Jewish Thought" (2-3). Both articles will be discussed later in this chapter. This issue included world news, followed by news about Jews around the world, and specifically news about Israel.

It is interesting to note what the editor considered newsworthy for a 1921 Hebrew publication in Baghdad. Here are examples of their world news topics: the Turkish supreme commander called for a meeting in order to discuss the status of Turkey and the Peace Agreement that he opposed; Austria and Serbia entered into a Peace Agreement; the Italian government recommended that factory owners make concessions in favor of their workers; in Egypt there were problems with delivering telegrams and with supplying gasoline; and American politicians held opposing positions regarding the liberation of Ireland.

There was also news from the Jewish world. The official publication of the Protestants in London powerfully protested the negative attitude of the Catholic Cardinal toward the Zionist movement. Protestant writers admonished Catholics for their hatred of Jews and Zionism, because the Catholics forgot the biblical prophecies about returning the land of Israel to the people of Israel. The Greek government objected to the suggestion made by the Turkish Sultan to hand over the monitoring of Christian holy sites to the king of Italy.

Sason Afendi, a Jew from Baghdad, was elected to be treasury minister of Iraq. In Poland, there were three days of pogroms. Many Jews were killed, fifteen hundred houses were burned down, and more than six hundred women were raped. In Hungary and Yemen, there were similar incidents. In Germany, hatred against Jews escalated, and a struggle took place to remove Professor Albert Einstein from his academic position. America restricted immigration.

There was specific news from Israel. The High Commissioner visited Galilee. Jews and Arabs welcomed him warmly, and he "was very happy when he saw the love and brotherhood that existed between Jews and Arabs." In Jerusalem, he launched an Exhibit for the Construction of Cities. The construction of a new port was initiated in Haifa.

Ezra Haddad published a poem (2-5) in this issue. He was an author (Baghdad, 1903, Israel, 1972), an educator, and an educational administrator. He published articles in Arabic newspapers and translated into Arabic the book, *The Travels of Benjamin of Tudela*. He translated poems ("Ruba'iyat") of Omar Al Khayam into Hebrew. After he immigrated to Israel, he was sent on a number of missions (Ben-Yaacob, 1979, 307-308; 1970, 418-419. See also Haddad, Ezra).

Ezra Haddad's poem is a love poem composed of eleven stanzas, which is written with meter and rhymes (abcb). In various instances, Hebrew love poems were interpreted as allegories for the love between God and the people of Israel ("Keneset Yisrael"). In this poem, there are various elements that may lead one to draw such an interpretation: departure, wandering, covenant, exile, quandaries, opening of the gates, encouragement for the future, and others. This terminology is frequently used in liturgies when the speaker describes God's departure from the Jewish people and their departure from their land, their wanderings in the world, the covenant God had with them, their quandaries, and their supplication for God to open the gates of heaven for mercy. Such liturgies may close with hope and encouragement. It seems to me, however, that this is a love poem between a man and a woman, written in a religious society restricted by traditional values.

In the first stanza, the speaker addresses the woman and reminds her of their passionate previous time together in the forest. In the following three stanzas (2-4), the speaker describes in detail nature's scenery where they first met. The characters in the poem interact with nature. The focus of the poem shifts over to elaborate on the couple's feelings, detailing their experience of affection (stanzas 5-6). In stanzas 7-9, the speaker strives to awaken the woman's love and affection and asks her (stanzas 10-11) to accept him endearingly.

The poem begins with the speaker addressing the woman directly: "Wouldn't you indeed remember, sister, the twilight we longed for / in the midst of the forest trees on the mountain of myrrh / When we sat in union holding hands / our souls are joined together by the same creed."

In these lines, readers hear the echo of biblical verses ("the twilight we longed for," Isaiah 21:4, "our joyous party," "in the midst of the forest trees on the mountain of myrrh," The Song of Songs 4:6). The language used at the opening of the poem is repeated with some variation in three stanzas (7-9): "Wouldn't you indeed remember me." The repetition reminds readers constantly of the speaker's desire to continue with his experience of love. The descriptions of nature are not literal. Rather, they are metaphors for the man and woman in the poem. For example, "Love nightingales flew over our heads / they sang for the sun parting songs. / It was nightfall, / the moon shone and its melted silver coated every pasture and river;/ nature was asleep, but the rushing of the river stream, cedars and their leaves / disrupted its silence by their humming," and it was at that moment that the adored woman had ravished the speaker's heart (The Song of Songs 4: 9), and (continuing with the tradition of medieval Hebrew poetry) "the arrow's light from your eyes flew into my heart," and his thoughts "floated on the ocean waves of your fondness."

The woman entered into a love covenant with the speaker to never depart from each other. However, she broke his heart, causing him to forlornly wander from one place to another. He reminds her of the day their hands picked a rose of love and their lips sang love songs. He wonders how is it that she does not give him her hand nor open her gate for him. He urges her to be with him forever and face the splendid future together. The poem was written in a religious society that internalized romantic feelings. The poem is influenced by Hebrew love poems of its time and the Enlightenment era.

The poem is far less sensual than medieval Hebrew poems of passion, but here too, like in medieval Hebrew love poems, the lips of the woman drip honey, she alienated him, her eyes shoot arrows at the speaker's heart, and the heart of the loving man is broken.

Yeshurun presents the 1921 religious, traditional reader with a secular poem that expresses an individual's feelings of love, longing, love's grief, and love's joy. The speaker is not inhibited. He balances strict tradition with artistic liberty.

The Third Issue

In this issue, the second section of the article discusses the Jews of Babylon (1-2). Additionally, this section includes the articles, "The Losses in Jewish Thought" (3-4), international news, and news from the Jewish world (5-6). Readers find (5) the poem *Deliverance*, written anonymously (Ben-Yaacob ascribes the poem to Ezra Haddad, see Ben-Yaacob, 1970, 472, No. 956). The poem carries a nationalistic message. Keneset Israel (the gender is female, representing the people of Israel) supplicates for the speaker in the poem to bring her to the land of Israel. The female image of Keneset Israel is detailed; her trembling, skinny hand caresses the speaker's hair, her sharp gaze pierces, her heart is warm, her body trembles from the cold, her face glares, and she is fatally wounded and can only find a cure in her homeland Israel. She repeats her plea: "Oh! Rescue rescue [me]," because she is fatally wounded, and the time for curing her is of the essence. The rhymes in the poem are grammatical suffixes that do not demand artistic creativity.

In this issue, the third and final part of the article appears, "The Losses in Jewish Thought" (No. 1, 3-5; No. 2, 2-3; No. 3, 3-4). The article's style is clear. It is well structured, and the ideas are well presented. It is based on general ideas that are applied to specific periods and places in Jewish history that lead to a discussion over the phenomenon of assimilation. The author distinguishes between "a loss that will be returned" and "a loss that will not be returned." For example, the Jews in Egypt were—despite the will of the Egyptians—a loss of the first kind, because they kept their identity until they returned to their homeland and God (the real owner of the "loss"), unlike the lost ten tribes. The Jews of Babylon experienced periods of comfort, but they kept their identity and remained "a loss that will be returned." Persecutions in Jewish history did not cause Jews to assimilate and become "a loss that will not be returned." On the contrary, they only strengthened the identity of the Jews. Assimilation can be the result of suffering or comfort. There are Jews that maintain a distance from their Judaism, either because of their suffering as Jews or because they enjoy their freedom. They should be encouraged to return to their people and become a loss that is returned.

News from the world includes news from Turkey, Greece, Spain, Morocco, Portugal, France, Belgium, Germany, China, Russia, Japan, and others. This news is brief, yet important. As to news from the Jewish world, U.S. President Wilson expressed his sorrow over the riots against Eastern European Jews. In Greece, the Greek College decided to include Hebrew language and literature in its curriculum. In Iraq, a new association was founded to provide financial aid to needy travelers passing through Baghdad, particularly those on route to Israel.

The Fourth Issue

This issue begins with the third and final part of the article, "The Jews of Babylon." It includes an article about "The Boundaries of Israel" (3-4); it continues with a story that began (4-6) in the first issue, followed by presenting the latest news.

The article "The Babylonian Jews" (No. 2, 1-2; No. 3, 1-2; No. 4, 1-3) was discontinued after publishing its third installment. The article describes the Babylonian Jews and their way of life during that era. There were fifty thousand Babylonian Jews in 1921. The articles provide information about their Jewish synagogues, Babylonian Jewish education, their places of residence, men and women's clothing, their economic condition, and their occupations.

The articles portray the many important roles Jews played in Babylon, the public offices they held in all fields of public service, the Sabbath atmosphere and Sabbath customs, including prayers and meals, Sabbath walks and post-Sabbath travels by car, horse, and carriage, and the coffee shops. The article depicts how community life changed since the death of Rabbi Yosef Hayyim and the influence of religion and prayer in daily life. It describes the marriage process for two different brides starting with the matchmaker, continuing with the betrothal and the role the parents play, explaining the dowry, and ending with a description of the wedding ceremony. The article is a treasure of information and a most thrilling reference source to help understand the spiritual world of Babylonian Jews during this period.

By presenting the main details from this article, it will enhance readers' knowledge of the social, religious, and economic context in which Hebrew creativity took place. The article focuses on the 50,000 Jews living in Baghdad during this time. In 1920, there were about 87,000 Jews in Iraq, including 50,000 in Baghdad. There were 6,000 to 7,000 Jews in each of the towns Mosul, Basr,a and Diwaniya (in 1930, there were 120,000 Jews in Iraq, including some 80,000 in Baghdad). The article reports that there were more than thirty synagogues at that time (in Baghdad). There were very few Jews who were illiterate; the elderly people were familiar with some Jewish traditional literature. The new generation spoke foreign languages. The older generation was more religious. Most of the Jews lived in a Jewish quarter, except for the few wealthy Jews who lived in beautiful homes along the Tigris River.

In 1917, Britain conquered Iraq at the end of World War I. The British Mandate in Iraq occurred between 1920 and 1932. The article notes that since the British conquest, more Jews left the Jewish quarter and found housing in other parts of Baghdad, due to the shortage of rental property in the Jewish quarter.

Most Jews were middle class Jews, but there were some wealthy Jews and a few impoverished Jews. Many of them were business people; there were Jews in all areas of craftsmanship, particularly shoemakers and silversmiths.

Most of the Jews wore European clothes, a few wore local clothes, and the sages wore a distinguished headdress. Women wore a variety of clothing. The young women wore Arabic women's cloaks ("Abbayah") and concealed their faces with a veil. The older women wore jewelry, including ankle bracelets and hair ornaments made of gold. The old women wore silver embroidered fancy hats. A few women wore nose rings embedded with sapphires.

The Jews assumed important roles in daily life. They were active in the stock market, they were clerks, accountants, attorneys, translators, and police officers. Baghdad became a quiet city on the Sabbath. On the Sabbath, after the evening prayer and final Sabbath meal, the Jewish families went out. Some went for a walk while others left the city by car or carriage. They went to coffee shops. Women attempted to see people through their veil. Other women wore more liberal clothes, in spite of the rabbis' admonitions. It seems that the religious authorities lost some of their power. The article states, "Obviously there are those [women] that want to be seen. Many times there was a directive by the spiritual leaders that forbade such an appearance. But who listens [to them]? In the past, the rabbis delivered sermons in the synagogues and many people went to listen, but at a later stage, since the death of Rabbi Yosef Hayyim [1909] the Big Synagogue was closed. This is the synagogue that could have contained one thousand people. It drew in many of the crowds in modern times on Saturdays, during the long summer days."

Men went to pray at the synagogues three times every day and stayed there until evening. The Babylonian Jews preserved their traditions and religion. One of the customs they kept was the engagement process. Sometimes, the young man and woman did not know each other at all, only the matchmaker knew about them. However, sometimes the woman or man rejected the choice that was made for them, which resulted in turmoil in the Jewish religious court.

Prior to the wedding, decorative wedding invitations were sent. They were written in Judeo-Arabic, with Hebrew lettering. A Jewish band performed and workers assisted the guests to their assigned seats. Women, single women in particular, struggled to get as close as possible to the bride. A children's choir sang songs of love about Jerusalem. On the Sabbath following the wedding, many women went to the newlyweds' home to visit the couple.

At the time the article was written, the brides were given away with large dowries. During World War I, the British brought luxuries to Jewish life. Girls learned about decorating, cosmetics, and the latest European fashions. The article states, "There was not even one single girl who wore a dress that was not made according to European fashion." They received patterns from Europe, copied them, and "Their fathers screamed 'Oh alas!' and 'Alack!' The girls became accustomed to expensive luxuries. In the first years after the War money flowed into their pockets like water. Consequently, when commerce started to die and income diminished, fathers and daughters were scalded." Due to the awful economy, they suffered a great deal. Young men demanded a large dowry, which inflicted troubles on the life of the poor families with daughters. Poor men married young. Educated men waited until they were at least thirty years old or older. Rich men enjoyed their life and remained single until they grew old. Men did not precede their sisters in marriage (those who were of age to marry). Rather, they waited until their sisters were betrothed.

The author of the article is informative. However, his remarks reflect a moral position whenever possible, in addition to expressing his own opinion about various customs. There is no attempt on his part to beautify reality or to conceal or ignore any part of it. He looks at the situation with some perspective, and his article seems reliable. For example, he writes about women who wanted to see the people and to be seen after the Sabbath: "Obviously there are those [women] who want to be seen. Many times there was a directive by the spiritual leaders that forbade such an appearance. But who listens [to them]?"

It seems that since there was no religious authority of the greatness of Rabbi Yosef Hayyim, the author feels that rabbinical authority was not as binding as before—a situation he regrets. As for imitating European fashion and a luxurious lifestyle, he calls them "corrupt luxuries." He clearly opposes the custom of engagement. As to the women's custom of standing in line to enter and visit the home of the newly wedded couple during the first Sabbath after the wedding, the author tells us "many people complain about this bad custom, but who will listen?"

The author of the first part of another article (which was discontinued), "The Boundaries of Israel" (3-4), claims that this issue was neglected for many years, and it deserves the attention of the Jewish people. The Bible is evidence that Israel was given to the Jews by God, and as to the exact borders, we should study them from history and the geography of Israel. The fact that there are many sources that discuss the question about Israel's boundaries is a cause for confusion, speculation, and differences of opinions.

Another article initiated in the first issue (7-8) continues in this issue (4-6). It is about meeting Galician and Hungarian Jews who were prisoners of World War I. After the capture of the Galician city Przemysl (pronounced Pshe-meshel) by the Russians, numerous prisoners of war were brought to Turkistan, many of whom were Jews. When the author of the article first met them, he thought they were eccentric, and he was afraid of them. Out of mercy, he gradually befriended them. He visited them daily and listened to their conversations. He found out that they were distinguished, one from another—some of them were Hasidim (a sect of pious Jews), some were opponents of pietism, and others were Enlightened Jews. There were orthodox Jews and secular Jews among the prisoners, and they did not get along with each other. Sometimes, they gathered and argued. The author participated in their arguments and was liked by all of them, because his opinions were moderate. He succeeded in bringing them closer to each other. The reader learns how different Eastern European Jews seemed in the eyes of a Baghdadi Jewish man due to their looks (such as sideburns and very long beards).

The Fifth Issue

The main article in this issue (1-5) is about the Jews of Buckara. There is news from the Jewish world and news about lectures and activities in the field of Hebrew in Baghdad.

The life of *Yeshurun* was brief, but it provides more evidence for the existence of secular Hebrew culture in Iraq. There was a group of authors who were ready, able, and willing to contribute to the Hebrew periodical. Financial difficulties plagued this undertaking from beginning to end, to publish a Hebrew periodical in Iraq over eighty years ago.

Chapter 11: *Shemesh*: An Anthology of Poems and Compositions from the Students of the *Shammash* School

Shemesh was a school newspaper that was published in Baghdad from 1930-1933. This publication reflected the Hebrew culture of its time by reporting on field activities, Hebrew libraries, Hebrew education, lectures, teachers, and achievements in each field. My purpose in introducing this publication is to add another element that portrays Hebrew society in Babylon by presenting the literary works of the young people who were immersed in that culture.

Shammash was a boys' school established in 1928. It was named after its founder, Benjamin Shelomo Shammash, who donated property to the school, which included seventeen stores, a pharmacy, and an inn. Until 1942, it had an elementary school. Until 1949, it had a middle school. However, from 1949 onward, it only maintained a high school while the rest of the students were transferred to another school. Most of the students who graduated from this school successfully passed the British High School examination, the "London Matriculation." Beginning in 1935, *Shammash* admitted a limited number of girls to the school. In Iraq, girls and boys did not study in the same school. In Jewish schools, however, they studied together until the third grade. In 1946, *Shammash* had a day program consisting of twenty-eight teachers and thirteen classes. *Shammash's* evening program had sixty students, nine teachers, and three classes. The number of teachers and classes for students increased over time.

For two years, *Shammash* also had an evening business college, which closed in 1947 when a public college for business and economics was established.

The editor of the first and second issues was Salih Mkammal (see Bibliography), who co-edited the fourth issue with Yitshak Haddad. Abdallah Ezra was the illustrator for these issues. The third issue was co-edited by a group of students and illustrated by Na'im Ezra. Students also contributed illustrations to these issues.

Shemesh noted the names of various teachers in the field of Jewish education in Baghdad. Among them were Avraham Rozen and Adolph Brothman. Avraham Rozen came from Israel in 1929. He encouraged the students to organize a group to promote Hebrew language and literature and to publish a Hebrew paper. Brothman came to Baghdad from London and was appointed, in 1926, to be the educational advisor for the Board of Supervision for Jewish Schools that was established in 1920. He also lectured in Baghdad's medical school. He lacked teaching experience and did not speak Arabic. Consequently, the board was dissatisfied with his work. In 1931, he returned to London.

Sixty years after the publication of *Shemesh,* Salih Mkammal, who became well known for his public service, spoke about his first impression of the teacher Avraham Rozen, who was sent from Israel to teach in Iraq (Myshlish, 9). Mkammal said, "[Rozen] was intense but not arrogant…His approach was sincere." Mkammal took the work upon himself—soliciting and gathering the students' works, editing and bringing the issues to print at the British Consulate in Baghdad, and ultimately delivering them to the Dangur Hebrew press for its final printing.

The first issue was initially printed in regular Hebrew fonts for the younger generation. Thereafter, it was reprinted in Rashi script for adults. Salih Mkammal was also one of the founders of the Baghdad Zionist group "Ahiever" that established a Hebrew library in the Talmud Torah school. He died in Toronto, in 1997.

The First Issue

The editor stated that he could not print all the well-written creative pieces that were submitted to him. Readers find in the first issue seven poems and a variety of prose. The poems are based on various themes (the issue is without pagination), including the son, an orphan child that a generous man adopted, love of a son for his mother, gratitude to a teacher, the winter in cold countries, the beauty of the garden, and the celebration of Purim (the Jewish festival commemorating the deliverance of Jews in Ancient Persia). The poetic style is quite rich and the poems are written with rhymes. I will use as an illustration the poem of Yehezkel Seti, "My Mother":

בְּלִי קֶשֶׁת וְשֶׁלַח
בְּלִי מָגֵן וְחֶרֶב
אִמִּי לִבִּי כּוֹבֶשֶׁת
בְּכָל בֹּקֶר וּבְכָל עֶרֶב.

כּוֹבֶשֶׁת אֶת לְבָבִי
אֵין לִי כֹּחַ לְהָגֵן,
קָשְׁתָה הִיא חִבָּתִי
לֹא יוֹעִיל נֶגְדָּהּ מָגֵן.

Without a weapon and a bow
Without a shield and a sword
My mother captures my heart
Every morning and evening

She captures my heart
I don't have the power to defend
My admiration for her is so commanding
A shield cannot thwart it.

This same author wrote another poem in this issue, "The Teacher," in which he equated the teacher to a king and the students to his soldiers, whose objective is to attain wisdom for the sake of the nation. Another student, Anwar Shaul, wrote a poem based on a call to the students to go to the garden that is full of roses, butterflies, and birds. Another student wrote a jolly poem calling on the students to happily celebrate Purim near the Tigris River adorned in Purim costumes.

In these poems, as well as in other creative pieces printed in this issue, Jewish life of the young and old is reflected authentically. One can draw conclusions about the advanced level of Hebrew knowledge that was attained in Baghdadi Jewish schools in those days.

Salih Mkammal, the editor, contributed two pieces. One of them relates his thoughts about the relationship between two people to a few words of wisdom: "Don't throw a stone into a well from which you drank water," "do not return evil for good," and "cast thy bread upon the water, for thou shalt find it after many years" (Ecclesiastes 11: 1). He concludes, "How beautiful are these words for a person who understands their significance, and how good they are for a person who has the merit of practicing them. Every person must try to do good all his life, otherwise what will he take with him if not his good deeds?"

In another charming piece, Mkammal writes about "Friday in Baghdad." He describes the preparations for the Sabbath and how three generations—himself, his mother, and grandmother—shared the work. He describes the markets on Friday, cleaning the house, the early return of his father from work to his home, going with his father to the synagogue, the prayer, the food table, the Sabbath clothes, the blessings, and the festive spirit.

Na'im Basri described "A Walk on the Sabbath Day" near the Tigris River, blossoming flowers, bird songs, people singing near the river, fruit trees, a meal in the garden, a walk along the river, the ducks, and the sight of people sailing along the river.

Students attempted to write short stories. One story, written by Ya'acov Perets, was about "How to Find Grace in the Eyes of People." In another piece, a student described in detail the Purim costumes in Baghdad. Another student wrote two short stories, both based on the interpretation and pronunciation of biblical verses. Still another student wrote a letter requesting to correct a textbook, which described the Jews of Babylon facing eastward during prayer, toward Jerusalem, while they actually faced westward toward Jerusalem.

In the school news, special attention was given to Hebrew culture, including the school acquisition of Hebrew books from Israel, the Hebrew teacher, and school parties that included singing in Hebrew and reciting Hebrew poetry.

The Second Issue

Most of the publications in first issue were republished in the second issue. One student (Meir Haddad) published a short story. The narrator described his walk along the Tigris River, contemplating the importance of spiritual possessions and the insignificance of material possessions. He managed to talk a woman out of her suicide attempt after her husband deserted her and her son died. This is what he taught her: "The Lord is the poor people's hope / No man will rescue them / Only the Lord will see their grief / And will break happy news for them."

Another student described the final examination environment at the school as a stressful time, taken seriously by everyone. In addition, the issue includes a new poem (by Salim Masha'al) about the mysteries of nature and a poem about the significant impact the school had on the life of the students.

The Third Issue

This issue includes poetry, memoirs, essays, and short stories. The age range of the contributors is greater than those of previous issues; it includes works of elementary school students, too. Yehezkel Seti wrote a lyrical poem with rhymes, describing the beauty of nature at dusk while walking along the Tigris River. He describes the sunset, the clear stream of the river, the boats sailing on the river, the palm trees on both banks of the river, the birds, and the burning sun that swelled in a cloud. This poem also gives us a taste of the students' Hebrew style:

בְּיוֹם צַח וּבָהִיר יָצָאנוּ
לְטַיֵּל עַל שְׂפַת חִדֶּקֶל
עֶרֶב וְהַשֶּׁמֶשׁ–וְהָעֵת
שׁוֹקַעַת שָׁם מֵאֲחוֹרֵי הַדֶּקֶל.

מַחֲזוֹת קֶסֶם!–וּלְפָנֵינוּ
הֲדַר הַטֶּבַע הַדּוֹמֵם
מַיִם זַכִּים, שׁוֹטְפִים בְּנַחַת
הַכֹּל נָע, חוֹלֵף, זוֹרֵם.

וְשָׁם בַּמֶּרְחָק הָמוֹן סִירוֹת
עוֹגְנוֹת וּמְחַכּוֹת לְמַשָּׂאוֹת
וַאֲחָדוֹת לִבְנוֹת מִפְרָשׂ
חֶרֶשׁ בִּדְמָמָה שָׁטוֹת.

דְּקָלִים וְשִׁקְמִים נִרְאִים
מִשְּׁתֵּי שְׂפוֹת הַנָּהָר
הַצִּפֳּרִים מְנַתְּרוֹת
מֵהַתְּאֵנָה אֶל הַתָּמָר.

וְהִנֵּה נִגְלוּ רָזֵי עוֹלָם
וְהַשָּׁמַיִם הִתְאַדְּמוּ בַּמַּעֲרָב.
הוֹ! כְּמוֹ תַּבְעֵרָה שָׁם בַּמֶּרְחָק
הַשֶּׁמֶשׁ נִבְלְעָה בְּתוֹךְ הֶעָב!

On a clean and clear day we went
To the banks of the Tigris River
It was evening and the sun
Was setting behind a palm tree.

And in front of us – enchanting scenes!
The grandeur of Nature's silence
Pristine water flowing serenely
Everything is in motion, drifting, streaming.

And there, afar, scores of boats
Anchored and waiting for freights
And some, with white sails,
Silently and tranquilly set sail.

Palms and sycamores are seen
From both river banks
The birds hop
From a fig tree to a palm tree.

And behold the world's secrets were revealed.
The sky turned red in the west.
Oh! How much flame is afar
The sun swelled in the cloud!

Naim Basri wrote an historical poem about a shepherd boy, who paid with his life for protecting Jews from the Romans. The use of a far-off historical event might be a safe way to write a didactic poem that could apply to the time the poem was written and carry nationalistic messages. Another student (Avigdor David) wrote a poem about the homeless, noting that only God hears their cry.

Georgy Yitshak Abbudi wrote an essay about the Hebrew language. The student's zeal for the Hebrew language conveys the positive impact of Jewish education in Iraq:

> The Hebrew language is the sacred language, which our forefathers spoke in their holy land. It is the language that every man who has in him a drop of Jewish blood has to speak in. It is the language in which our holy Torah, for which our forefathers fought for many years, was written in.
>
> […] Would a Jew forget his language… Would a Jew mock his brother who wants to teach and promote his forefathers' language among his brethren in the Diaspora? Would a Jew refuse to study his language that he has already forgotten?

Ya'acov Y. Zluf wrote an essay about his travel and stay in India. In Rangoon, Burma, he studied in a Jewish school. This school had over two hundred students who shared ten teachers. It also housed a synagogue, a grove with fruit trees, and a flower garden. Another student, Yosef Meir, wrote about "My Dream Country and My Real Country." In the country of his dreams all people are equal.

They pray, work, and thrive in a natural setting. The king is God and the president is the judge, and all the people are police officers. The parents are the teachers who train their children to live off their own labor with justice and compassion for all. The discrepancy between his real country and his dream country caused him to cry and to ask bitterly, "When will the real country be like the country of my dreams?"

Meir Haddad wrote a tragic didactic story about a disloyal and defiant son. Ya'acov Perets wrote about visiting, particularly during Shavuot (Feast of Weeks, Pentecost) the holy tomb in Babylon of the prophet Ezekiel. When train transportation was unavailable, Jews traveled up to a certain point by carriages, horses, camels, and donkeys. From there they continued by boat. When transportation was simplified, Jewish visitors to the tomb increased. They traveled by train or by bus and toured various places on their way. The maturity in style is particularly apparent in those paragraphs where the student reflects on the transient nature of vigor and glory. Here is what happened when travelers toured historical sites:

> There, a person will remain standing wondering and astonished, remembering Babylon and its prominence and thinking in his heart: Where is Nebuchadnezzar [King of Babylon, the conqueror of Jerusalem]?! Where is Nebuzaradan [the commander of Nebuchadnezzar] that burned the temple down and exiled thousands of Jews to Babylon in accordance with his king's order. [The visitor] remembers our forefathers who came to this country and left their country desolate without inhabitants, and will turn his face back and forth seeing mounts and ruins and imagines his old country as if in a dream.

The student details the visit to the tomb. Some of these details include bathing near the gravesite in a well containing pure water, entering the tomb calmly and purely, going around the tomb to sit and read the Psalms, and writing wishful notes and inserting them into the wall. In the evening, the women and children join in singing and celebrating. Behind the main tomb room, there is another room that holds five tombs of the Gaonites.

Salih Mkammal wrote about "Passover in Baghdad," describing the preparations for the holiday, cleaning the house and baking matsot (unleavened bread) without ovens, and making wine and haroset (date juice with a mixture of ground nuts). He includes references to special Passover melodies, prayers, travels, special holiday food, and more, writing, "It is an old custom that we have in Baghdad to visit the relatives and friends during the holidays and therefore the streets of Baghdad get filled during the holidays and the Jews reciprocate and visit their Muslim friends during their holidays." Also, "the Passover holiday is very abundant with flowers, countless bouquets of flowers are sold during the holiday. There is no house that is not decorated with roses and other flowers." The holiday is felt throughout the city: "All the banks are closed…most of the stores in the city are closed, the markets are empty and it is as if all Baghdad is celebrating with us."

Regarding school life, students performed in three Hebrew plays for the various holidays. There were Hebrew singing events. Students and teachers lectured in front of the entire school in Hebrew. Hebrew books were acquired from Warsaw. A group for the promotion of Hebrew books was established at the school. They contacted publishers and institutes in Israel. Ezra Haddad (see *Yeshurun*, above), the vice principal, translated Omar Al Khayam into Hebrew. Student groups, such as the sport teams, were conducted in Hebrew.

Additionally, this issue included reactions to this publication.

The Fourth Issue

This is the final and most interesting issue of *Shemesh*. It includes poetry, stories, and news. Hebrew creativity ceased in Iraq after Operation Ezra and Nehemiah (1950-1951, see Introduction). Had creativity continued to flourish, there was a forthcoming generation that held promise for new creative Hebrew writing.

Y. Pinhas published a poem under the title "Bahofesh" ("In the Vacation"), in which he described his return to his childhood village after six years of studies elsewhere:

יוֹם אֶחָד יָצָאתִי
מִבֵּית־סִפְרִי לָרְחוֹבוֹת
אֶל כְּפָר קָטָן הִגַּעְתִּי
בְּאֶרֶץ תלאובות.

'שָׁלוֹם לָךְ מוֹלַדְתִּי!'
אָמַרְתִּי לַכְּפָר בִּצְחוֹק.
'הִנֵּה כִּי הִתְגַּעְגַּעְתִּי,
בָּאתִי מֵרָחוֹק!'

חַלּוֹנִי כְּבָר פָּרַח
שֶׁקֶט מִסָּבִיב
גַּם הַשֶּׁמֶשׁ זָרַח
עִם רוּחַ הָאָבִיב.

הַאֵינְךָ מַכִּיר אוֹתִי
חֲבֵרִי הַיָּקָר?
הֲלֹא מִמְּךָ נִפְרַדְתִּי
זֶה מִזְּמַן עָבַר!

שֵׁשׁ שָׁנִים לָמַדְתִּי
בְּבֵית־סֵפֶר בַּבִּירָה
עֲרָבִית אַנְגְּלִית
וּשְׂפָתֵנוּ הַיְקָרָה!

וְעַתָּה גָּמַרְתִּי
אֶת לִמּוּדַי בְּשִׂמְחָה,
אֵשֵׁב לִי בַּמּוֹלֶדֶת
וְאֶטְעַם אֶת הַמְּנוּחָה

One day I went out
From my school to the streets,
I came to a small village
In a parched land.

"Hello my home village!"
I said to the village laughingly.
Behold, because of my yearning
I came back from afar."

My window has already blossomed
It is silent all around
The sun shone too
With the spring wind.

Don't you remember me
My dear friend?
I have departed from you
A long time ago.

Six years I studied
In a school in the Capitol
Arabic and English
And our precious language!

And now I have completed
My studies happily
I will sit in my home village
And enjoy the leisurely life.

The verses rhyme (abab). Some rhymes are grammatical suffixes. The style is rather rich.

Another student, Moshe Seti, wrote a poetic adaptation of the legend about Moses (Shemot Rabbah, b). When Moses was a shepherd, a lamb scampered off, and Moses followed it. The lamb stopped near a pool of water and began to drink. Moses said to the lamb that he did not know that it ran away because of thirst. Moses hoisted it on his shoulder and walked back. God said to Moses that because Moses showed compassion in tending to the flock, he would become the shepherd of Israel (see Bialik, *The Book*). In his poetic adaptation of the story, Setti remains faithful to the details of the story and adds details that do not conflict with the ideas and spirit of the story.

Avigdor David published a poem "Dear Moon!" in which the speaker asks the moon what it can see from up above: "Does it see shameful, sorrowful, terrifying scenes?" In this poem, one finds echoes of the poem "El Ha-Kokhavim" ("To the Stars") from the Hebrew poet Mikha Yosef Levinsohn.

Salim Kthuri wrote a short story entitled "Abayah" ("Arab-cloak"). The wife of an Arabic young man decided, like other women during her time, to stop wearing the traditional abayah. The husband asked her time and again to wear the abayah, but she would not listen to him. In a moment of anger, he murdered her and their son. The dramatic story is told in a restrained style, until the end when the narrator erupts, "He was a savage!!!" And the narrator treats with contempt the reaction of some people to the murder—"he did the right thing"—and the concluding words of the murderer from jail—"it is better to live among the mice than to see a wife without an abaya."

The story includes dialogues in which the author translates idioms from Arabic to Hebrew, such as, "whatever happened is in the eye and in the head," an idiom expressing full acceptance of a situation. In the story, the narrator presents various points of views and voices. For example, the husband "was angry with his accursed wife"—the words are from the narrator, but the point of view is from the husband. Some parts of the story are detailed, such as admonishing the husband. Other parts are brief and dramatic: "And in resolute speed he took out his sharp knife and attacked the woman."

The issue includes a piece written by Salim Bekhor about the "Worshippers of Satan," includingtheir number, location, beliefs, and traditions. Georgy Abbudi wrote about "The Story of One Journey" to the Euphrates. From his account, the reader learns about the intellectual curiosity and the interest of the Jewish youth of Iraq in anything novel and pioneering in fields such as cinema, sports, travel, and politics. He specifically tells readers about a trip that he and his friends took by train. The songs they sang made him imagine various places that were far away from him—New York, Paris, Hollywood, Los Angeles, London, and, particularly, Tel-Aviv, the new city with "the air of our homeland…ocean breeze." He and his friends thought with love and yearning about Israel.

Ya'acov Perets wrote two legends of the Jews of Baghdad about the tomb of the prophet Ezekiel. In both legends the tomb is associated with miraculous powers. Salih Mkammal wrote memories from his childhood, when he was five-years-old. Here one finds an authentic description about the life of a little Jewish boy in Baghdad, with the spirit of the Jewish school ("heder"), the love and cares at the parents' home, the coffee shops, the fireplace with the pungent and fragrant tea in the teakettle, and the story telling at home in the evening. I will present this translated piece not as an illustration of a literary achievement of an author, but for the world and way of life it portrays:

> It was evening and the streets of Baghdad were cold and chilly. The streets were empty of people, and only one narrow street, in the middle of the city,

is full of little children. When they left their school, [a few] words rang in their ears: "Run immediately to your homes." And it was as if they were not merely said by a teacher but by an angel.

Each one of the little children runs to his home in the same winding road, in the same place, and at the same late hour...

The wind carried me and I held my Bible, running in the empty streets of Baghdad. It was chilly all over, my feet trembled, and I ran further. I was happy because my home was not far away from the school. But I faced another trouble, my hands trembled and I could not knock on the door. I stood perplexed, because there was no one else who would knock for me, and at last I entered my home miraculously.

And here, inside the house, the situation improved. The house was warmer than the outside, daddy just came back from the coffee shop, and he was sipping the brewed tea.

And into that same narrow room, in the same place that we gather everyday, I entered that day, too. What a pleasure! The room was very warm, my mother was sitting, and near her was my little brother—the two-year-old—the fireplace in the middle, and the pungent and fragrant tea on it.

"Good evening!" greeted my mother. "How red your cheeks are! Come, come here my son, put your book down, take your hat off your head, and come and warm up near the fireplace."

The pleasant welcome comforted me a bit, and without enthusiasm I sat down to sip the pungent and fragrant tea.

"Listen well, my son," my daddy said to me, "tonight I will tell you a wonderful story, on the condition that you will not fall asleep in the middle. It is a story about one Sheikh who lived in Baghdad, at the time of Haron Al Rashid. This Sheikh was called Sheikh al Muntafak. He had slaves and servants and plenty of cattle and herds." And here my eyes closed, and I was half asleep.

"Wake up, big liar!" daddy said. "You have already fallen asleep? And in one night the Sheikh encountered a disaster..."

My eyes closed again, my ears did not hear anything any more. I fell asleep, and my sleep was sweet...

Meir Haddad wrote about Omar Al Khayam. Meir Haddad's poems and quoted poems from Khayam were translated from Persian to Hebrew by Ezra Haddad. The translation style is excellent and includes poems with themes such as praise of music and wine, disbelief in the world to come, and belief in God. The translator, Ezra Haddad (1903-1972, see Haddad, *Sofer*; and Ben Yaacob, 1979, 307-308 and 1980, 379-381), was an author, a Hebrew poet (see *Yeshurun*), a scholar, an educator and a principal, a journalist in Arabic newspapers, and a public figure. He was one of the editors of a Jewish weekly that was published in Arabic (*Al Hasid*, 1929-1939). He translated eight books into Arabic. Among them (in 1945) was an annotated translation of *The Travels of Rabbi Binyamin of Todela* with an introduction and a translation of a 1956 novel about the Sephardic Hebrew author Yehuda Burla, *Naftuleh Adam* (*A Man's Wrestling*). He authored three Hebrew books; one was a Hebrew textbook that he published in Iraq and two were about Babylonian Jews (see Haddad) that he published in Israel. In Israel, he continued to be a public figure, and because of his meticulous knowledge of six languages, he was sent on various missions. At the time *Shemesh* was published, he was vice principal of the *Shammash* school.

S. Mkammal wrote in this issue about "The Spoken Arabic Language of Iraqi Jews." The main difference between Judeo-Arabic and Arabic is that it includes many words in Hebrew and Aramaic. The Hebrew vocabulary is used often in religious, cultural contexts, greetings, and includes Hebrew idioms. Sometimes, the idioms are partially in Hebrew and partially in Arabic.

Goerge Shviru wrote a touching piece about the death of a student at his school, and Yitshak Sason wrote about the death of another student.

The news from the school is intense and dynamic. I will mention some of the lectures delivered to the entire student body: "Funny Math"; "The Importance of Hypnosis in Science"; "Contemporary Arabic Literature"; "Espinoza and Plato"; "The Cinema"; "Anti-Semitism and its Causes"; "Modern Hebrew Literature"; "The Jews During the Persian Era"; and "The Importance of Reading." These lectures were conducted in one of three languages: Hebrew, English, or Arabic. School activities included the production of plays in Hebrew and in Arabic, the completion of a beautiful tennis court, organized trips, sport matches between Jewish schools, and news about the school's Hebrew library that grew in readership and increased their book volume.

Responses to *Shemesh*

Some responses to the students' publication were published. Students from the Beirut Jewish school wrote in Hebrew, "After we read the entire journal we felt as if a new creation affected our imagination. And you truly gave us great pleasure by your gift" (see *Shemesh*, N. 3). School students from Jerusalem wrote (*Haverenu*, Tahkemuni, No. 87, Heshvan-Kislev *trtsa*) in their own Jerusalem journal:

> [...] This journal [*Shemesh*] shows that the sun of the Hebrew language started to rise in Baghdad again. The Hebrew language that was forgotten there since the closing of the big Yeshivot [Talmudic colleges] is revived and we hope that soon all our brethren, young and old, will be fluent in the Hebrew language. In the first issue were published poems and stories that are written with emotions: From them we know the strong love that is planted in the heart of the young generation for everything, which is precious and holy.

In Europe, Aharon Lubishatski, an editor (of *Ha-Kokhav*) wrote about *Shemesh* a short essay in the book *The Teaching of Writing and its Value for the Child Development*, (Polland, 1931):

> Among the students' journals that were sent to the editorial board of Ha-Kokhav during the last year from various places, excels in particular the publication *Shemesh*, published by Hebrew school students from Baghdad. It is not a big collection; it includes literary attempts and essays from the above-mentioned school life that is apparently administered by expert teachers with style. The names of the young authors seem to us, the Jews from Europe, a little strange (Na'im Basri, Salih Mkammal, Anwar Mash'al, Khthuri Cohen, Abdallah Ezra etc.) but their language - is the Hebrew language, fresh and vivid, and all the above-mentioned publication is a warm greeting for us from our far away brethren on the banks of the Tigris River...
>
> ...These three samples from the journal of the Jewish students demand our understanding. First of all they proved to us, that also in the sites of the Tigris and Euphrates Rivers the Hebrew language wrestles with its two competitors: The Arabic and the English, nevertheless the Hebrew language was not flawed in the Hebrew school there as in the other countries and the style of the students is evidence that the students are not translating their thoughts and reflections from a foreign language into Hebrew. Secondly, the young students from Iraq came to us without hiding behind heavy clouds and without any unnecessary pretensions; they just experiment in the expressions of their reflections and give us a picture of their life at the rabbi's school, at their home and in the market place – and to works such as these there is undoubtedly a positive educational value. Thirdly, the minor errors

> that we find in the above-mentioned publication prove, that most of its editing work was done by the young authors themselves and the influence of the teachers was limited to their early management—and this is in praise of the teachers.

Several points that may be drawn from these specific welcoming responses are worth making. There was a presumptuous, erroneous attitude due to the absence of information about Hebrew culture in Iraq: "The Hebrew language…was forgotten there since the closing of the big Yeshivot was revived" (*Haverenu*, Tahkemuni, No. 87, Heshvan-Kislev *trtsa*). The Jews of Iraq, as one may see from our accounting, did not forget the Hebrew language. The Hebrew language was the correspondence language between Jews in various parts of the world. European Jews were not even accustomed to the names of Jews from the Middle East, unlike many of the Jews from the Middle East who were familiar with many aspects of Jewish European life. The level of Hebrew in Jewish schools in Baghdad was notable in contrast to Jewish schools elsewhere.

Shemesh was not presented here as evidence of the existence of notable literary works in Iraq. It was presented in order to illustrate the Hebrew culture in Iraq and the importance of Hebrew in Jewish education and life. The flow of Hebrew productivity from one generation to another depends to a large extent on the place Hebrew occupies in the educational system. The reader of *Shemesh* can have a solid sense of the advanced level of Hebrew education achieved at that time in Baghdad. He can also have a tour of Jewish life in Iraq—their values, ideals, desires, beliefs, priorities, their life at home, in the school, in the market, and their relations with Muslims. The spiritual and materialistic cultures find a spontaneous, innocent expression written in the Hebrew language.

Shemesh expresses the interests, sensitivities, knowledge, and solemnity of the students. One can also assess the achievements in the field of Hebrew education at that time. The students demonstrate the use of a rich Hebrew vocabulary and the ability to produce clear, attention-grabbing, pensive poetry and prose. Their achievements also provide evidence of the importance of Hebrew in Jewish education during this era. Additionally, it clarifies readers' understanding of the inseparable tie between Jewish studies and Hebrew—guided parents, educators, community leaders, and students.

While searching for evidence of Hebrew knowledge among school students in Baghdad, the reader is exposed to their love for Israel and the Hebrew language and their concern for maintaining high standards and preserving Jewish values. The reader is also exposed to curiosities about the world and its respective Jewish communities.

The adult Hebrew authors were involved in Jewish education. They did not look down on teaching, but related to it with care, passion, and pride. The schools provided Hebrew knowledge, the motivation for self-expression in Hebrew, and the educational framework to achieve that purpose. The fact that the school promptly ran out of the first issue of *Shemesh* and decided to republish it is significant. The first issue was originally printed in regular Hebrew fonts for the young generation, and then it was republished in Rashi script for the adults. This is indicative of the interest in Hebrew, in Hebrew education, and in the world of young students. Hebrew could flourish among the students in an environment in which their achievements were highly valued in a community that was interested in their Hebrew culture.

Passion for the Hebrew language itself and the fact that its literature was highly valued by these people may explain why a small Jewish community that experienced economic and political difficulties attained this kind of achievement. Large and affluent Jewish communities today do not attain this level of achievement. One witnesses the shortcuts taken and devices used in our current culture to justify the allegation that Jewish studies do not require a thorough knowledge of Hebrew. We mourn the shallowness that has replaced yesteryear's dedication and love for learning a language. Such dedication is a fundamental prerequisite for comprehending Jewish studies.

Chapter 12: *Derekh He-Haluts*: The Journal of the Movement Counselors

In a previous discussion about the poetry of Rabbi Menasheh Saliman Shahrabani and Shelomo Salih Shelomo, I presented poetic responses to the "Farhood." In response to the pogrom, young Jews joined the He-Haluts movement.

After the 1941 pogrom against the Jews of Iraq, they realized that assimilation, participation in Iraqi nationalism, communism, and donations to Israel would not resolve their problems. However, an exodus to Palestine would bring resolution. The Zionist movement was legal in Iraq during the 1920s. The movement continued underground in the 1930s and reorganized between 1940-1941.

As a result of the 1941 pogrom, several societies were founded in Iraq whose focus was based on Jewish nationalism. In 1942, emissaries arrived from Baghdad to Palestine and began organizing Zionist activities. Groups from the He-Haluts movement were organized. They conducted Hebrew classes, distributed Hebrew books among the movement members, and educated the members about Palestine and the Zionist movement. The members of the movement were young, some as young as fifteen. A junior movement was formed called He-Haluts Ha-Tsa'ir ("The Young Pioneer").

Hebrew instruction and Jewish studies were taken to higher level. There was a new Hebrew library, instruction in Hebrew songs, trips, physical training, conventions, and instruction in dealing with emergency situations. In 1942, there were 300 members in the He-Haluts movement. In 1946, there were 1,000 members, and in 1948, there were 2,000 members and 120 counselors. The members had underground nicknames, and their towns were named after Palestinian settlements.

This movement was established in 1942. Its goals were to inculcate and promote the Hebrew language among the younger Jewish generation and to teach them about Israel, provide them with a Zionist education, familiarize them with the use of firearms, and organize their flight to Israel. In 1948, the seventeen branches of the movement were composed of two thousand members. The movement published two journals in Arabic and two in Hebrew. The two Hebrew journals were *Niv*, that provided information about the activity of the underground movement, and *Derekh He-Haluts*, which was published between 1945-1950.

The contributors to *Derekh He-Haluts* used underground nicknames. They also used nicknames to identify their geographic locations, in order to disguise the site of their movement's branch. My presentation will point out that during this era, Babylon had young Jews who could write a quality piece of Hebrew literature. They had the ability and the need to express themselves in Hebrew. Their main creative urge was a consequence of their love for Israel. Through this journal the reader is exposed to the world of these young, idealistic women and men who were enthusiastic and willing to pursue their dreams.

Literary works composed by women are presented in the first chapter of *Derekh He-Haluts.* As a general rule, the Hebrew education and knowledge expected of women was less than the Hebrew education of men. Hence, the contribution of women to Hebrew literature was uncommon. One should keep this in mind when assessing the contribution of women to Hebrew literature in Babylon.

During the Enlightenment, women participated in Hebrew literature, even at the outset of the movement (Rahel Morporgo). However, their participation was uncommon. Frequently, a woman's proficiency in Hebrew was the result of her being an only child, in which case Hebrew knowledge, unable to pass from father to son, passed from father to daughter. This situation changed when the center of Hebrew literature moved to Palestine where women's daily language was Hebrew and where women were essential participants in all the aspects of life. Rahel and Devora Baron were among the important women who immigrated to Palestine and whose contributions to poetry (Rahel) and prose (Baron) were prominent.

I will not speculate as to whether this group would have produced Hebrew poets and writers had they stayed in Babylon. Rather, I will present what they produced.

Derekh He-Haluts expresses the national-social role these young people assumed, their willingness to sacrifice their life for the sake of their nation, and their commitment to building the state of Israel. They identified with the pioneers in Israel by forming an opinion about a person based on his or her social conduct and attitude toward Zionistic, humanistic, and socialistic values about the land of Israel. The needs of the individual are identified with the needs of Israel and its people. The basic values of the movement members are identical with those of the characters from the War of Independence Generation (Hakak, 1993, 79-87). The general feeling that is imbued in this journal is one of decisiveness, heroism, idealism, and anticipation.

The First Issue

In this issue of *Derekh He-Haluts*, readers find a song from "Yoav" (13). Yoav Biron (Katan) became one of the first volunteers in 1948 to join the well-known Golani Brigade. Thereafter, he was known as a judge and author of a book, *Lehavot Ba-Galil* ("Blazes in the Galileo," Bibliography, Biron). He sent his poem from "Haifa" (i.e. Basra). It is a romantic melodious rhyming song of love, separation, and longing that was sung by many:

זִכְרִי אֶת יָמֵינוּ הָרְחוֹקִים
וְלֵילוֹת אַהֲבָה אֲרֻכִּים
כָּל שִׁיר, כָּל נוֹף מַזְכִּיר לִי
בְּחִירַת חַיַּי, אֲהוּבָתִי.

כַּחֲלוֹף פַּלְגֵי נַחַל זוֹרְמִים
כָּךְ חָלְפוּ יָמֵינוּ הַמְּתוּקִים:
נִשְׁאַרְתִּי רַק אֲנִי לְבַדִּי
וּבְלִבִּי שִׁירֵי עזב נִשְׂרָפִים.

Remember our faraway days
And the long loving nights
Every song, every scene reminds me
Of the chosen one of my life, my beloved.

Our delightful days vanished the same way
That the streaming brooks pass away.
Only I remained alone
And in my heart was burning parting songs.

One observes here the connection between movement members and Hebrew literature of their time.

Carmela B (Berta Sofer. For keys to the real names of cities and authors, see Bibl, Vol. 2, 793-797. Some of the names could be decoded in spite of my use of these keys) and Eliahu, both of whom were from "Tel-Aviv" (Baghdad), published in this issue responses to the first poem (1891, Bialik, *Selected Poems*, 3-7) of Hayyim Nahman Bialik (1873-1934). Bialik was a Hebrew poet, storywriter, essayist, translator, and editor. He was considered the greatest Hebrew poet of modern times who strongly influenced modern Hebrew culture. Bialik's first poem was addressed "To the Bird," and there were two parts to the question. First, "What was the bird's response?" This question was presented to the movement members in the context of a seminar about the movement.

In his poem, Bialik wonders what happened "in the fairer, warmer climate" of the land from where the bird came, which is Israel. Here are some quotations from Bialik's "To the Bird": "Do they [in Zion] guess what heavy sorrows / I must suffer here?"; "Do they know and could they picture / How many rise against me, / How their hatred swells?"; "...Now I am fading / Now my strength is gone!"; "And the laborers, my brothers - / Have not those who sowed with weeping / Reaped with song and psalm?"; "In this far, cold land, no singing, / Only sighs and lamentations, / Only groans and woe"; "Shall I tell my tale of sorrows / [...] Of the present, or the others / That are yet to strike?"; "For if beside me you linger / You, too, singer, will be weeping / For my destiny"; and "Yet all lamentations and moanings / Will not heal my anguish, / Will not cure provide. / I have seared my eyes with weeping, / I have filled with tears the chalice, / And my heart is dry / Gone all tears, and gone each hinted / Year of Messianic tiding, / All is gone but pain..."

Sofer writes a missive to Bialik, (who immigrated to Israel in 1924 and was deceased at the time Sofer "addressed" him) in which she encourages him to change his poetic views. Here is the opening paragraph from this missive:

> What's the matter with you, good poet, why all this despair and tears, suffering and grief? Were the talents of an excellent poet given to you just in order to be a poet of tears and despair? You should be a poet of encouragement, a poet of life and hope.
>
> What is the grief and despair aren't they the weapons of the weak and cowards? Be comforted, man, fill your heart up with faith in the future, be strong against any obstacle and pain, because the time came for your redemption and for the end of your grief. There is no gain in crying. Crying will bring death, not life. The life is in your return to your warm, beautiful country. There is life and liberty there, future and hope. The work there is the elixir of life and happiness, the source for blessing and peace for the people on earth.

In the mid-1940s, readers can see that women were important participants in the ideological Jewish life of Iraq. They were regular contributors to this publication. The author of this piece is familiar with Bialik's work (the single poem represents a viewpoint which is typical of other poems). The author expresses Zionist-socialist views, emphasizing the value of labor, pioneering, and commitment to national goals. She writes with an eloquent, poetic style. Here is how she ends her piece:

> And now, my friend, you should know that your hard working brethren are harvesting, are reaping in joy what they sowed in tears. The flowers that you planted did not wither, but are fully blossoming. You too did not age, and were not weakened. Push the despair away from you. The memory of your homeland will save you from your bitter destiny. The homeland is awaiting and yearning impatiently for your return.

> And now, my friend, let's go to the homeland, to do the work, let's go to the new world, a world of delight and illumination.

Eliahu from Baghdad wrote another response to the same poem:

> Greetings to you, poet, from the uninhabited, bewildered and ruined Zion. Malaria swamps cover your homeland and limbs were amputated from its body [...] the hands of the enemy destroyed our homeland one generation after another. Few and lonely are now the Jewish hands that break new paths and construct. The eyes of a few are anticipating newcomers, those who will continue the work; they are waiting for the entire nation. [...] Get up and go back to your home. You will hear a song of a bird brightening the wilderness and the sound of liberation from above the ruins. [...] Open your eyes, man, and choose the road to life. With an upright head and courageous steps march forward, eastbound, toward the liberation.

Both pieces represent the same values as those found in Hebrew literature written during the early years of struggle to establish the state of Israel and continued through its early years as a state. Focus was placed on the collective problems and experiences, and their system of that generation's values was clearly defined. It emphasized a positive attitude toward Zionism, pioneering, humanism, socialism, devotion to the land of Israel, and the struggle to build it. The attitude was optimistic, the characters were positive and proud to represent the Jewish nation, and they believed that the struggle would lead to a positive outcome. "We" was stressed more than "I," and social rules were accepted as a matter of course. Emphasis was placed on friendship, obedience, struggling against the enemy, group cohesiveness, and direction to socially toe the line.

The Third Issue

Yoav (Katan) from "Haifa" (Basra) published two poems in this issue. One poem is a love poem, and the other poem, "My Poetry," is about the nature and origin of his poetry. "My Poetry" was influenced by a Jewish poet from Spain, Solomon ibn Gabirol (*Melitsati Be-Da'gati Hadufah*). "Shimshon" from "Tel-Aviv" (Baghdad) wrote about the poetry of Yehuda Halevi, a Jewish poem from Spain, emphasizing the autobiographical elements in his poetry.

Hertseliyya (Violet Ben Porat) from "Tel-Aviv" notes her reaction to a poem by Bialik (*Yada'ti Be-Lel 'Arafel*, "I Knew in a Day of Fog," 1906) in which he denounced the world for its crimes against the Jewish people. The poem was written after the 1905 Russian revolution and after the pogrom episode against the Jews in Russia. The poetic speaker knows that he and his nation's "wrath shall smolder like a crater / Whose flames have fallen," their cry will "pierce the heavens, everlastingly / Withholding the redemption of the world," and it will represent eternal evidence of the evil world. It continues, "And when, at the end time, the sun of guile / And counterfeited righteousness shall rise / [...] the sun / shall redden to an orb of your pure blood / To brand the mark of Cain upon the front / Of all the universe, to testify..."; "Until the Lord of Vengeance, stung to wrath / Shall rise and roar and with His sword unsheathed / Go forth to strike" (Bialik, *Selected Poems*, 195-196). I will present a paragraph from what Hertseliyya wrote:

> In this poem Bialik was elevated to the stature of a prophet. It is as if he felt the calamity that awaited the Jewish people. This bitter day, which he prophesied, indeed came. Our people were annihilated all over Europe, and all the nations kept silence and there is no nation that remembers our annihilated people, our big graves that filled the earth in Europe.
>
> This is sad. And I think: Aren't we human beings? Our blood is free for every murderer? The number of our murdered people is larger than the number of the murdered people of any other nation, and our grief is greater than the grief of any other nation. The unfaithful and the destroyers of justice are more successful than the faithful Jews. We are more oppressed than all the wicked people. If only our sadness could penetrate the heart of the world, go deep into its soul and ferment its blood, if only our cry will reach the heaven, will agitate the hearts of people, and the blood of our pure people will "pierce the bottomless abyss of darkness and eat away the foundations of the putrefying earth" [H.N. Bialik, *On the Slaughter*], in this world which is full of malevolence, injustice and inequality [...]
>
> A day will come and there will be an end to the world of deception and inequality. After a great deal of labor and bloodshed of war there will be

> a world justice and with it will come justice and happiness to our nation among the nations.

This piece again illustrates the participation of Jewish women in the ideological deliberations of their time and their advanced level of Hebrew. Additionally, readers observe that the young men and women of this movement were familiar with modern Hebrew poetry.

The Fourth Issue

Rina (Rina Dlumi Sason) wrote about the immigration of a movement member to Israel. She expressed her spirit of willingness to participate in the founding of Israel and to take the necessary responsibilities to meet this goal:

> [...] By their pioneering work they [the movement members who immigrated to Israel] will show and prove to the veterans in Israel, that our Jewry is no less capable than others to participate in the war for independence and redemption, in spite of the fact that our participation in building and fighting is only a few years old.

Another woman, Tsviyah, wrote a poem about love and longing for Israel. In The Song of Songs (5:8), readers note, "I am lovesick," while in Tsviyah's poem, the speaker states, "I am homesick." "Home" and "love" are synonymous. Yoav from "Haifa" (Basra) wrote a poem in which the speaker begs not to be awakened from his dreams to avoid facing his sorrowful reality. In another piece, Shimshon wrote about the life and poetry of Abraham ibn-Ezra, another medieval Jewish poet from Spain.

The Fifth Issue

The voice of women highlights some issues of *Derekh He-Haluts,* even though the majority of contributors were not women. The women's voice presents new viewpoints, and they tackle difficult issues.

Shulamit from "Haifa" (Basra) wrote about "The Life of a Young Woman in the Diaspora." She described the traditional, conservative way of life of a young Jewish woman in Babylon that limited her social, educational, and emotional life and expressed hope for change. I will present some selections from this piece because it may well explain why the voice of women in Babylonian Hebrew literature was not heard until now.

Young women describe their situation in Babylon as they report their viewpoints in the fifth issue of *Derekh He-Haluts*:

> I cannot portray for you a full picture about the life of the young woman here. True, people feel how hard her situation is, but you don't know her life conditions the same way she knows and feels them. The young woman lives a dark life; she feels she is in jail. Her father is the superintendent of her jail. Her suffering is hard, all her life she is humiliated, oppressed, and discriminated against.
>
> Her father, particularly when he is conservative, does not allow her to stand in front of him and argue with him, and she sees him not as a father but as a cruel judge; he controls her and her freedom. There are very few young women who have a little freedom.
>
> There are fathers here that do not allow their daughters to acquire even a little bit of education. They force them to leave school and stay at home and work. When a girl asks her father to allow her to graduate, her father responds by scolding and screaming at her. When she leaves her father's home, the situation does not change. She does not find her freedom, but she goes from darkness to humiliation. Her husband uses the same system her father did, closes the doors on her, and does not allow her to go out. Most of the people consider the woman to be a heavy burden, when a girl is born there is mourning, the father is angry at the mother, and when the time for marriage comes, it is hard for the father to pay the big dowry to the groom who demands a high amount without mercy. This results in quarrels in the woman's home. Her father thinks and worries all day and night about how to obtain the money. And she, the girl must sit idle, without saying anything about the man she has to live with all her life. And she did not even know him nor conversed with him.

> This is how the young woman lives. She is bought and sold. But now there are some young women that are awakened and feel their terrible situation. They want and look for someone who would save them from this slavery, and they know that there is in the world a different way of life. They wait impatiently for the day of deliverance, when they see a new light, where they can see the wide world and participate with a man in all aspects of life, in work and toil, and in creating a new world in which there is no difference between a man and a woman, between the strong and the weak.
>
> And I feel the progress of the young woman in our movement; she is progressing because she can see with her own eyes her future in the movement, free of shackles, working together as a partner with the men for women's liberation, for the liberation of her people, of mankind.
>
> A light shone upon us from Israel. Only a few sparks reached us, but we, the women and men who are members of the movement, will rekindle them to a big flame, a flame of freedom and liberation that will shine and give light in our forefathers land.

It is typical for these idealistic pioneering movement members to view Israel as the place where all the problems they faced will be resolved.

Uziel (Uziel Levy) from "Tel-Aviv" (Baghdad) wrote about "Bialik, the Castigating Poet" (7-8). He wrote about Bialik's national poetry, which he loved and understood. Yehoshafat (Yosef Meir) wrote an essay entitled "I found My Goal" (9-10). Neither people nor books helped him find an answer to his question "What are my goals?" Then, one day he understood that his goal was to fight against ignorance and darkness and to improve the human condition. He understood that he must join the movement in order to participate in the national Jewish struggle. Shoshana (Shoshana Arbeli Almuzlinu, later a minister in the Israeli government) wrote about her "Dream" (10) to be in Israel and work in the kibbutz.

Other women authored various pieces in this issue, among them Rina (Rina Dlumi Sason) and Carmela. Rina expresses appreciation for the contribution of the movement to her life, specifically in helping her define her goals. She expressed pain over the suffering of European Jews, appreciation to the Zionist movement, and admiration for the rebels of the Warsaw ghetto. She wrote, "Due to the fact that the big world did not come to the aid of our miserable nation, we the members of the Zionist movement in the world have to learn the lesson that there is no real power that will save us except our own, the power of everyone of us to save himself and others..."

Carmela recorded her thoughts about the 1894 poem "I Believe" of Shaul Tchernihovski. The speaker in this poem expresses his personal dreams as well as dreams for his people and the entire world. He believes in the woman that he is speaking to, he believes in man and mankind, he believes that a day will come and "man shall rise to heights of glory, / vanity's fetters from him shed; / the worker will starve no longer, / spirit-freed, and hunger-fed." The speaker believes in friendship, in the future, in world peace, and that his "people, too, again will blossom." The Jews will be "living, working, doing, / on the earth alive indeed, / not hereafter—hope of heaven,/ not content with an empty creed." (see Silberschlag, 95-96).

In response to the poem, Carmela wrote:

> O my dear, the poet Tchernihovski, how wonderful are the dreams you dreamed. What a great impression your dreams made on me! [...] I have already read poems of Bialik and Rahel, but your short and simple poem affected me profoundly.
>
> My dear poet, you dreamed many dreams, and I believe that the day will come and they will materialize [...] such a day will not come if the young woman will not be liberated. The young woman is weak in the world; this is how nature created her. And you young male members of the movement have to understand us and know our situation, the young women of the Middle East.
>
> Do know it young men: Our fight is difficult, and I am not exaggerating if I say that we are more pioneers than you are. The young man is always free everywhere in the world, but the young woman is the one who is shackled, particularly in the Middle East.
>
> How do you want us to help you and work shoulder to shoulder with you while we are still in a bad environment? Come to our help, let's shatter together our iron vanity shackles, and see the light together...

Hebrew literature was a source of inspiration and guidance for these young people. They not only related to it aesthetically, but also ideologically. They did not read poems for the sake of art only, but drew from them ideas and incorporated their messages into the central goals of their very existence. They either responded to what they read with acceptance or reservation. Additionally, they either applied their discoveries to their personal lives or to their community relationships.

Eliezer (Ya'acov Eliezer) from "Basra" wrote a poem (8) about longing for Zion, wishing he had wings so he could fly to his homeland and rebuild it. Yoav, another member of the movement, published a poem about the elusive butterfly and his hope of catching one.

The Sixth Issue

In this issue, Avraham from Baghdad wrote another response to Bialik's poem "To The Bird." His response is optimistic and encourages the reader to immigrate to Israel and to participate in building it. Israel is idealized and described as the place in which all problems will be solved. In Israel, there are no "afflictions, only happiness and work," the Jews there "are happy in their homeland," the country blossoms "and the Valley of Sharon is dressed in green clothes; The Jews became people like all the other people," and "The Jews from their homeland suggested to me / Get Thee out of thy country [Genesis 12,1] and go there / they are fighting for liberty and freedom / hurry up and join them." Unlike this poem, which responds with an answer by identifying the destination, in Yoav's poem (10), his lifeboat wanders and rocks as he searches for a peaceful shore. Yoav also wrote (9-10) about the mighty thoughts that evoked Nineveh, the capital of Assyria near Mosul. He wrote, "I climbed up one hill and looked around, piles upon piles, I went up on all the piles, my feet stepped on all the great kings of Assyria... But the Jewish people still exist... The mighty Nineveh dies and the Jewish people are still alive. And I, the eternal Jew, am walking on the ruins of Nineveh shouting: The Jewish people are alive!"

Tova (Chitayat) from Baghdad wrote (10-11) a vibrant and colorful description about the market environment on Friday.

The Eighth Issue

In this issue, literature has an extensive section, including a play, an article, and a short story. Amnon (there were four members of this underground movement named Amnon) from "Baghdad" wrote the play.

There are four characters in the play: a wandering Jew, the Jewish National Fund that is personified as a beautiful girl, Elijah the Messiah, and a boy who is not Jewish. The play contains lucid symbols.

The Jew is lost in darkness. He cannot find the way that leads to his destination. He is hungry, injured, and needs the spiritual and practical support of people and God, but he does not have any support. The gates of heaven are shut in front of him, and he cannot count on anyone except himself. He encounters hungry beasts—nations that threaten his existence—while heaven is silent, and one can only see the shadow of stars. The "spirit" (wind) threatens him; it is the spirit of his time, and at the same time thorns and thistles prick him as he faces endless obstacles. It was as if nature, heaven, and people joined together to make his path difficult to tread. Indeed, the Jew is "the Chosen one"; he was chosen to labor and to live in quandary. The homeland in the play appears as an image of a mother who is calling her son to return to her. In the homeland, the Jew feels "a generation long hunger for food and peace, for creativity and love."

The Jew tries to get help from some of his own people—the rich and the orthodox. The rich turn him down, and the orthodox do not listen to his argument that he came to build the homeland, which they pray for daily. He turns to the world for help, but he is denied.

In his despair, while he is in a life and death struggle, he hears the voice of the prophet Elijah telling him that the time for redemption has arrived, and he should no longer feel detached and subdued, because the gates of heaven are open to him. The Jew has modest requests: "I do not know how to pray. I do not know how to talk to you, give me a strong hand to take bread out of this earth, give me a strong hand to defend myself from the many wolves." He wants to make his living from this Earth and to overcome "the voices that tempt him" to emigrate from his country. The temptations are materialistically based—gold and wealth, a life of peace, and nobility overseas tempt him to emigrate from Israel. However, he is decisive: "My plough is my gold and my happiness, and God is my wealth and my peace." Besides the materialistic temptations, there are other temptations—the possibility to acquire education and scientific knowledge overseas is also tempting and provides an incentive to assimilate: "I am the world... Forget your Judaism and come to me... I will give you light and science and everything else."

The Jew, however, wants his own light for his new small home (homeland). He returned "to the source of happiness, life, and love," to the Earth that is the source of strength for all nations, and it invigorates the Jewish people in their country. The other nations who want to inflict death on the Jews recoil when they see a new, strong Jew, who is connected to the earth, on the site of the Jewish National Fund. The Jew understands that life and happiness "are hidden in the earth," and he can find them by digging with his hoe. He dedicates his life to Mother Earth to remove its thistles, to make the desert bloom, to end poverty, and to make Israel the garden for all Jews wherever they are. After that, the time arrives to sing "the song of peace, love, and blessing." This way the Jewish people will be part of creating a new world, and they will not hold a grudge against their enemies.

This is a didactic play, in which the author expresses Zionist-socialist views, devotion to the land of Israel and to the struggle of building it, emphasizing values such as labor, pioneering, commitment to national goals, and humanism. The outlook is one of optimism. The characters are willing to represent the Jewish nation, and they believe that their struggle will lead to a positive outcome. The center of the individual's thoughts is "we" (not "I"); an emphasis is placed on readiness to work hard for the sake of the nation and on the justification for towing the social line. The "tie" of the pioneers to the Earth is demonstrated in this play not only metaphorically; The Jewish National Fund (a beautiful girl) uses a rope to tie the pioneer to his land. It is only after he is bound that he stands upright and is paid respect by all nations.

"Yoael" (Yehuda-Yoel Shohet) from "Baghdad" published (13) a short story entitled "Justice, Justice Shalt Thou Follow" (Deuteronomy 16:20). The story is about a young man in China who worked hard in order to become an attorney, and indeed, he became a successful attorney. His goal was not to become rich but to pursue justice, and when he could not find justice in his immediate environment, he searched for justice elsewhere.

Ten years later, he came back to his hometown disappointed, poor, and old but full of wisdom and love for mankind. He dedicated his life to providing free education to poor children and guiding them to appreciate love, peace, and equality. His government executed him because he was considered to have a bad influence on young people who might refuse to go to war. His students, however, carried a tombstone for him in their hearts.

In this story, readers observe the values that were emulated by the movement members—love, peace, equality, public service, courage, and being goal-oriented. The undefined time of the events, the setting of the plot in China, and the names (the character's name is Menashas and his town is Sabbakin) are devices to conceal the applicability of the story's moral to the time and place in which it was written. The Hebrew style of this didactic story is fluent and colorful. Here is the opening of the story:

> There are two kinds of people: one who burns his clothes in order to light the road for other people and who will also end up burning his thin, naked, body, and one who burns down towns in order to light the hidden nooks

> of his dark heart. The latter one is the admired and praised hero in front of whom everyone will kneel. And on his head will be a glistening crown.

"Ehud" (Menasheh Katsir) published a story about a young woman who suffered from hostility and mockery because of her corrupt sister. The movement embraced the good sister and provided her with the appreciation and understanding she craved.

Immanuel from "Baghdad" wrote (7-8) about a conversation he had with a friend one Sabbath evening regarding the movement. He describes his attachment to the movement:

> How beautiful and tempestuous is life in the movement when you consider the great revolution it created in you. Beforehand you lived in a gloomy, dark world, and now you are marching along a lit road towards an exalted goal. You went astray in the wilderness and struggled to find your way and you found an intersection and chose your road. You raised your eyes and you saw the flaming bonfire on the horizon.

One of the movement members wrote a poem (6) about admiration and lamentation in memory of those who sacrificed their life for Israel.

Another member wrote (8-9) a memoir about his experience in the Iraqi jail and the experience other movement members had while in jail as punishment for their membership in a Zionist movement. He received a letter from his brother in Israel. Consequently, he was detained and questioned. Then, he was sentenced to three years in jail. Five prisoners shared a small room without a roof and slept on the concrete floor.

Then they encountered a jail warden. This man was born in jail and spent twenty-eight out of thirty-two years of his life in jail. He was a wild man who could do whatever he wanted to the Jewish prisoners and go unpunished. He assaulted the author and took his money. He awakened three times every night. Each time he awakened, he admonished the prisoners for not dousing themselves with urine and excrement from a nearby can. He invented various ways of torture, along with verbal and physical abuse, as detailed in this memoir.

Bribery was common in jail. The movement members were helpful to each other. Jews were not allowed to visit a doctor. One Jewish prisoner who asked to see a physician was beaten, put in solitary confinement, and bound with a heavy chain. Another time an old Jewish man was put in solitary confinement for wearing sunglasses in the jail courtyard. That day it was hot, and it was evident if he stayed there for a few hours he would die. The prisoners paid a bribe, and the old man was released from solitary confinement.

The Ninth Issue

In this issue, Oved wrote about the "Mother" (14), describing her motherly beauty, love, and dedication, and then about the homeland as "mother":

Mother! How enjoyable is the word mother!
Mother is the holiest word in all the languages. It is the first word that a baby says when he begins to talk.
The little child cries and calls for his mother! The young soldier is killed in the war, rolling in his blood, he blesses his country in the word that he loves: "To life mother!"
And you, buddies! We, are the happy ones because of our mothers, can we feel the sorrow of a person who does not have a mother? We that shout for joy in the morning and call: "Mom!" We, that fill our eyes with the splendor of our mothers' faces every day, can we feel the significance of the word "mother" for a person who does not have a mother, and who cannot call during his lifetime: "Mother!"
Can any nation in the world feel the anguish of the Jews because they lack a mother for the nation – a homeland?
Or can that rich man, who lives in a palace and is dressed in silk, feel the pain of the farmer who dwells in a cabin, and who covers his thin body with rags?
Mother is the symbol of every beautiful thing in the world. She is a symbol of love. A symbol of care. And he who lacks a mother is destined to live without someone caring for him, without love. He rolls in his pain without feeling, without crying out. Because who will hear him? Who will listen?

Oved also wrote a piece about "The Chained Freedom of Speech" (15):

They cut their tongues!
But wouldn't the pencils continue revealing the guilty ones?
They broke the pencils!
But would this prevent their hands from engraving in the stones?
They amputated the hands!
Wouldn't their eyes glow with the fire of rage?
They gouged their eyes out!
And their breathing, why are you emitting sighs?
They cut off their breathing!
They still will not succeed; those who will follow through will come!

The Tenth Issue

Some movement members contributed poems to this issue. Oved wrote a poem inspired by Greek mythology about people conducting themselves like "worms" when they encounter powerful people. However, he hints at the ability a man has to subdue the one who tramples over people. In another poem (20), Oved describes a resilient man emerging from his painful childhood years. The injured heart of flesh and blood produces an iron man whose hopes and love are different from those of his youth. Trumpeldor from "Baghdad" wrote a poem (19) calling on "forgetfulness and inattentiveness" to free him from his bad memories. Dan from "Baghdad" published a poem (19) that included a prayer to fertilize the soil of Israel with his bones and fearlessly break the cuffs of his life's experiences regardless of the outcome. Yigal from "Baghdad" wrote a poem (23) about his own poetry, which he wrote during the silent evenings.

Closing Remarks about *Derekh He-Haluts*

Derekh He-Haluts shows how modern Hebrew literature and the ideology of the pioneers in Israel were part of the creative work of young people in Iraq. In *Derekh He-Haluts*, readers find national and social themes, Zionist values, love for Israel, willingness to sacrifice for it, care for the nation, passion for pioneering, and a spirit of heroism and courage. The young members of the movement were familiar with the literature and ideology of the pioneers in Israel.

The themes about which they wrote were expanded and secular. A wide range of themes found expression in the Hebrew creativity of the young people who participated in writing in this journal. They were not influenced by the long, rich tradition of religious Hebrew poetry authored in Iraq. They did not look up to Hebrew authors in Iraq or to medieval Hebrew poetry. Rather, they were inspired by the ideology and literature that was widespread in Israel.

For the first time, women became equal participants in Iraq's Hebrew creativity. Women did not only play an important role in publishing their Hebrew works in the journal, they also expressed a new, liberated spirit. They acknowledged their status courageously and demanded equality.

The language used in *Derekh He-Haluts* is modern Hebrew that includes biblical and rabbinical vocabulary. It is not a creative language that is based on allusions. Rather, it is a flowing, living language, the same language that was used at that time in Israel. The authors were not influenced only by ideas from Israel, but also by the Hebrew style.

Had Hebrew creativity continued in Babylon, one would have more poetic forms and influences from contemporary Hebrew literature in Israel. The young participants in this journal did not look to biblical Hebrew as the source for their expression. Their ideological world and writing style paralleled that of the pioneers in Israel.

Epilogue

Hebrew creativity is an essential part of Jewish culture. It is important that we recognize Hebrew creativity wherever it took place. It is important to determine the information, the description, and the aesthetic evaluation of secular Hebrew creativity, including places where we mistakenly thought that Hebrew creativity did not exist, as was the case in Babylon.

Herein I have presented Hebrew poets who wrote important secular Hebrew poetry that was aesthetically compatible with Hebrew poetry of its time. Yet, their poetry was not part of the tapestry of classical Hebrew literature as it should have been. This poetry is valuable not only in and of itself, but also because it is a link in the history of Hebrew literature and should be recognized in this manner. Ezra Habavli, for example, is a poet who writes with a powerful style and astonishing poetic language. His poems, however, are not mentioned by any Hebrew literature historians.

When the majority of Babylonian Jews immigrated to Israel (1950-1951 Operation Ezra and Nehemiah), it was not the conclusion of the Babylonian Jews' secular Hebrew creative contributions. This creativity had a long tradition. Some of the authors mentioned here, such as Menasheh Saliman Shahrabani and David Tsemah merely continued their expression of Hebrew creativity in Israel.

Hebrew writing was part of Jewish education. The rabbis possessed a thorough knowledge of Hebrew, and Hebrew writing was part of their work. In later years, Hebrew writing and Hebrew creativity became part of the life of the younger generation who were influenced by the Hebrew literature written in Europe and Israel. The poetic themes were extensive. Poets such as Shaul Yosef and David Tsemah were strongly influenced by medieval Hebrew poetry. However, poets such as the Mani brothers were strongly influenced by modern Hebrew poetry and less by medieval Hebrew poetry.

Derekh He-Haluts (1945-1951) reflects the influence of modern Hebrew literature on the themes of Hebrew writing in Babylon. The voice of women was heard in *Derekh He-Haluts* together with the voice of men. The involvement of women in Israeli creativity and pioneering encouraged and inspired the young women in Babylon to write for *Derekh He-Haluts*.

Besides Hebrew poetry, the Jews of Babylon wrote journalistic articles in Hebrew, poetic missives, research articles, short stories, and a play. Their poetry was significantly richer than their prose, and one wonders why. They purchased Hebrew books from Israel and Europe, including periodicals, and they were aware of fictional prose. Did they have the talent to write fictional prose? Their Hebrew was rich, and they created rich folk literature and poetry. They employed sophisticated literary devices in their folktales.

The tradition of writing poetry in Babylon was well established. Many poets who wrote religious poetry also wrote secular poetry. An author who wanted to write poetry had a long tradition of poetry in Babylon to inspire him. However, he did not have a local tradition of Hebrew novels, short stories, and plays to draw from. Rather, he had a long tradition of religious writings including sermons and preaching, folktales, biblical interpretations, prayers, compilations of Jewish law, and Jewish mysticism. The environment was better suited for this type of creativity than for fictional prose.

Another reason for the lack of fictional prose in Iraq is because Hebrew was in competition with Arabic and Judeo-Arabic. Arabic and Judeo-Arabic had authors and readers, and both of these languages competed with Hebrew.

Babylonian Jews were not secular; they strove to be religious and did not accept non-religious communities. The secular movement in Babylon related to religion considerately and respectfully. It was not an easy task to write and publish a Hebrew book in Babylon that was fictional prose with modern-secular content and draw a sufficient local audience.

It seems to me that if Hebrew creativity continued in Babylon, it would lead to fictional prose with an emphasis on the local color—the life in Iraq (with themes similar to those in *Shemesh* and *Derekh He-Haluts*).

With all its shortcomings, Babylonian Hebrew literature was significant and fascinating. It should be designated as an essential branch of literature that can be used to depict the history of Hebrew literature.

Questions

Introduction

A. A Brief History about the Jews in Babylon

1. Please explain the following terms: Amoraites, Tania, Midrash, Babylonian Talmud, Saboraites, Yeshiva, Gaonites.

2. Illustrate times in which Jews lived in peace with Muslim Arabs. In your opinion, can this happen now?

3. When was Baghdad built? Who built it?

4. In the twentieth century, the Jewish community in Iraq had many synagogues, charitable organizations, social clubs, and rabbinical courts. Compare this with Jewish community centers in the United States today.

5. What is "Farhud"? Why did the Los Angeles Holocaust Memorial Museum recognize "the Farhud" as a Holocaust pogrom?

6. What were the ways in which the Jews of Iraq hoped to prevent future pogroms?

7. Expound on the case of Shafik Adas. What are your thoughts about the case?

8. How does the knowledge of a people's history help us understand their culture and literature?

B. The Essence of the New Hebrew Creativity in Babylon

1. Describe some of the difficulties of Jews who decided to write Hebrew literature in Iraq in modern times. What motivated them?

2. How can we distinguish between secular and liturgical Hebrew poetry?

3. How did the Jews of Iraq interact with Jews from far away communities? How did modern technology impact the interactions between communities that are far away from each other?

C. Jewish Education in Babylon
Compare the Jewish educational system in Iraq with the Jewish educational system in the United States today.

D. Hebrew Teaching and Hebrew Knowledge in Babylon
Compare the status of the Hebrew language in Babylon with its status in the United States today.

E. The Hebrew Press in Babylon
Compare the Hebrew press of nineteenth century Iraq with the Hebrew press in the United States today. Why did a smaller Iraqi Jewish community print more Hebrew books then than a larger United States Jewish community today?

F. The Hebrew Creativity of The Near Eastern Jews and the History of Modern Hebrew Literature
What argument is made about the need to rewrite the history of modern Hebrew literature?

Part 1: Poetry

Chapter 1: Pathfinders and Explorers in the Eighteenth and Nineteenth Century Hebrew Poetry in Babylon
What translation of poetry appeals more to you—a literal translation or one that keeps the general content of the original but focuses on its metrical structure and rhymes?

Rabbi Ezra Habavli: The Debate of Man and his Earth
1. What would the reader miss in Habavli's poetry if he is not aware of its biblical allusions?

2. Are Habavli's ideas individualistic, national, or universal?

"A Man Must Get Tipsy": The Call of Rabbi Moshe Hutsin
When do you find it acceptable that a spiritual man becomes whimsical, funny, and mischievous?

Didactic Poetry: Rabbi Salih Matsliyah

Can a poet write an instructive poem with a moral without compromising the aesthetic aspects? Illustrate your answer with the poems of Rabbi Salih Matsliyah.

Rabbi Nissim Matsliyah: Playful Poetry
What are the effects of the use of homonyms in a poem? Illustrate by using an Americam poem known to you.

Rabbi Sason Ben-Mordekhai: "I am Sason a Small Minded and a Short Tongued_Man."
1. How does the fact that the poetic speaker includes his biographic name in his poem affect you?

2. How does the fact that the poetic speaker addresses you in the second person affect you?

3. "The love of pleasure is sweet / But its evil is awfully grave." Illustrate the validity of this statement nowadays.

Rabbi Mordekhai Ben Sason: His Pals Disappointed Him
The statement "and my soul says, this is for the good" is ambiguous. Please suggest how to interpret it. What are your thoughts about poetic ambiguity?

Rabbi Sason Yisrael Gives Advice: "For Who will You Collect Silver and Gold?"
The poem, except for its first few words, is a monologue of its author. Write a response to the addressee in the first part of the poem.

Chapter 2: Four Poets of Babylonian Origin
Shaul Yosef: An Enlightened Poet
1. Illustrate the use of poetic overstatement in Shaul Yosef's poem. Further expound on how these overstatements affect you.

2. Do you hold a bias toward the critic or toward the author of the poem because of his criticism of another poet?

Rabbi Saliman Menahem Mani: From the Bonds of the Conventional to the Personal Articulation
Compare the poem "If Tarshish" by Saliman Mani with Sason Yisrael's poem.

A Lyrical Poet Who Died While Still in his Prime: Rabbi Avraham Barukh Mani

Avraham Barukh Mani died of an illness when he was twenty-seven years old. Would you factor this into your analysis of his poem or comment without including this external influence on his work?

Rabbi Ezekiel Hai Albeg Carries his Legacy Overseas

Read the biblical story (Genesis 4) about Cain and Abel and Albeg's poem "Cain." What elements from the biblical story are incorporated into the poem?

Chapter 3: The Twentieth Century Poets in Babylon

The Renaissance Poet Aharon Sason

Find out about the ideas and the goals of the Enlightenment period in Hebrew literature. Do you find similar ideas in the poems of Aharon Sason?

***The School Poems* of David Hai Abbudi**

There are language instructors who think that the best method of teaching a foreign language is by combining the teaching of a language with singing in that language. What is your opinion about this method?

Shelomo Yitshak Nissim, a Member of the Hebrew Association in Babylon

What are the values that the poet promotes in his poems? Do you think that they are universal?

***The Vineyard Poems* by Rabbi Shelomo Ben-Salih Shelomo Gabai**

Compare the historical background of the 1903 Hayyim Nahman Bialik's poem "On the Slaughter" with the 1941 poem of Shelomo Gabai and the positions of the poetic speakers toward the victims of the pogroms.

About the Holocaust and the Massacre: Rabbi Menasheh Saliman Shahrabani

How does the use of allusions in Menasheh Shahrabani's poem "I will Shiver and Quiver" support the sense of Jewish unity?

"And they Pierced their Heads with Nails": Rabbi Yitshak Nissim Mourned, Rabbi Moshe Ventura Condoled

Write about some of the stylistic differences between the poet's account and the historical record describing the same event.

The First of the Social Protester Poets: David Saliman Tsemah

Compare the tone and the position of David Tsemah's poem about the hookah with Mosheh Hutsin's poem about wine drinking.

Part 2: Folktales, Reportage, Epistles, Research of Literature, and a Story

Chapter 4: The Folktales of Rabbi Yosef Hayyim
Please choose one of the folktales and write about the literary devices employed in the story.

Chapter 5: Rabbi Shelomo Bekhor Hutsin (Rashbah): The World of an Enlightened Jew
Should a journalist write with an emotionally involved style or merely report the facts? What was Rashbah's style of writing, and what is your opinion about his style?

Chapter 6: An Epistle as a Literary Work: Rabbi Ya'acov Hayyim's Letter to Farha Sason
Do you think that Ya'acov Hayyim rambled too much and that we should analyze his epistle without introducing external evidence?

Chapter 7: Shaul Abdullah Yosef: A Scholar of Medieval Hebrew Poetry
Illustrate the ways in which a scholar's own life experience may enrich the quality of his research. Why did Shaul Yosef feel that he had an advantage in understanding Medieval Hebrew poetry?

Chapter 8: Rabbi Saliman Mani: Hebron, Gaza, and the Demons
Should art—including literature—be recruited in order to promote or demote certain ideas? Do you think that this story contributed to a progression of Jewish life in Palestine?

Part 3: Hebrew Periodicals in Babylon

Chapter 9: *Ha-Dover:* The First Hebrew Journal in Babylon
Search for the story of *Hadoar,* which was a publication in the Hebrew language in America (see http// hadoramerica.com). What could be learned from the story of Hadoar about Hebrew periodical publication hardships in 1863 Iraq?

Chapter 10: *Yeshurun*: "The Newspaper is the Heart of the People"
Do you agree with *Yeshurun* about the great importance ascribed to newspapers? Do newspapers hold the same power now, when we have radio, television, and Internet?

Chapter 11: *Shemesh*: An Anthology of Poems and Compositions from the Students of *Shammash* School
Please write a letter to a contributor of *Shemesh.*

Chapter 12: *Derekh He-Haluts*: The Journal of the Movement Counselors
Compare the dreams of the Movement Counselors with the dreams of young people now in the United States and Israel.

Epilogue
You have read literature that to a great extent was derived from previously unknown sources. What is the most important thing that you will remember from this study?

Index of Authors

Bibliography

Abbudi, David Hai. *Shireh Bet-Ha-Sefer*. Booklet A. Baghdad: El Samueliah Library, matbaat G. K. Yisraeliyyat, 1930.

Agasi, A. *Husham Mi-Baghdahd—Ma'asiyyot Bavliyyot*. Tel-Aviv: Am Oved, 1960.

——. *Ha-Mikhtav Shenislakh Im Ha-Ruuah—Sippureh Am shel Yehudeh Bavel*. Tel-Aviv: Am Oved, 1979.

——. *Ha-Yafa Bat Ha-Ruuah, Sippureh Am Bavliyyim*. Tel-Aviv: Yariv-Hadar, 1980.

Albeg, Hai Ezekiel. *Kenaf Ha-Arets*. Jerusalem, 1936.

——. *Kenaf Renanim*. New York, 1942.

——. *Mizmor Shir*. New York, 1960.

——. *Me-Aram Naharayim Li-rushalayim*. New York, 1963.

——. *Massa Ninveh*. New York, 1980.

——. *Ir U-Mmigdal*. New York, 1980.

——. *Megillat Sefer*. California, 1983.

——. *Divan*. Encino, California, 1983.

——. *Asara Rishonim*. Encino, California, 1987.

Aruaeti, Ezra. *Makedonia—Salaeh Derekh*. Tel-Aviv: Eked, 1973.

——. *Hovesh Ha-Kova Ha-Kaful*. Tel-Aviv: Eked, 1995.

Attal, Abraham. "Germania Ha-Natsit Ba-Shira Ha-Amamit shel Yehudeh Tunisia." *Pea'amim*. no. 28 (1986): 126-130.

Avishur, Yitzhak. "Ha-Sifrut Ha-Amamit shel Yehudeh Bavel Be-Aravit Yehudit." *Pe'amim*, no. 3 (1979): 83-90.

——. *Ha-Sippur Ha-Amami shel Yehudeh Iraq* I and II. The University of Haifa, 1992.

——. "Shiddud Maarakhot Sifrutiyyot U-Temurut Leshoniyyot Be-Kerev Yehudeh Iraq Ba-Et Ha-Hadasha (1750-1950)." *Mi-Kedem U-Miyyam* 6 (1995): 235-254.

Ben-Yaacob, Abraham, collected and selected. *Shira U-Fiyyut shel Yehudeh Bavel Ba-Dorot Ha-Aharonim*. Jerusalem: Ben-Zvi Institute, The Hebrew University of Jerusalem, 1970.

——. *Yehudeh Bavel Mi-Sof Tekufat Ha-Geonim ad Yamenu*. Jerusalem: Kiriat Sefer, 1979.

——. *Yehudeh Bavel Be-Erets Yisrael Me-Ha-Aliyyot Ha-Rishonot ad Ha-yom*. Jerusalem: Reuven Mas, 1980.

——. *Ha-Rav Yosef Hayyim Mi-Bagdhdad*. Or-Yehuda: The Baylonian Jewry Heritage Center, 1984.

——. *Otsar Ha-Shirim, Ha-Hibburim Ve-Ha-Derashot Ve-Sippureh Ha-Ma'asiyyot shel Ha-Rav Yosef Hayyim*. Jerusalem: Makhon Ha-Ketav, 1994.

——. *Perakim Be-Toldot Yehudeh Bavel* I and II. Jerusalem: Olam Ha-Sefer Ha-Torani, 1989.

——. Ha-*Otsar—Hamishim Sippureh Am Ve-Aggadot*. Tel-Aviv: Yavneh, 1969.

——. "Millu'aim Le-'Hadefus Ha-Ivri Be-Artsot Ha-Mizrah.'" Jerusalem: Kiryat Sefer, 22nd year, no. 1.

Berg, Nancy E. *Exile from Exile: Israeli Writers from Iraq*. New York: State University of New York Press, 1996.

Benayahu, Meir. *Sefarim She-Nithabberu Be-Bavel U-Sefarim She-Neaetku Bah*. Or-Yehuda: Yad Ha-Rav Nissim and The Babylonian Jewry Heritage Center, 1993.

Bezalel Yitzhak, ed. "Ha-Paam Be-*Pe'amim*." *Pe'amim*, no. 26, (1986): 1.

Bialik, Hayim Nahman and Ravinitzky, Yehoshua Hana. *The Book of Legends: Legends from the Talmud and Midrash*. Translated by William G. Braude. New York: Schocken Books, 1992.

——. *Selected Poems*. Translated by Israel Efros. New York: Bloch Publishing Company for Histadruth Ivrith of America, Revised edition, 1965.

Bezalel, Itzhak, ed. *The Sephardi and Near Eastern Jewry at the Time of the Holocaust*. *Pe'amim*, no. 27 (1986).

——. *Pe'amim*, no. 8 (1981): 21-91.

Bibi, Mordekhai, collected and edited. *Me-Arba Kanfot Ha-Naharayim: Eduyot Ve-Sippurim al Ha-Mahteret Ve-Ha-Haapala Be-Iraq*. Tel-Aviv: Hakibbuz Hameuchad, 1983.

——. "Ha-Mahteret He-Halutsit Be-Iraq." *Pa'amin*, no. 8 (1981): 92-106.

——. *Ha-Mahteret Ha-Tsionit He-Halutsit Be-Iraq, 1942-1945: Mehkar Te'audi* 1, 2. Jerusalem: Makhon Ben-Zvi, Yad Tabbenkin, 1988.

Biron (Katan), Yoav. *Lahavot Ba-Galil*. Tel-Aviv: Hakibbuz Hameuchad, 1994.

Cohen, Hayyim Y. *Ha-Peailut Ha-Tsiyonit Be-Iraq*. Ha-Sifriyya Ha-Tsiyonit al yad Hanhalat Ha-Histadrut Ha-Tsiyonit. Jerusalem: Ha-Oniversita Ha-Ivrit—Ha-Makhon Le-Yahadut Zemanenu, 1969.

Dangour, Ezra, ed. *Sefer Ha-Shirim*. Baghhdad: Ezra Dangour Printing House, 1906.

Derekh He-Halutz: Itton Madrikheh Ha-Tenuah, no 1, Sivan *Tshah*, 1945.

——, no 3, Elul *Tshah*, 1945.
——, no 4, Kislev *Tshu*, 1945.
——, no 5, Adar Bet *Tshu*, 1946.
——, no 6, Sivan *Tshu*, 1946.
——, no 8, Elul *Tsht*, 1948.
——, no 9, Heshvan *Tshia*, 1950.
——, no 10, Shevat *Tshia*, 1950.

Eldar, Dan. "Teguvat Ha-Yehudim Be-Artsot Ha-Mizrah al Ha-Medinniyut Ha-Antishemit Be-Germania." *Pe'amim*, no. 5 (1980): 55-76.

Gaon, Moshe David. "Emunot U-Terufot Elil Be-Kerev Yehudeh Ha-Mizrah." *Yeda Am* 4, no 1-2 (1957): 36-37.

——. "Hartsubbot Ha-Indulko." In *Hahme Yerushalayim: Mivhar Maamarim*. Sephardi and Near Eastern Jews Council, 1976.

Gilbowa, Menuha. *Lexicon Ha-Ittonut Ha-Ivrit*. Tel-Aviv: Mosad Bialik with The Hayyim Resenberg School for Jewish Studies, Tel Aviv University, 1992.

Guthaf, Yehuda. *Ittonut Yehudit She-Hayeta*. Tel-Aviv: Ha-Iggud Ha-Olami shel Ha-Ittonaim Ha-Yehudim, 1973.

Haddad, Ezra. "Divreh Hagut Ve-Sippur," in *Sofer U-Mehanekh Mi-Bavel: Dappeh Zikaron Le-Ezra Haddad*. Tel-Aviv: Ha-Histadrut Ha-Kelalit shel Ha-Ovdim Ha-Ivrim Be-Erets Yisrael, 1973.

——. *Alfa Beta*. Baghdad, 1947.

——. *Avneh Derekh*, Tel-Aviv: Irgun Yotsaeh Iraq Be-Yisrael, 1970.

Haddad, Heskel M. *Jews of Arab and Islamic Countries: History, Problems, Solutions*.

New York: Shengold Publishing, Inc., 1984.

——. *Flight From Babylon*. New York: McGraw-Hill, 1986.

Ha-Havatselet, no. 25 (1841).

Hakak, Balfur, ed. *Shoah Ba-Mizrah*. Jerusalem: Ministry of Education and Culture, 1981.

——. *Ve'az Be-Kets Ha-Yohasin*. Jerusalem: Shalhevet, 1987.

Hakak, Herzl. *Teudah Nishkahat*. Tel-Aviv: Shalhevet, 1987.

Hakak, Lev. "Yotsaeh Iraq Ba-Sifrut Ha-Ivrit." *Massah* (3 September 1976) 14. Reprinted in *Hedim*, no. 18 (October 1976) 18-19.

——. "Kakh Neelma Yahadut Iraq." *Ma'ariv* (17 September 1976) 39. Reprinted in *Leket Le-Divreh Bikkoret* (30 September 1976) 15-17.

——. *Im Arbaah Meshorerim: Avraham Ben-Titshak, Amir Gilbowa, Natan Zakh, Shelomo Zamir.* Jerusalem: Eked, 1977, 165-192.

——. "Terumatam Shel Yostaeh Iraq La-Sifrut Ha-Ivrit Ba-Arets." *Itton* 77, no. 5-6, (November-December 1977) 22-23.

——. "Al Arbaah Shirim Shel Shelomo Zamir Ve-Al Kamma Aspektim Poetiyyim Ve-Tematiyyim shel Shirato." *Shevet Veam* (April 1978) 476-496.

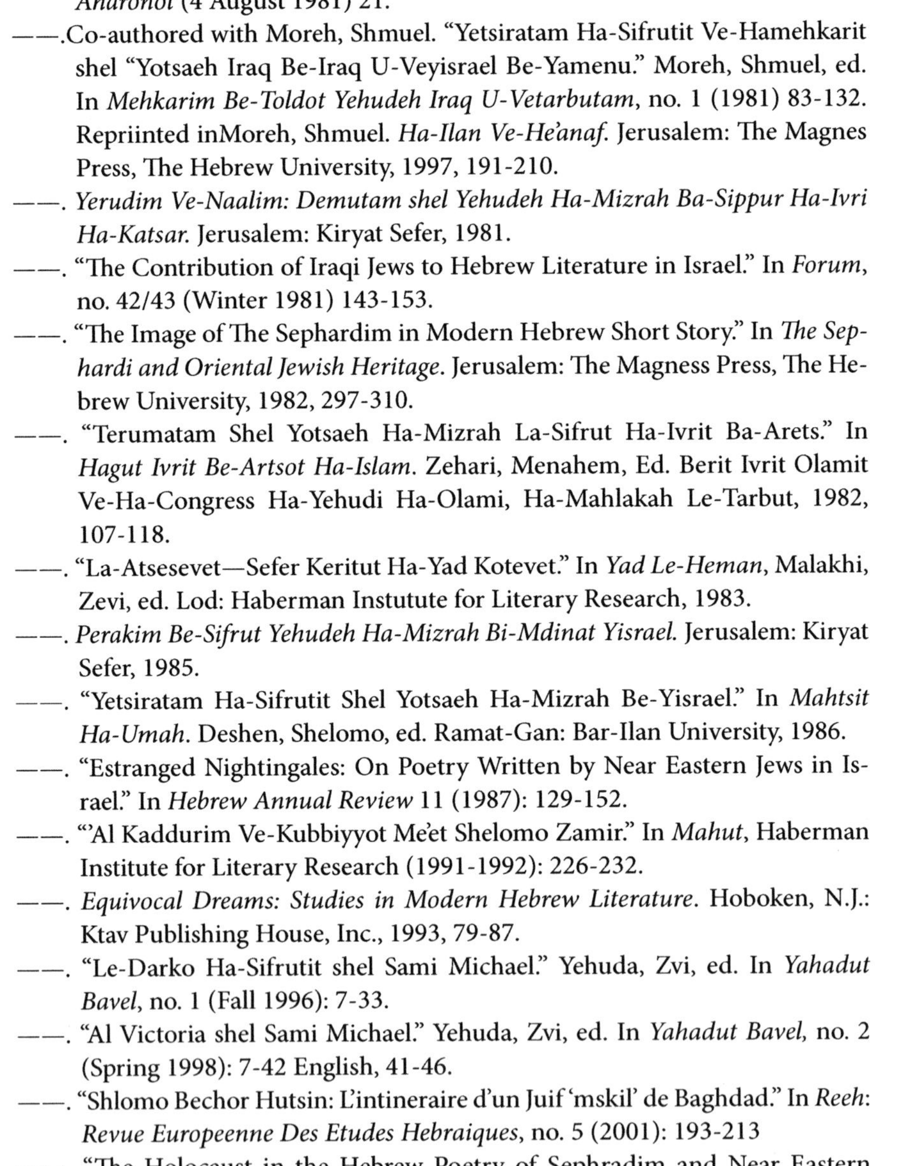

——. "Gam Be-Iraq Hayetah Sifrut Ivrit." Lev Hakak, interviewed by Hayyim Nagid. *Ma'ariv* (7 July 1978) 37.

——. "Demut Yehudeh Ha-Mizrah Ba-Sippur Ha-Ivri Ha-Katsar." *Shevet Ve-Am* 9 (1980) 149-158.

——. "Shiratam shel Yehudeh Ha-Mizrah Bi-Medinat Yisreal." *The Eighth World Congress For Jewish Studies*, Jerusalem (1981) 283-288. Reprinted in *Yediot Aharonot* (4 August 1981) 21.

——.Co-authored with Moreh, Shmuel. "Yetsiratam Ha-Sifrutit Ve-Hamehkarit shel "Yotsaeh Iraq Be-Iraq U-Veyisrael Be-Yamenu." Moreh, Shmuel, ed. In *Mehkarim Be-Toldot Yehudeh Iraq U-Vetarbutam*, no. 1 (1981) 83-132. Repriinted inMoreh, Shmuel. *Ha-Ilan Ve-He'anaf*. Jerusalem: The Magnes Press, The Hebrew University, 1997, 191-210.

——. *Yerudim Ve-Naalim: Demutam shel Yehudeh Ha-Mizrah Ba-Sippur Ha-Ivri Ha-Katsar.* Jerusalem: Kiryat Sefer, 1981.

——. "The Contribution of Iraqi Jews to Hebrew Literature in Israel." In *Forum*, no. 42/43 (Winter 1981) 143-153.

——. "The Image of The Sephardim in Modern Hebrew Short Story." In *The Sephardi and Oriental Jewish Heritage*. Jerusalem: The Magness Press, The Hebrew University, 1982, 297-310.

——. "Terumatam Shel Yotsaeh Ha-Mizrah La-Sifrut Ha-Ivrit Ba-Arets." In *Hagut Ivrit Be-Artsot Ha-Islam*. Zehari, Menahem, Ed. Berit Ivrit Olamit Ve-Ha-Congress Ha-Yehudi Ha-Olami, Ha-Mahlakah Le-Tarbut, 1982, 107-118.

——. "La-Atsesevet—Sefer Keritut Ha-Yad Kotevet." In *Yad Le-Heman*, Malakhi, Zevi, ed. Lod: Haberman Instutute for Literary Research, 1983.

——. *Perakim Be-Sifrut Yehudeh Ha-Mizrah Bi-Mdinat Yisrael.* Jerusalem: Kiryat Sefer, 1985.

——. "Yetsiratam Ha-Sifrutit Shel Yotsaeh Ha-Mizrah Be-Yisrael." In *Mahtsit Ha-Umah*. Deshen, Shelomo, ed. Ramat-Gan: Bar-Ilan University, 1986.

——. "Estranged Nightingales: On Poetry Written by Near Eastern Jews in Israel." In *Hebrew Annual Review* 11 (1987): 129-152.

——. "'Al Kaddurim Ve-Kubbiyyot Me'et Shelomo Zamir." In *Mahut*, Haberman Institute for Literary Research (1991-1992): 226-232.

——. *Equivocal Dreams: Studies in Modern Hebrew Literature*. Hoboken, N.J.: Ktav Publishing House, Inc., 1993, 79-87.

——. "Le-Darko Ha-Sifrutit shel Sami Michael." Yehuda, Zvi, ed. In *Yahadut Bavel*, no. 1 (Fall 1996): 7-33.

——. "Al Victoria shel Sami Michael." Yehuda, Zvi, ed. In *Yahadut Bavel*, no. 2 (Spring 1998): 7-42 English, 41-46.

——. "Shlomo Bechor Hutsin: L'intineraire d'un Juif 'mskil' de Baghdad." In *Reeh: Revue Europeenne Des Etudes Hebraiques*, no. 5 (2001): 193-213

——. "The Holocaust in the Hebrew Poetry of Sephradim and Near Eastern Jews." *Shofar* (Spring 2005).

——. *Nitsaneh Ha-Yetsira Ha-Ivrit Ha-Hadasha Be-Bavel.* Merkaz Moreshet Yahadut Bavel, 2003.

——. *Iggerot Ha-Rav Shelmo Bekhor Hutsin*: Collected, Wrote an Introduction and Lists of Abbrivations and Publications. Hakibuz Hameuchad, 2005.

Harashovski, Binyamin. "Ha-Im Yesh La-Tselil Mashmaut?" *ha-Sifrut* 1, no. 2 (Summer 1968): 410-420.

Halkin, Shimon. *Modern Hebrew Literature, Trends and Values.* New York: Schocken, 1950.

Halevi, Yosef. "Ha-Meshammerim Hevleh Shav...Megamot Maskiliyyot Ba-Sifrut Ha-Ivrit Ba-Mizrah Ha-Muslemi: Iyyun Be-'Emek Ha-Shedim' le-Rabbi S"M Mani." *Mehkereh Misgav Yerushalayim Be-Sifruyot Am Ysirael.* Jerusalem: Misgav Yerushalayim, 1987, 33-60.

Hayardeni, Galia. Collected, annotated and wrote an introduction. *Sal Anavim.* Jerusalem: Mosad Bialik, 1967, 45-53.

Hasan-Rokem, G. "Iyyun Bi-Mkorot Sippurch Ha-Am shel Yehudeh Babvel. Pitgamim Be-Sippurim." *Mehkarim Be-Toldot Yehudeh Bavel U-Vetarbutam* 1 (1981): 187-196.

Hayyim, Yosef. *Sefer Rav Pealim* 2. *Hoshen Mishpat.* Jerusalem, 1903, 5, 11, 24. Bene Berak: Agudat Shetile Zetim vVe-T.T. Shai (1979 or 1980).

—— and Yosef Chayim Chacham. *Parables from Baghdad.* Adapted by Nehama Conuelo Nahmoud. Brooklyn: Lightbooks, 1981.

——. *Niflaim Maasekha.* Jerusalem, 1912. Jerushalayim: Y. ben D. Salem; T.A. (z.o. Tel-Aviv): Hafatsah rashit, A. Barzani (1985 or 1986).

——. *Mashal Ve-Nimshal.* Jerusalem, 1913. Yitshak Bakkal, 1948.

——. *Niflaaim Ma'asekha.* Siyyah Yisrael, Jerusalem, 1988, 5 Volumes.

Holtz, Abraham. "Prolegomenon to a Literary History of Modern Hebrew Literature." *Literature East and West* XI, no. 3 (1968): 253-270.

Hutsin, Shelomo Bekhor. *Ha-Levanon*, 6th year, no. 12 (18 March 1869): 95-96.

——. *Sefer Talmud Katan* (1850).

——. *Ha-Tsefira*, 16th year, no. 217 (1890): 891.

——. *Ha-Tsefira*, 16th year, no. 278, 1145.

——. *Ha-Maggid*, 7th year, no. 11 (12 March 1863): 84.

——. *Ha-Maggid*, 6th year, no. 48 (December 1862): 377.

——. *Ha-Levanon*, 6th year, no. 12 (18 March 1969): 95-96.

——. *Ha-Maggid*, 12th year, no. 49 (16 December 1868): 387.

——. *Ha-Maggid*, no. 34 (26 August 1863).

——. *Ha-Tsefira*, 16th year, no. 278, 1145.

——. *Ha-Maggid*, 7th year, no. 11 (12 March 1863): 84.

——. *Ha-Levanon*, 6th year, no. 12 (18 March 1969): 95-96.

——.. *Ha-Maggid*, 12th year, no. 49 (16 December 1868): 387.

——. *Ha-Maggid*, 6th year, no. 48 (December 1862): 377.

——. *Ha-Maggid*, no. 34 (26 August 1863): 268.

——. *Ha-Maggid*, no. 28 (16 July 1873).

——. *Ha-Maggid,* no. 48 (December 1862): 377.
——. *Ha-Maggid,* no. 23 (9 June 1874).
——. *Perah,* no. 45 (4 May 1883): 271.
——. *Perah,* no. 8 (3 August 1883): 44.
——. *Ha-Maggid,* no. 39 (10 October 1877): 356.
——. *Ha-Tsefira,* 28 Shevat, no. 12 (1887).
——.*Ha-Levanon,* no. 7 (11 February 1870): 54-55.
——. *Ha-Maggid,* no. 34 (26 August 1863): 208.
——. *Ha-Maggid,* no. 32 (31 August 1866): 252.
——. *Ha-Levanon,* no. 11 (31 August 1866): 83-84.
——. *Ha-Maggid,* no. 46 (28 November 1866): 363-364.
——. *Ha-Tsefira,* no. 11 (16 September 1874): 83-84.
——. *Ha-Levanon,* no. 13 (25 June 1869): 102-103.
——. *Ha-Tsefira,* no. 11 (September 1874): 83-84.
——. *Ha-Maggid,* no. 11 (12 March 1863): 84.
——. *Ha-Tsefira,* no. 16 (25 April 1866): 124.
——. *Ha-Maggid,* no. 16 (25 April 1866): 124.
——. *Ha-Maggid,* no. 34 (29 August 1866): 268.
——. *Ha-Maggid,* no. 41 (21 October 1863): 325.
——. *Ha-Maggid,* no. 50 (26 December 1866): 396.
——. *Ha-Tsefira,* no. 9 (1877): 67.
——. *Ha-Levanon,* no. 20 (24 January 1872): 158.
——. *Ha-Tsefira,* no. 42 (1879): 331.
——. *Ha-Maggid,* no. 11 (12 March 1863): 84.
——. *Ha-Havatselet,* no. 25 (1880).
——. *Ha-Levanon* (18 March 1869).
——. *Ha-Tsefira,* 16th year, no. 217, 891
——. *Maasim Niflaim.* Hutsin Printing House, 1890.
——. *Maasim Mefoarim.* Hutsin Printing House, 1890.
——. *Maaseh Nissim.* Hutsin Printing House, 1890.
——. In *Ha-Levanon,* March 18, 1869.
——. In *Ha-Tsefira,* 16th year, no. 217, 891.

Jason (Yazon), H. "Ha-Sippur al Har Ha-Shemesh—Ha-Degam shel Ha-Hikkuy Ha-Koshel." Mehkarim Be-Toldot Yehudeh Iraq U-Vetarbutam 1 (1981): 169-185.

——. *Sippureh Am Mi-Pi Yehudeh Iraq.* Or-Yehuda: The Babylonian Jewry Heritage Center, 1988.

Kattan, Naim. *Farewell, Babylon.* Translated from the French by Sheila Fischman. Toronto: McClelland and Stewart, 1976.

Katav, Shalom. *Al Gedot Ha-Naharayim.* Tel-Aviv: Eked, 1973.

——. *Mishereh Shalom Katav.* Tel-Aviv: Eked, 1980.

Kressel, G. *Guide to the Hebrew Press.* Switzerland: Inter Documentation Company Ag Zug. Switzerland, 1979.

Levin, Yisrael. "'Zeman' Ve-Tevel' Be-Shirat Ha-Haol Ha-Ivrit Bi-Sfarad Bimeh Ha-Benayim." *Otsar Yehudeh Sepharad* 5 (1962): 68-79.

Mahberet Mivhan Ha-Talmidim, 56 religious questions. Baghdad: Ezra Dangour Press, 1913.

Mani, Saliman. "Be-Emek Ha-Shedim." *Ha-Tsevi*, no. 31 (1885): 134-135.

——. "Be-Emek Ha-Shedim." *Ha-Tsevi*, no. 32 (1885): 137-139.

——. "Be-Emek Ha-Shedim." *Ha-Tsevi*, no. 33 (1885): 141-142.

——. "Be-Emek Ha-Shedim." *Ha-Tsevi*, no. 34 (1885): 147-148.

——. "Be-Emek Ha-Shedim." Reprinted in Galia Yardeni, collected annotated and wrote an introduction. *Sal Anavim*. Jerusalem: Mosad Bialik, 1967.

——. "Hevron t." *Ha-Tsevi*, no. 25 (1885).

——. "Massa le-Aza." *Ha-Tsevi*, no. 7 (1886).

——. "Efneh Ve-Aeraeh Tsel Temunati." In Mani, Eliahu. *Siyah Yitshak*. Jerusalem: Hevrat Ahavat Shalom y.k.b., 1975.

——. "Ir Kodesh Hebron Kiryat Arba." In Medini, Hayyim Hizkiyyahu. *Sedeh Hemed*, VI. Warsaw, 1896.

——. Two Poems. In *Perah*, no. 10 (1888).

Mani, Avraham Barukh. *Sefer Barukh Avraham*. Jerusalem: Makhon le-Hotsa'at Sefarim ve-Khitveh-Yad "Ahavat Shalom", 1987.

——. "Barukh Mi-Banim." In Mani, Eliahu, *Zikhronot Eliahu* I (1936).

——. "Mavo Ve-Hearot La-Sefer *Gay Hizzayon*" (at its end the Lamentation "Ekha Neaetma Erets Ha-Tsevi") I, by Avraham Yagel, 1880.

——. Two responses in the book of Franco, Rahamim. *Sha'areh Rahamim* II (1902).

——. "La-Ben Ki Nolad." In *Heshek Shelomo*. Le-Rabbi Shelomo Ha-Mekhunneh M"V Babba Gohn ben M"V Pinhas from Samarkand. Jerusalem, 1907.

Mattityahu, Zion. *Kol Ba-Alatah*. Tel-Aviv: Alef, 1973.

Mattityhu, Margalit. *Hatser Harukha*. Tel-Aviv: Eked, 1988.

Mizrahi, Moshe Barukh, ed. *Ha-Dover* (Later *Dover Mesharim*). 1863-1868, 1870-1871.

——. *Ha-Maggid*, no. 15 (1869): 119.

——. *Ibid*, no. 31 (1869): 248.

——. *Ibid*, no. 33 (1869). Signed Berakhya Ben-Yedidya.

Mkammal, Salih, ed. *Shemesh: Osef Shirim Ve-Hibburim shel Talmideh Bet-Sefer Shemesh*. no. 1 (1930). Illustrations by Abdallah Ezra.

——. no. 2 (1930).

——. no. 3 (1931). Edited by a school class. Illustrated by Naim Ezra.

——. no. 4 (1933). Editor and illustrator as no. 1 above.

Moreh, Shmuel. "Pera'ot Hag Ha-Shvuo't tash"a Bi-R'ei Ha-Sifrut." In "Sina't Yehudim U-Fra'aot Be-Iraq." Moreh, Shmuel, and Yehuda, Zvi, eds. Or-Yehuda: The Babylonian Jewry Heritage Center, 187-210.

Murad, Ezra. *Nofeh Yaldut Mi-Bet Abba*. Stavit, 1985.

Myshlish, Dalia, interviewed. "Sippuro shel Bitta'on Ivri Be-Baghdad." *Nehardea*, no. 18 (November 1996): 9-10.

Neimark, Efrayim. "Erets Ha-Kedem: Mass'a." *Ha-Asif*, Warsaw, 5th year, 1889, 39-75.

Nissim, Shelomo Yitshak. "Shuddedu Mi-Bet Megurehem." Baghdad: Ezra Dangour, 1917. Reprinted in *Hamesh Taaniyyot*, Jerusalem, 1956, 19-191.

——, and Yehezkel, Shmuel. *Lekah Tov* I, Baghdad: Ezra Dangour, 1912.

——. *Derekh Tovim, Kovets Imreh Shefer*. Baghdad: Ezra Dangour, 1938.

Noy, Dov. *Ha-Narah Ha-Yefifiyyah U-Sheloshet Beneh Ha-Melekh, 120 Sippureh Am Mippi Yehudeh Iraq*. Tel-Aviv: Am Oved, 1965.

Obermeyer, Jacob. *Modernes Judentum im Morgen - und Abendland*. Kaiferl. u. ronigl. Hof-Buchdruckerei und Hof-Verlags-Buchhandlung Carl fromme. Vienna nad Leipzig, 1907.

Ozer, Yosi. *"Farhood."* In Hakak, Balfur, ed. *Shoah Ba-Mizrah*. Jerusalem: Ministry of Education and Culture, 1981, 22-23.

Pagis, Dan. *Shirat Ha-Hol Ve-Torat Ha-Shir Le-Moshe ibn Ezra U-Vne Doro*. Jerusalem: Mosad Bialik, 1970.

Rejwan, Nissim. *The Jews of Iraq: 3000 years of History and Culture*. London: Weidenfeld and Nicolson, 1985.

Sason, Aharon. *Sefer Shireh Ha-Techiyya*. Baghdad: Elisha Shohet, 1936.

Sason, Yisrael. *Shireh Sason*. Baghdad: Elisha Shohet, 1939.

Schayyik, Shaul. "Morim Artsi-Yisraelim Be-Iraq (1825-1935)—Moked Le-Hinnukh Ivri Leummi." In *Yahadut Bavel*, no. 2 (Spring 1998): 141-148.

Shelomo, Salih Shelomo and Gorgy, Moshe. *Ha-Mathil*. Baghdad: Ezra Dangour, 1912.

Shilowah, Amnon. *Ha-Massoret Ha-Musikalit shel Yehudeh Bavel: Mivhar Piyyutim Ve-Shirim*. Or-Yehuda: The Babylonian Jewry Heritage Center, 2003.

Shireh Rinna, Shirim Ve-Tishbahot Madrasat Talmud Torah, (twenty-six liturgies in Hebrew and eight liturgies in Arabic). Baghdad: Ezra Dangour, 1906.

Shohet, Nir. *Sippurah Shel Golah*. Jerusalem: Ha-Agudda Le-Kiddum Ha-Mehkar Ve-Ha-Yetsira, 1981.

——. *The Story of an Exile*. Zilkha, Abraham, translated and edited. Association for the Promotion of Research, Literature and Art, 1982.

Shtahl, Avraham. *Yahadut Ha-Mizrah—Sefarim, Homer Hazuti Ve-Orkoli*. Medinat Yisrael, Misrad Ha-Hinukh, 1989, 167-169.

Silberschlag, Eisig. *From Renaissance to Renaissance (Hebrew Literature 1492-1970)*, New York: Ktav Publishing House, 1973.

——. *Saul Tschernichowski: Poet of Revolt. Translations by Sholom J. Kahn and Others*. Ithaca, N.Y.: Cornell University Press, 1968.

Stillman, Norman A. *The Jews of Arab Lands*. Philadelphia: The Jewish Publication Society of America, 1979.

Tsion, Refael Ben Shelomo. *Al Neharot Bavel*. Jerusalem: Refa'ael Hayyim Printing House, 1937, 19-20.

Ventura, Moshe. *Ivrit Be-Ivrit*, 4 Volumes. Baghdad: Ezra Dangour, 1919.

Woolfson, Marion. *Prophets in Babylon: Jews in Arab World*. London and Boston: Faber and Faber, 1980.

Yea'ri, Avraham. *Ha-Ddefus Ha-Ivri Be-Artsot Ha-Mizrah* 2. Jerusalem: Ha-Hevra Le-Hotsa'at Sefarim al Yad Ha-Oniversita Ha-Ivrit, 1940.

——. "Tosafot Le-*Ha-Defus Ha-Ivri Be-Artsot Ha-Mizrah*." *Kiryat Sefer* XIV, 1947, 71-72.

Yehuda, Zvi. *Mi-Bavel Li-Rushalayim: Kovets Mehkarim U-Teudot al Ha-Tsiyonot Ve-Ha-Aliyya Me-Iraq*. Or-Yehuda: The Babylonian Jewry Heritage Center, 1980.

——. *Bateh Sefer Yehudiyyim Be-Baghdad, 1832-1974*. Or-Yehuda: The Babylonian Jewry Heritage Center, 1996.

——. "Yehudeh Bavel Ve-Shinnuy Tarbuti Bi-Fculatah shel Kiy"h." *Yahadut Bavel*, no. 1 (Fall 1996) 45-59.

——. "Iraqi Jewry and Cultural Change in the Educational Activity of the Alliance Israelite Universelle." In Goldberg, Harvey, ed. *Sephardi and Middle Eastern Jewries: History & Culture in the Modern Era*, Indianapolis: Indiana University Press, 1966, 134-145.

——, ed. *Ha-Rav Yosef Hayyim: Pirkeh Mehkar Ve-Iyyun Bi-Melot Tishim Shana Li-Ftirato*. Or-Yehuda: The Babylonian Jewry Heritage Center, 1999.

——. "Temurot Ba-Yishuv Ha-Yehudi Be-Baghdad Ba-Meaot ha-12-18." In *Mehkarim Bekorot Yehudeh Bavel U-Vetarbutam*. Or-Yehuda: The Babylonian Jewry Heritage Center, 2002.

Yellin, David. *Torat Ha-Shira Ha-Sepharadit*, 1940. 2nd edition. Jerusalem: The Magnes Press, The Hebrew University, 1972.

Yosef, Shaul Ben Abdullah. *Giv'at Shaul, Interpretations to the Poems of Yehuda Halevi*. Samuel Krauss, ed. Vienna: Ungar, 1923.

——. *Mishbetset Ha-Tarshish, Perush Le-Sefer Ha-Tarshish shel Moshe ibn Ezra*. Samuel Krauss, ed. Vienna: E. Goldston, 1926.

——. *Gan Ha-Meshalim Ve-Ha-Hidot: Osef Shireh Todros ben Yehuda Abulafia al pi Ketav Yad Shaul ben Eved-El Yosef* I. Proofread, organized, interpreted, and edited by David Yellin. Jerusalem: Defus Ha-Sefer, 1932.

——. *Gan Ha-Meshalim Ve-Ha-Hidot: Osef Shireh Todros Ben Yehuda Abulafia al pi Ketav Yad Shaul ben Eved-El Yosef* II. Proofread, organized, interpreted, and edited by David Yellin. Jerusalem: Defus Weise, 1936.

——. "Kol Ha-Sirim tahat Ha-Shir." *Ha-Tsefira*, 14th year, no. 79 (1887): 3; no. 83 (1887): 3-4; no. 84 (1887): 3-4.

"Kol Ha-Sirim tahat Ha-Shir." *Ha-Tsefira*, 16th year, no. 214 (1889): 3; no. 215 (1889): 2.

——. "Kol Ha-Shirim: Rabbi Yaacov ben Elaazar Ha-Meshorer." *Ha-Tsefira*, 18th year, no. 133 (1891): 541-542; *Ha-Tsefira*, 18th year, no. 139 (1891): 565-

566; *Ha-Tsefira*, 18th year, no. 146 (1891): 593; *Ha-Tsefira*, 18th year, no. 156 (1891): 633-634; *Ha-Tsefira*, 18th year, no. 158 (1891): 641-642.

——. "Kol Ha-Sirim tahat Ha-Shir." *Ha-Tsefira*, 28th year, no. 214 (1901): 938-939; 28th year, no. 235 (1901): 943; 28th year, no. 238 (1901): 954-955; 28th year, no. 239 (1901): 959; 28th year, no. 240 (1901): 963; 28th year, no. 241 (1901): 963-967; 28th year, no. 242 (1901): 971; 28th year, no. 245 (1901): 982-983; 28th year, no. 246 (1901): 987; 28th year, no. 248 (1901): 995; 28th year, no. 249 (1901): 999; 28th year, no. 251 (1901): 1007; 28th year, no. 252 (1901): 1010-1011; 28th year, no. 253 (1901): 1014-1015.

——. "Ha-Yehudim Be-Hong Kong U-Veaerets Sinim." *Ha-Tsefira*, 14th year, no. 286 (1887): 1-2.

——. *"Ha-Yehudim Be-Erets Sinim: Mikhtav A." Ha-Tsefira*, 15th year, no. 20 (1888): 3.

"Ha-Yehudim Be-Erets Sinim: Mikhtav B." *Ha-Tsefira*, 15th year, no. 63 (1888): 3-7; *Ha-Tsefira*, 15th year, no. 64 (1888): 5.

——. "Rea'eh Zeh Hadash Hu." *Ha-Tesifira*, 22nd year, no. 193 (1895): 741; no. 194 (1895): 44-45; 22nd year, no. 287 (1896): 1138.

Shelomo ben Salih Shelomo. *Kerem Ha-Yeladim, Poems*. Baghdad: Elisha Dangour, 1925.

Shenhar, Aliza. "Ha-Sifrut Ha-Amamit shel Yehudeh Bavel Ve-Zikkatah Le-Sifrut Ha-Agadah." Mehkarim Be-Toldot Yehudeh Iraq U-Vetarbutam 1. Or-Yehuda: The Babylonian Jewry Heritage Center, 1981.

Sofer, Moshe Azuri, and Nissim, Yaacov Tsion Mualim Nissim. A) *Mesillat Ha-Limmud* B) *Meshalim Melukatim Le-Talmidim*, 1927. Baghdad: Published by Rahel Shahmoon School, 1927.

Zamir, Ya'acov. "Sefarim Shenidpesu Be-Vateh Defus Yehudiyyim Be-Baghdad ve-enam Nizkarim be-Sifro shel Avraham Ye'ari." *Yahadut Bavel, Merkaz Moreshet Yehudeh Bavel*, no. 2 (Spring 1998): 163-168.

Zamir, Shelomo. *Ha-Kol Mi-Baad La-Anaf*. Tel-Aviv: Sifriyat Poalim, 1960.

"Mr. S. A. Joseph of Hong Kong," *Israel's Messenger* 3, no. 10 (August 1906): 7.

"The Literary Remains of the Late S. A. Joseph of Hong Kong." *Israel's Messenger* 6, no. 12 (September 1926): 13.

ספר

תוכחות מוסר

בקושטאנדינא

Tokhehot Musar by Ezra Habavli, 1735.

ספר

קול ששון

פה ליוורנו יע"א

Kol Sason, Sason Ben-Mordekhai, 1859.

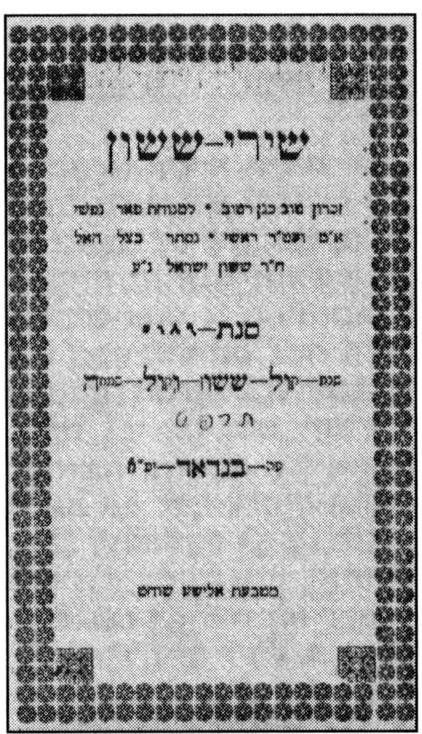

שירי-ששון

זכרון טוב כגן רטוב ‧ למנוחת פאר נפשי
א"מ ועט"ר ראשי ‧ נכתר בצל האל
ח"ר ששון ישראל נ"ע

Sason Yirael, Shireh Sason, 1929.

ערבית של שבת

יהוה

A page of a Baghdadi prayer book, illustrated by Rahamim Sehayik, 1906.

Nuriel School.

Shammash School.

Talmud Torah School, Baghdad.

כתאב

יחוי ﭏ ראודיה . מלאחי ערביה

קטף ׳ ותרתיב ׳ ותעריב ׳ ותאליף ׳

דאוד ס׳ צמח

צאחב מכתבת ﭏ ראודיה קרב דרבונת

שיך יצחק נפרה וז—ע״ז ו׳ וינטלב מנהא

וכל חק מחפוץ לדו

קסם ﭏ אול

מן לם ישתרי ﭏ נצאייח מגאנן אאכדהו

יכלפהו ﭏ נדם ג׳לי

פרח

בגדאד יע״א

The cover of David Tsemah book.

גליון א׳ שנה ראשונה Yeshurun

ישרון

No. 1

שבועון עברי

יוצא בכל יום ששי

על ידי האגודה העברית הספרותית

התכן :

חסן ישעות חכמת ודעת

ישעיה לג׳

פהרסת

The first issue of *Yeshurun*, 1921.

The Babylonian Heder.

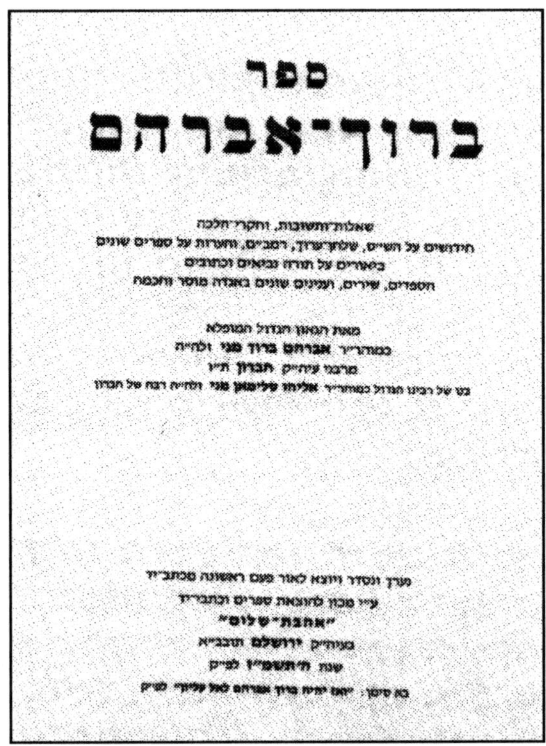

ספר

ברוך־אברהם

שאלות־ותשובות, וחקרי־הלכה

חידושים על הש"ס, שלחן־ערוך, רמב"ם, והערות על ספרים שונים

באורים על תורה נביאים וכתובים

הספדים, שירים, ועניינים שונים באגדה מוסר וחכמה

מאת הגאון הגדול המופלא

כמוהר"ר אברהם ברוך מני זלה"ה

מרבני עיה"ק חברון ת"ו

בנו של רבינו הגדול כמוהר"ר אליהו סלימאן מני זלה"ה רבה של חברון

ערוך ונסדר ויוצא לאור פעם ראשונה מכתב־יד

ע"י מכון להוצאת ספרים וכתבי־יד

"אהבת־שלום"

בעיה"ק ירושלם תובב"א

שנת [illegible] לפ"ק

The book *Sefer Barukh Avraham*, by Avraham Barukh Mani.

מזמור שיר

שירים ופזמונים

מאת

יחזקאל חי אלבג

MIZMOR SHEER

POEMS AND LYRICS

by

EZEKIEL H. ALBEG

Mizmor Sheer, by Rabbi Ezekiel Hai Albeg.

A class in Rahel Shahmoon School.

Teachers in Gan Menahem Daniel School.

Teachers at Alliance School, Baghdad, 1931.

Teachers at Shammash School, 1933.

Hebrew teachers in Baghdad.

שירו ליי שיר חדש

ספר

שירה לאל

מכיל בו שירות ותשבחות. לימי החול ולימי
מנוחות. וגם בו רצוף ידידות כנסת ישראל
לאל אלהי הרוחות. ונחמות ללבבות משמחות.
ותהלות ותפלות ותחנות ליוצר כל היצורים.
עם איזה מוסרים. אשר ללב מעוררים. למען
ילך בדרכי טובים וישרים. ועוד ככל בו
פתגמים על סדר האב טובים ונעימים
וסדר תחנה ובקשת רחמים. בעד שארית
הגשמים. וה׳ לא ימנע טוב להולכים בתמים:

מאת הצעיר

מנשה בן לאא סלימאן שהרבאני ס״ט

אשירה ליי בחיי אזמרה לאלהי בעודי

אשירה ליי כי גמל עלי

שירו ליי ברכו שמו

Poetry Volume by Rabbi Menasheh Saliman Shahrabani.

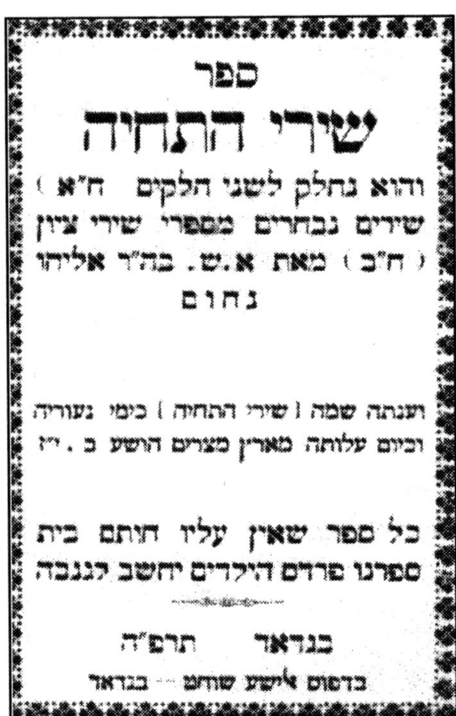

ספר

שירי התחיה

והוא נחלק לשני חלקים ח"א)
שירים נבחרים מספרי שירי ציון
(ח"ב) מאת א.ש. בה"ר אליהו
נחום

וענתה שמה (שירי התחיה) כימי נעוריה
וכיום עלותה מארץ מצרים הושע ב. י"ז

כל ספר שאין עליו חותם בית
ספרנו פרדס הילדים יחשב לגנבה

בגדאד תרפ"ה

בדפוס אלישע שוחט -- בגדאד

The cover of Aharon Sason's book.

A class in Gan Menahem Daniel School.

Physical Education Class in Gan Menahem Daniel School.

הדובר

The cover of *Ha-Dover*, the first Hebrew journal in Babylon (1863-1868).

The cover of the third issue of *Shemesh*, 1931, a collection of Hebrew poems and compositions written by the students of Shammash school.

Images courtesy of The Babylonian Jewry Heritage Center.